391
.01 ✓
DeM

De Marly, Diana.
    Working dress : a history of occupational clothing
/ Diana de Marly. -- London : Batsford, 1986.
    191 p. [8] p. of plates : ill. (some col.), ports. ; 26
cm.

Bibliography: p. 183-187.
Includes index.
02992884   ISBN: 0713450282 :

1. Work clothes - Great Britain - History. 2. Labor
and laboring classes - Great Britain - History. I. Title.

WORKING DRESS

Diana de Marly

WORKING DRESS

A History of Occupational Clothing

B.T. Batsford Ltd
LONDON

ISBN 0 7134 5028 2

Typeset by Servis Filmsetting Ltd, Manchester
and printed in Great Britain by
The Bath Press Ltd
Bath, Somerset
for the publishers
B.T. Batsford Ltd
4 Fitzhardinge Street, London W1H oAH

Contents

Acknowledgements
6

1   **Before 1600**
7

2   **The Seventeenth Century**
21

3   **1700–1795**
47

4   **The Industrial Revolution 1795–1845**
76

5   **The Heavy Industrial Age**
105

6   **Into the Twentieth Century 1900–1945**
137

Appendix 1: Range of occupations, 1500–1700
173
Appendix 2: Some women warriors
175
Glossary
176
Notes
177
Bibliography
183
Index
189

Acknowledgements

Black and white photography: Reproduced by Gracious Permission of Her Majesty the Queen 6; British Library 1, 2, 3, 4, 5, 26, 31, 32, 33, 39, 40, 42, 57, 69, 85, 87, 88; British Museum 8 (photograph John Freeman); Hereford County Museum 47; Institute of Agricultural History & Museum of English Rural Life, Reading University 29, 64, 71; Coll. Mrs Loudon 18; Museum of London 11, 12, 14, 15, 16, 34, 35, 36, 37, 38, 48, 50, 51, 52, 53, 54, 55, 60, 68, 70, 72, 73, 74, 75, 76, 77, 84, 86, 89, 91; National Gallery of Scotland 21, 22, 23, 24, 25 (photographs Tom Scott); National Museum of Wales 41; National Portrait Gallery, London 7; Portsmouth and Sunderland Newspapers 78, 79, 80, 81, 82, 83, 84, 90; Museo del Prado, Madrid 13; Rijksmuseum, Amsterdam 17; Royal Museum of Scotland 9, 45, 63, 65, 66, 67; Trinity College, Cambridge 49, 58, 59, 61, 62; Victoria & Albert Museum, London 10, 19, 20, 27, 28, 30, 43, 44, 46, 56. Colour photography: HM Government Art Collection 1; Manchester City Art Gallery 4, 5, 6, 7; National Museum of Wales 2, 8; Walker Art Gallery, Liverpool 3.

The author is grateful to the Pasold Research Fund for a travelling grant which enabled her to study around the country.

ONE

Before 1600

Agriculture

Working dress can be defined as anything which anyone wears to work in. For most of history, however, agricultural labourers were too poor to own more than one outfit, so the clothes they wore to work in and at home were one and the same.

The food industry is the oldest profession in the world, starting with hunting and then the discovery of how to grow crops; any claims that prostitution is older are nonsense, for all human activity depends upon the food to fuel it! The oldest working garment was composed of the skins of animals who were hunted for food, and endured longest as the clothing of shepherds and goatherds. The antiquarian John Aubrey wrote of the Ancient Britons: 'the inhabitants [were] almost as salvage as the Beasts, whose Skins were their own rayment. They were perhaps 2 or 3 degrees, I suppose, less salvage than the Americans.'[1] (By Americans he meant the Red Indians.) Sheepskin cloaks or mantles remained the mark of the shepherd into this century along the Danube, and in Afghanistan. The long shaggy skirts worn by Babylonian men, with hanks of wool in horizontal tiers, show the sheepskin being converted into a garment, but this urban development did not affect shepherds and goatherds, who wore the natural skin for thousands of years.

Protection from thorns and bushes was necessary, and Homer described such garments in the *Odyssey*, when Odysseus finds his father:

. . . clad in a filthy coat
Patched and unseemly; and around his shins
Were laced a pair of mended ox-hide leggings

To save him from scratches, and he wore
Gloves on his hands by reason of the thorns,
And on his head he had a goat-skin cap.

There is a difficulty with translation as Sir William Marris here used the term 'coat', which did not come into existence as a buttoned garment until the thirteenth century. 'Tunic' might be nearer the original. Nevertheless the dirty, patched outfit and the skins are a good picture of the ancient farmworker.

In the Middle Ages Langland described in *Piers Plowman* the hero setting out in sheepskin:

In sumer seson when soft was the sonne,
I shape me in shroudes as I a shepe were.[2]

This was the most ancient form of dress, but the sheepskin shorn of the wool became leather, and in the past this was the best waterproof covering known to man. Leather was used for boots, shoes, capes, tunics and hats, and regular applications of fat or grease were considered to keep it supple and to help keep the rain off. Nowadays leather is an expensive item of fashion, but in the ancient past it was the sign of outdoor workers and travellers.

The oldest man-made fabric is probably felt, produced by the pressing and pounding together of the hairs of sheep, goats or dogs into a thick cloth which offered good protection against rough weather. The popularity of felt garments lasted longest in the Steppes of Asia, where there was no wood to make looms. Protection from the weather was also given by the straw capes worn when it rained, not only in China and Japan but in Spain and Portugal down to the present day. Rushes could be used in this country.

The first woven woollen fabrics survive in the Bronze Age tombs in Denmark, and were not made into garments but into imitation 'skins', as wraps that went round the body, and mantles over the shoulders. A woman's jacket with sleeves had appeared in the middle of the Early Bronze Age around 1200 BC, worn with a string skirt, as we know from a grave at Egtved. The woollen cloth was of course rough and hairy. Such a tailored garment continued to be very rare, for the Late Bronze Age women wore skin capes and plaid skirts, or else a long piece of cloth tied and pinned like the Greek *peplos*. Fitted garments were always a luxury. The majority of country wear was made loose, as the first kind of ready-made garment which could fit anybody, and be passed on to the next generation. Durability was always the prime consideration, so the cloths were woven thicker and heavier than today, with the additional advantages of warmth and weatherproofing.

Only barbarians wore trousers – such was the opinion of the Greek and Romans about their Germanic and Asiatic neighbours, but once the Roman legions reached Caledonia they found *braie*, breeches, very convenient in cold climes, and adopted them as *bracchae*. When Germanic, British, and Dacian tribesmen were recruited into the Roman army they were allowed to keep their native trousers, worn with a Roman-type tunic. The Scythians had fitted jackets, but it was another thousand years before fit became the fashion in Western Europe, and took a couple of hundred years more for it to percolate down to the level of labourers. Trousers became established as rural wear hereafter in various forms as tight pantaloons, as loose garments tucked into boots, and as footless trews, completely separate from court fashion which ignored trousers until the Regency.

The simple classical tunic in linen or wool became established as the garment for working men, since its knee length was very practical and kept out of the mud, whereas the upper class was denoted by its long tunics, right down to 1300. The hood was another classical garment that lasted well into the Middle Ages and can be seen on the ploughman in the Luttrell Psalter of *c*.1340, illus-

1. Christophe Weiditz, 'A Castilian Shepherd', 1529. The smock frock began as this simple shape in Castile then spread north to the Netherlands and England, made of linen. The shepherd also wears trousers, and carries a branch as his crook, and his scrip or bag.

trated in East Anglia. The oxen driver wears a double layer, with a *guarnache* over his tunic as a sort of loose overcoat. By now the law was deciding what farm labourers could wear. The Romans had had *leges sumptuariae* which were aimed principally at restricting the amount spent on luxuries and banquets, although the Lex Julia of Augustus did ban men from wearing silk. The Middle Ages, however, while trying to restrict spending, also restricted what people at all levels could wear. In 1337 Edward III required his subjects to wear only English wool, and in 1362 he issued a statute restricting yeomen and handicraftsmen to cloth costing not more than £2 the piece. Carters, ploughmen, oxherds, cowherds, swineherds, shepherds, and dairymen were restricted to undyed blanket cloth or russet at one shilling a yard, so that they and their wives had to wear a uniform colour of brown or creamy wool. Finer fabrics and the new buttoned cotes were forbidden. A century later Edward IV in 1463 allowed them a price increase, in that they could now buy cloth costing two shillings a yard. Their womenfolk were not to wear coverchiefs costing over one shilling. Foreign coverchiefs would result in a fine of one mark, 13/4. Yeomen were allowed only a lining in their doublets, and no padding, on pain of the fine of 6/8. In 1482 Edward IV imposed a fine of £10 for wearing foreign cloth, and Henry VIII repeated it in 1510. In particular, the lower orders were not to wear the extremely short doublets which exposed the buttocks and codpiece, although their 'betters' could. This seems rather unfair, for this immodest fashion had been copied from the peasants working outdoors in summer in only their underwear, which by the fifteenth century meant a doublet-waistcoat to

which the hose were laced, or else the shirt and breeches, discarding the tunic which was worn over them. The court took up the idea of wearing only doublets, not tunics, and tried to restrict the fashion to itself.

An important statute for the unemployed was issued by Edward III, the *Anno XXV Edwardi III statuta prima, cap.1.* on labourers, of 1350. It ruled that haymakers could be paid only one penny a day, reapers twopence a day in the first half of August, and threepence in the second half. Mowers could receive fivepence an acre. The statute directed all carters, ploughmen, drivers of the plough oxen, shepherds, swineherds and servants that, if

2. Agostino Ramelli, 'Le Diverse et Artificiose Machine', 1588. This design for a one-peasant-powered flourmill shows the basic ancient peasant dress of tunic and trousers which stretches back to Roman times. Homespun or second-hand, in linen or wool, a peasant's wardrobe was rarely more than one outfit. In summer the trousers could be left off and straw gaiters worn. Tight hose were another alternative.

workless, 'all workmen bring openly in their hands to the merchant towns their instruments, and there shall be hired in a common place and not privy'. The statute did not require them to stand for hire at fairs, contrary to later assumptions, but was mainly about fixing pay. The 'instruments' were to indicate the trade: picks, shovels, crooks, sickles, scythes, and whips, while women wore aprons to indicate domestic or farm work. The idea of the unemployed standing at statute fairs did not develop until after 1700, and then was mostly in southern England to begin with.

Probably the oldest garment that is donned only for work is the apron. In 1307 'naperonne' meant a linen napkin or nappy, and was pronounced 'apurn' in the 1500s, but Shakespeare wrote 'apron'. The earliest illustration of an apron seems to be that in the Luttrell Psalter of 1340 which shows it worn by a woman who has milked some sheep. Women wore it for many activities indoors and out, but it was not exclusive to the sex. Farmers used aprons to carry seed when sowing, and both sexes found them useful for carrying chickens, ducks or a piglet. Wood cutters and carpenters adopted aprons to protect their other clothes from being stained, which influenced other workers to follow suit.

Still better protection for clothes evolved in the sixteenth century: the smock frock, which combined the word 'smock', meaning a woman's shift in linen, and 'frock', the long gown worn by clergymen. This religious aspect is still retained in the term to 'unfrock' a priest. Thus a long, loose linen gown was a smock frock. It seems to have begun in Spain, where a loose garment to work in heat would have been very practical, and in 1529 Christophe Weiditz drew a Castilian shepherd in a sleeveless smock down to his calves. From Spain the costume would have been carried to the Spanish Netherlands and so across the Channel. Dutch and Flemish shepherds, cowherds, and chimney sweeps were wearing smock frocks by 1600, which influenced the English to copy them. These early smock frocks were plain, without the elaborate smocking that began in the middle of the eighteenth century. They were adopted by farm labourers, herdsmen, wagoners, drovers, ostlers and brickmakers, for smock frocks protected their suits at both the back and the front better than any apron could. Their other advantage was that they were simple to make, with no shaping or waists to bother about, and the undyed linen was easy to wash, so the wives and mothers who made the clothes at this level in society favoured them, particularly as the clothes underneath would not have to be washed so often.

Clothing terminology is rarely precise, and in southern England smock frocks were called gabardines; they were also called cassocks by some. In the sixteenth century 'cassock' meant a loose riding coat, but in 1666 Pepys described his brother, a clergyman, as wearing a cassock, and it could also mean a smock frock. In 1698 flesh-coloured vests were said to be 'like brickmakers' frocks', so the terminology was fluid, for 'frock' could also mean a frock coat or a priest's gown.[3]

Coping with the weather was always a problem for country workers, especially on the west side of Britain which gets more rain than the east as it faces the Atlantic. Keeping the feet out of the mud had been answered in the Middle Ages by wearing wooden pattens over the shoes, but they do not appear in art until the fifteenth century.

A country wife had an enormous amount of work to do. Her duties were described by John Fitzherbert in his *Book of Husbandrie* of 1555. After housework, feeding the children, and the farm labourers' breakfast, dinner and supper, she was in charge of the dairy, looking after the cows and calves, doing the milking, making cream, butter, cheese, tending the chickens and collecting the eggs. She had to take the corn and malt to the mill, check the measure to ensure the miller was dealing fairly, plus baking the bread, brewing the beer and making the cider. In March she should sow the flax and hemp, and in summer harvest them to make sheets, shirts, smocks, towels, and aprons from the former and sacks from the latter. The husband had to rear the sheep and shear them, but the wife had to spin the wool into yarn, and either weave it into cloth or take it to a weaver, and then make the family clothes from the cloth.

Thomas Tusser in *The Points of Huswifrie* in 1575 said she should also serve the feasts in the farming calendar: Plough Monday, Shrovetide, Sheep-shearing, Wake Day and Harvest Home, when she should bake seed cake, pasties and serve furmenty pot. In 1598 the German visitor Paul Hentzner saw a Harvest Home near Windsor, where the last cartload of corn was decked with flowers and topped by a figure of Ceres, with the men and women harvesters cheering and shouting all the way to the barn. He was very surprised to see no binding: 'The farmers here do not bind up their corn into sheaves, as they do with us, but directly they have reaped or mowed it, put it into carts and convey it into their barns.'[4] It took another century before that continental practice appeared over in England, so Breughel's harvest scenes will not do for England.

The clothes of country women were always shorter than the mode out of necessity. A simple home-made dress with a bodice, skirt and sleeves was the basic form for centuries, although the poorest women workers had little more than a shift and mantle. Some ready-made clothes were sold at fairs and markets, along with second-hand and stolen clothing, and the pattern of farm labourers going to the fair to buy an item or two lasted into this century as an annual event. For many it was the rough homespun, home-made linen and cloth garments.

The Dutch consul Emanuel van Meteren was impressed by how well English women, including the peasants, protected their complexions with hats and veils, and their hands with gloves. Straw hats in particular covered the heads of both sexes out in the fields, right back into antiquity.

Farm labourers began to face serious unemployment from the enclosure acts starting in 1490, which turned crop land into grazing for sheep, thus putting all but shepherds and weavers out of work. Queen Elizabeth I tried to help with the Poor Laws of 1601, putting the responsibility on to the parish, but parishes would drive off 'vagabonds' from elsewhere. The drift of country folk to town began and has continued ever since.

Artisans and professionals

The idea that artisans should be identifiable by their clothes and tools spread to the towns, as Shakespeare makes clear at the start of *Julius Caesar*, where the tribunes Flavius and Marullus rebuke 'a rabble of Citizens':

FLAVIUS: Hence! home, you idle creatures, get you home.
    Is this a holiday? What! know you not,
    Being mechanical, you ought not walk
    Upon a labouring day without the sign
    Of your profession? – Speak, what trade art thou?
CIT: Why, sir, a carpenter.
MAR: Where is thy leather apron and thy rule?
    What dost thou with thy best apparel on?

It was not an official holiday, so the workers could not have the day off, and the cobbler is told to get back to his shop and awl. That these citizens had any best clothes suggests a degree of prosperity, but for a lot of workers, a holiday simply meant leaving off the apron and wearing the same clothes underneath. Leather aprons had appeared for tougher jobs, but the cloth apron was still the widest form of working attire used by both sexes. The term 'mechanical' meant a worker with a handicraft, and the system of employment was revised in 1562 by *Anno Quinto Elizabethae cap.4*: 'An Act containing divers orders for artificers, labourers, servants of husbandry, and apprentices.' It ordered that staff must be engaged for a year in 'the sciences, crafts, mysteries or arts of clothiers, woollen cloth weavers, tuckers, fullers, clothworkers, sheremen, dyers, hosiers, tailors, shoemakers, tanners, pewterers, bakers, brewers, glovers, cutlers, smiths, farriers, couriers, sadlers, spurriers, turners, cappers, hatmakers, feltmakers, bowyers, fletchers, arrow head makers, butchers, cooks and millers'. Employees could not leave in under a year without a certificate. Wages were to be set by the justices of the peace and the sheriffs. Farm labourers' hours were from 5 a.m. to 7 or 8 p.m. in summer. Apprentices had to serve 7 years, and come from landless families to be trained by wheelwrights, ploughwrights, carpenters, mill-wrights, masons, plasterers, sawyers, limeburners, brickmakers and brick layers, tilers, slaters, tile makers, linen weavers, coopers, earthen potters, thatchers and shinglers. (See Appendix 1.)

Many of the modern professional posts began in religious foundations like hospitals of the saints, universities, and seminaries. While the Protestant movement closed down religious institutions like monasteries and Catholic schools, its own clergymen, doctors and teachers were expected to set a modest example by wearing black. University dons still had to be in holy orders, so they continued to dress like priests in gowns, and any teacher of any standing wore black to emphasize his respectability. University dress came under its own statutes at Oxford and Cambridge, with only the noble student allowed rich decoration to show his rank, with coloured gowns, and gold or silver buttons. Gentlemen commoners could have four dozen buttons, but servitor students who earned their place by working for the college were not allowed any buttons. Oxford kept the ban on buttons for yeomen from 1362 right into the seventeenth century.[5]

Swords were not to be worn in the City of London, and the livery guilds had their own rules as to what they considered correct dress. The Guilds of Merchant Tailors and Linen Armourers was licensed by Edward I in 1299, and from time to time it would fine or even imprison members of the fraternity whose clothes it found too shocking. In 1562 it sent Robert Maltby to gaol for wearing a shirt edged with silver, it fined a Mr Elliott for his rich cloak, and in 1575 it warned Richard Dysson that his habit was not fit for a tailor. In 1613 the Guild made a new ordinance which was approved by the Lord Chancellor: 'The ordynance for them that mysorder themselves in theire Apparell and Array'. It ruled that no member:

shall from henceforth take upon him to use or weare any costly array, Garments or apparell within this City, otherwise than shall be decent, meete and fit for his degree and calling and such as a Citizen and Merchant man ought to have and under such manner and forme as it shall be adjudged and deemed by the Maister, Wardens and other Assistant of the said fraternity.[6]

While James I did not issue a law about clothes, the guilds still felt that merchants should not dress better than their customers and so laid down rules to ensure that they did not. The legal approach of the Middle Ages to keeping people in their place had become a tradition which was given new strength by the rise of the Protestant Church and its strong belief in modesty and simplicity in dress. Worldly show was considered sinful, and its wearer an empty vessel not fit for any society.

The town's rules were proclaimed by the town crier, and city officials did not always wait for the government to take action over clothes. In 1532 the city of Coventry banned its common folk from wearing fox or lamb fur and silk or satin doublets, with a fine of £10. A traveller could find him or herself in trouble for wearing something in one city which was not legal at home. The people charged with arresting the guilty were the constables, but their numbers were few. By the end of the century their dress was a blue coat and hat, trimmed with red or gold. The chief constable had a staff with a silver top, but the petty constables and beadles had the plain truncheon. In the seventeenth century watching coats were available for the constables and town watch. These were very long to the ankle and made of rough woollen cloth, and were another version of the overall overcoat. The officers of the law were often made figures of fun by Shakespeare and latter playwrights, as in the *Merry Wives of Windsor* where they search the house for Sir John Falstaff, but fail to locate his hiding place in the laundry basket.

Modesty could be found among citizens' wives; the German merchant Samuel Kiechel from Ulm was very impressed on his visit in 1585:

Item, the women there are charming, and by nature so mighty pretty, as I have scarcely ever beheld, for they do not falsify, paint, or bedaub themselves as in Italy or other places; but they are somewhat awkward in their style of dress; for they dress in splendid stuffs, and many a one wears three cloth gowns or petticoats, one over the other.

This rather suggests that Kiechel made his visit in winter, for before the days of thermal underwear people had to add layer upon layer of clothes to keep warm. The Dutch consul expressed views similar to Kiechel's:

The women are beautiful, fair, well-dressed and modest, which is seen there more than elsewhere, as they go about the street without any covering either of huke or mantle, hood, veil, or the like. Married women only wear a hat both in the street and in the house: those unmarried go without a hat, although ladies of distinction have lately learnt to cover their faces with silken masks or vizards . . .[7]

he observed in 1599. This description, however, can only apply to the London area, for mantles were still being worn in Dorset a hundred years later. Foreigners were often surprised by the relative freedom of women in Protestant England and the Netherlands, where they were not shut up like Spanish ones, could go to market, visit friends, play cards, go to the playhouse, for walks, rides, christenings, churching and funerals. They could even be kissed by strangers by way of greeting. Van Meteren was not without some criticism, for he felt that the English and their servants were as lazy as the Spanish, and lacked the industrious drive of the Dutch and Germans. This could still be said to be true, for the German bureaucrat of today is at his desk by 7 a.m. and the English one not till 9 or even 10 a.m.; the English feeling that life is not only for work is a long-established one. The consul also felt that those wives with servants did not set a good example:

They are well dressed, fond of taking it easy, and commonly leave the care of household matters and drudgery to their servants. They sit before their doors, decked out in fine clothes, in order to see and be seen by passers by.

The annual fairs were the chief markets for cloth and clothes in the Middle Ages, and even the royal tailor would travel round East Anglia to buy his materials in 1200. The centralization of textile sales in London did not develop until the monarchs stopped travelling all round the country on progresses, which were still made in the reign of Elizabeth I. Royal garments were stored in the Tower, until Edward III bought Sir John Beauchamp's house on his death in 1359 and moved the Great Wardrobe there. It was the biggest clothing department in the country, making liveries for the household, personal clothing for the royal family,

mourning, hangings, state canopies, and state robes for ministers and English ambassadors, the royal heirs, and the Knights of the Garter. This creation of a permanent headquarters encouraged merchants to set up nearby at Blackfriars. There was of course an overlap, and fairs continued to be important while shops were increasing in the city.

Professional tailors were male, and they dressed both sexes. John Marreys was tailor to Edward III, Edward Joanes was tailor to Mary I, and Walter Fish tailor to Elizabeth I. Men were also the embroiderers and were required for royal and ecclesiastical vestments, hangings and canopy decoration, and the elaborate decoration of horse furniture. Aprons with pockets for threads and needles were the only specific working garment in these professions, and the master tailor strove to look fashionable, if not too rich.

An additional influence in making London a centre for clothing was the building of the Royal Exchange by Sir Thomas Gresham in 1567 for the convenience of merchants. It imitated the Bourse in Amsterdam with its arcade and square free of traffic. There were about 160 shops upstairs to rent at £2 a year. Most shopkeepers disliked this separation of the shop from the home, since most of them and their apprentices lived on the premises, but the international traders liked the Exchange, so the shopkeepers had to comply. It became the centre for luxuries, with fine fabrics, lace, fine linen caps, shifts, shirts, gloves, silk stockings, ribbons and gauze on sale.

Town maintenance was the responsibility of the councils. In 1375–6 the Mayor of Leicester reported that he had spent 4/6 on street cleaning and 5/– on mending pavements. In 1467, however, Leicester decided to put the cleaning on the citizens' shoulders, ordering:

all men and women that been inhabitauntes of this town that they clense the Kynges stretes every man before his place, as well withinne the gates as in the subberbys of the same. And they that hath muck and swepynges and othere fylthes and corripcions, withinne them do ordeyne a carte before to carye it away, and that they lye not owte at there dors past iii dayes at the most, in payne of imprisonment as long as the Mayre likes and fyne and raunsom to the Kyng.[8]

Doubtless there was much donning of aprons after this. Similarly, in December 1562 the Leet Jury ordered the citizens of Portsmouth to keep the gutters clean, and butchers to wash the market place after slaughtering. It complained about the number of pigs running about the town; the combination of that smelly animal with all the fish being gutted by the fishermen must have made the residents grateful for strong westerlies. The council strictly forbade washing upper and under-clothes in the wells, the moat and the springs, for fear it spread plague, so women had to carry their washing outside the walls.[9] Washing linen was called bucking, and was simpler to do than heavy cloth clothes, which were often shaken and not washed. In Shakespeare's *Merry Wives of Windsor* Mistress Ford sent her foul linen to the laundress at Datchet mead, for as homes had no piped water, washing was done in meadows and river banks, as can still be seen around the world in poor countries. Moorfields in London was a bleaching ground for laying linen in the sun. Washerwomen wore short skirts for wading, straw hats and aprons. The fewer the garments the better as they could get quite wet, so they avoided lots of petticoats. Beaches, ramparts, fields and bushes were all used for drying linen. In city tenements people hung clothes on poles out of the windows. Washing lines did not appear until the seventeenth century. In the *Odyssey* Nausicaa took the dirty clothes in a wagon to the stream and trod on them to get the dirt out, then laying them on the beach to dry: people still do this in some parts of the world.

The clothes of prostitutes did not often concern lawmakers. In 1355 it was ruled that such women had to wear red garments or else striped clothes inside out, to distinguish them from respectable women, but the statutes on dress in 1362, 1463 and 1482 do not mention them. Of course the ban on gold or silver girdles, expensive wimples and coverchiefs concerned prostitutes in that they affected all women of low degree, but these restrictions were not aimed at them exclusively. The City of London did not allow playhouses or brothels, so the South Bank of the Thames became the centre for such businesses. The Bankside brothels were said to have been built for use by the Knights Templar across the river. Henry VII reduced the number of houses to 12, but Henry VIII closed them down; his 'tender Conscience startled at such scandalous and open Lewdness', as Aubrey wrote drily. Individual prostitutes were excommunicated and could not be buried in hallowed ground. The Boar's Head, The Crane, The Cardinal's Hat, The Swan, The Bell, The Crosse-Keys, The Pope's Head, and The Gun, were the signs over the doors. The inmates were known for make-up, hoisted-up skirts and tawdry finery indoors where the law could not see.

For the poor the only chance for 'new' clothes lay in second-hand ones. The supply was greater near cities, where servants sold off the clothing their masters gave them. In the Middle Ages Hog Lane became a centre for such goods, to such an extent that by 1608 the name was changed to Petticoat Lane. This meant that the poor in London could follow the fashion in a way undreamt of by their country cousins, albeit a decade or two behind the mode. 'Cross dressing' was common at the bottom of society, since the poor wore whatever they could get their hands on, regardless of the sex of the previous owner. Itinerant old-clothes sellers were an ancient trade, trudging all over the country to markets.

A huge number of articles were sold in the street, from brushes to pies and pokers. A lot of street sellers were bundles of rags, with one holed garment over another equally gaping in places, as they carried firewood, twig brooms, lavender, wild flowers and fruits. Simplers were mostly women who slept rough in hedges or barns, collected wild herbs, blackberries, mushrooms and such, and then trudged 15 miles to Covent Garden to sell them to the herbalists, and 15 miles back out to the country. They were famous for their dirt, and the only sign of wealth they ever displayed was a fondness for brass bangles. Otherwise they were a jumble of brownish garments, in basic russet, or dirty undyed cloth. It was usual for street traders to walk 25 miles a day, six days a week, on regular routes so that customers would know which days to expect them. Itinerant musicians were another ind of ragged worker, very different to those in noble and ecclesiastical establishments who were given liveries or surplices.

There is some debate as to when ready-made clothes began, but the Roman Army would have been the biggest customer in antiquity, and thereafter huge orders for set types of clothes were common with later armies. In the Middle Ages markets sold some ready-made breeches, gloves, hats, mantles and shoes, for a maker would not come to a complete halt when commissioned orders ran out but would make something else to sell as ready-made, and when a customer returned a garment that too would be sold ready-made, so the trade must be very ancient.

Industry and the sea

Mining dates back to the Stone Age when men used antlers to dig for flints. Britain's mineral wealth was one reason the Romans came, and a Roman gold mine is preserved at Dolaucothi in Wales. The technique was to heat rock then throw cold water on to it to split it. Once gunpowder appeared in the late 1300s that was employed, but many miners were killed in the process. The earliest example of a miner's dress here is in Newland parish church on the Greyndour tomb of the fourteenth century. He wears a sweat cloth round his head, a conventional tunic belted in at the waist, and hose. His light was a stick held in his teeth with a candle at the end, to leave his hands free to carry his pick and his hod. Underground the tunic and hose would be stripped off, for it was traditional for miners to work naked, or almost. In the fifteenth century miners were wearing turbans, but by the 1550s a special costume had appeared in Germany, Flanders, Italy and France. It had a close-fitting hood and a tunic to the waist but at the back it dipped into a tail below the knees. Underneath went traditional hose or the new kneebreeches. The special tail could have been to protect the back of the legs when pulling a coal trolley along underground or to sit on when hacking at a coal face. In either case, it may have been padded. Queen Elizabeth invited

some German mining experts to England and they may have brought the costume with them, since it was so common in the continental mines of coal and ore. Women were employed underground too, and on the surface to sieve ore and coal, often wearing only shifts. When pulling coal trucks underground some started to wear kneebreeches, since the chain passed between the legs. There were no laws concerning safety clothing. Carpenters were much employed at mines to line the shafts, make the windlasses and the buckets, the pit props, the wagons and the wooden rails. They wore aprons of linen or sheepskin, often with the wool shaved but not shorn off completely, so that the surface would absorb paint and stains. Otherwise, they wore the standard tunic and hose, and the introduction of various kinds of kneebreeches like canions and Venetians did not completely oust hose until the seventeenth century.

Water made industry possible. Not only did it cool, clean and form a constituent part of industrial processes, but it powered the watermills, and carried the products by boat and barge to the customers. Watermills were common in Roman times, and the Domesday Book recorded 5,000 in southern England in 1086, preceding windmills. Monasteries had several watermills to sieve flour, grind corn, hammer cloth into felt, shine linen, turn fulling machines and tan leather. Water was the cheapest form of transport. Once the Romans left, the roads deteriorated and became impassable muddy quagmires in winter. A horse can tow 30 tons in a barge, but only pull a cart with five-eighths of a ton on a bad road, while a packhorse could only carry one-eighth of a ton, so improving the waterways was important. Da Vinci invented a mitred lock gate at Milan in 1497 and this was copied at Exeter in 1564. In 1600 England had 700 miles of navigable river, which was increased by 1760 to 1,300 miles through the construction of weirs, cuts and canals, before the Duke of Bridgewater appeared on the scene. There were no distinctive costumes here but the conventional tunics, hoods, and hose for the men, and short skirts for the women – this applied to all women working on or by water.[10]

3. Sebastian Muenster, 'Cosmographia Universalis', 1550. The special mining costume that was common across Europe, with its tail and hood. The miner at the right at the face uses his tail to sit on. Underneath go hose and a codpiece. This German metal mine has a wooden railway on the left, and a diviner goes in quest of other metals on top. The hammering of ore was often done by women.

The biggest industry was cloth. Regulations issued by Richard III in 1483 in *Anno Primo Ricardi III cap. viii* state that broadcloth must be two yards wide and 24 yards long, and be watered before sale. A half cloth should be 12 yards long. Streit cloth must be one yard wide and 12 yards long. Kersey cloth was to be one yard wide and 18 yards long. The weavers were either full-time workers, or else husbandmen farmers trying to supplement the income from their smallholdings. Women were the basis of the whole industry, because it was the spinster at home who produced the yarn from the wool, and five spinsters were thought necessary to keep one weaver supplied with yarn. Fine linen was imported from Harlem, which Fynes Morrison visited in 1593: 'The Citie makes great store of linnen clothes, and hath five hundred spinsters in it.'[11] The fact that the word 'spinster' came to denote a certain female status shows just how many women were involved in spinning. The spinning wheel was invented in the fourteenth century and had to be turned by hand, so it involved two operations, but the foot treadle appeared in the 1500s, freeing both hands to feed the yarn. Their dress was the apron, of course, together with the conventional dress of ordinary women: a simple frock with sleeves, and a linen cap, or coif, which was also worn widely by men in the Middle Ages. When spinning outdoors the women would don a straw hat or a hood for that essential protection of the complexion from the sun. A lot of cloth was undyed and formed the natural blanket cloth the law required ordinary folk to wear. Weavers were usually men but could be helped by their wives, and were not distinctive in their dress.

When smelting iron some form of protective clothing was desirable but not required by law, so it was left to the workers to devise their own, such as cloths round the face, and very loose tunics because of the heat, sometimes with hoods attached. Boots were probably common, though illustrations do not show them, but when liquid iron was being poured out some sturdy footwear would have been necessary to cover the hose. Leggings and gloves were probably also worn.

Women had to hammer the ore, usually outside, so they wore dirty old dresses, mantles, coifs and aprons.

The Roman navy had blue uniforms and blue sails as camouflage and this continued into the Byzantine navy, so blue for sailors goes back a long way. The best preserved Roman naval base is at the top of Portsmouth Harbour, at Portchester Castle (from the Latin *portus castra*). It was Alfred the Great who decided that the entrance to the harbour was preferable for high water and established his base across the water at Portesmutha. There was no distinction in England between sailors and civilians, and the latter were press-ganged into the fleet when required, unlike the Army. Britain being an island, the Navy needs dominated, and it grew or shrank enormously in war and peace, pressing men in their thousands and discarding them afterwards.

Fishermen, shepherds, labourers and tradesmen could be rounded up to serve on ships, wearing their own clothes until they fell to pieces, as no uniforms were supplied by the Royal Navy in the Middle Ages. Professional sailors onboard were outnumbered by soldiers and press-ganged men during wartime, since battles were mainly of a hand-to-hand kind. The Cinque Ports, however, did give their men a uniform, a blue tunic, drawers, stockings and shoes. Chaucer described his mariner or shipman 'all in a gowne of falding to the knee', which was a very rough cloth garment. Fifteenth-century manuscripts show some sailors in a gown with a hood, wide sleeves to the elbow, and slits at the hem to make it easier to climb the rigging, very similar in outline to the smelters' costume. Fishermen always copied sailors, as they both liked to consider themselves distinct from landlubbers, so they adopted these gowns. By the 1570s to 80s a very wide kind of kneebreech was beginning to appear, called 'galligaskins' or 'slops', which remained popular at sea into the nineteenth century. Equally popular were trousers, for when Christophe Weiditz sailed to Spain in 1529 he wore the sailor's tunic and trousers as the best protection for wet conditions, and trousers or slops became the distinctive mark of sailors for

Empire women in trousers were common, and the Moresco women in Spain wore kneebreeches which Weiditz saw in 1529, but they both covered themselves with mantles when going outdoors. In Western Europe, however, it was the sea which put women into trousers, albeit disguised as men to begin with.

Dockyards expanded once cannon were taken to sea and bigger ships had to be built to carry them, like the *Henry Grace à Dieu* and the *Mary Rose*. Carpenters, cannon casters, joiners, painters, ropemakers, iron workers, sailmakers, brewers and ships' biscuit bakers were all in demand. Aprons dominated, in leather, canvas or rough linen, as the common working garment worn over their one set of home-made or second-hand clothes. The most common headgear in docks and at sea became the Monmouth cap, a knitted cap in brown wool. Shakespeare described 'Welshmen, wearing leeks in their Monmouth caps' in *Henry V*, IV.iii, and Drake ordered 36 dozen caps in 1596 for his expedition to the West Indies. Given the proximity of Monmouthshire to Bristol, the Monmouth cap was exported in great numbers to the new American colonies, for settlers and slaves.[12]

4. Sebastian Muenster, 'Cosmographia Universalis', 1550. This smelting works has a waterwheel-powered bellows. The special costume gives more protection than the miner's outfit, but like it it has a hood. The side slits resemble those on sailors' gowns to allow for action. The boy with the wheelbarrow wears a miner's costume.

centuries. Canvas was also used for clothes; especially when a gale had torn the sails and sailors used them to make garments. Grease and tar were used to waterproof clothes; hence the term 'Jack Tar'. Leather doublets were worn by officers but would be too expensive for the crew. The very first women in trousers in Western Europe were those who went to sea, either in disguise as a man for adventure and higher pay, or else smuggled onboard as wife or girl friend but emerging to act as a nurse during action. Of course in the Turkish

Servants

The servant was often the best dressed and the best fed of all workers, particularly if he or she was employed in a great house, but the establishments were all male in the Middle Ages, except for a few ladies-in-waiting or nurses. The entire household of Edward II in June 1323 was a steward, a treasurer of the wardrobe, a chamberlain, a controller, a cofferer, a clerk of the counting table, the Clerk of the Privy Seal and his four clerks, the Clerk Purveyor for the Great Wardrobe, the Clerk of the Spicery, the sergeant under usher of the wardrobe and the porter of the same, a squire fruiterer and a sergeant chandler, two valets to work in wax, a confessor, a chief chaplain, an almoner, an under almoner and a valet of the almonery, a physician, a surgeon, a clerk of the market, a coroner of the household, infants who were wards of the king, the esquires of the king's mouth, esquires of the king's chamber and the valets thereof, the serjeants-at-arms, the Knight Marshal, the Knight Chief Usher and two serjeant ushers of the Hall, a fuer to strew rushes, two knights and two serjeants as Marshalls of the Hall, a Surveyor of the Dresser (where plate was displayed), assayers, esquires of the Hall, a Clerk of the Pantry and his underclerk, panterers, waferers, bakehouse men, a napper in charge of linen, a ewer in charge of water vessels, a launderer, the butlery, kitchen, larder, poultry, garbage, scullery, saucery and ports marshaly (transport) staffs, a serjeant valet warden or *herbejour* of the king's palfreys and carthorses, the huntsmen, ferreter, partringer, birdtaker, fisher, and messengers, trumpeters and archers. Nobody was allowed into the royal household unless in royal office and livery, under pain of imprisonment. The only females would have been among the wards.[13] Over the next three centuries women began to infiltrate the system because they were economical in that they were paid less and were not dressed in coats-of-arms. When a ruler or peer found himself in need of retrenchment he took on women servants instead of men. The situation so changed that by the time Celia Fiennes visited the West Country in 1685 she considered a Mr Newbey singularly whimsical as he would not employ women but had men to do the washing, the ironing and run the dairy – which by then had become a feminine occupation.

The term 'livery' included food, heating, and health care, and it was granted twice a year in kind, and by the fifteenth century in money. Thus references to livery in accounts do not mean clothing unless that is specified. The household book of Edward IV in 1461–82 gives the duties of the King's personal staff. The four esquires of the body waited on the King and received 'clothing with the household for winter and Somer, or els in keeping with this Court'. Another four esquires of the body had to dress and undress the King: 'Cloathing with the howshold winter and summer, or fortie shilling beside watching cloathing'. The four yeomen of the chamber had to make the beds,

5. Christophe Weiditz, 'Himself in sailor's costume', 1529. The artist dressed as a sailor for his voyage to Spain. The tunic and trousers are not very different from peasant wear, but sailors clung to trousers when peasants began to adopt kneebreeches in the seventeenth century, so that trousers became a sort of maritime identity for fishermen and sailors. An alternative was extra-wide kneebreeches from the 1580s, called slops.

set the hangings, and carry torches. They also received the household livery or 18s. and watching clothes. Twenty squires had to attend the King when he went riding, 'and clothing winter and sommer, of the Compting House, or else xi[s]. It hath ever bine in speciall charge to squires in the Court to weare the Colour of the Kinges livery Customably for the more glory'. Esquires also had to be able to entertain the court with singing, playing the harp or pipe, telling the chronicles of the kings, and talking about policies. If sick, esquires were entitled to the same allowance as knights with a bed to themselves. Sick yeomen were two to the bed, as in ordinary hospitals then.[14]

It seems that the Church had been granting too many liveries, for in 1411 Henry IV ordered that no archbishop, bishop, abbot or prior was to give livery except to their own menials and officers. Similarly, knights should not give livery cloth or hats to others than the members of their own household staff, or face a fine of 100s., and 40s. for the recipient. Royal esquires were given privileges, for Edward IV's sumptuary law of 1463 allowed them to wear satin damask, while the steward, the chamberlain, the treasurer, and the comptroller of the King's household were allowed to wear sables and ermine. In 1510 Henry VIII ruled that ordinary serving men could not have more than 2½ yards of cloth in their garments, and no hose over 20d. unless their master gave them better. Elizabeth I also expressed displeasure that some servants were not being dressed correctly and in 1559 ordered all lords to check which servants were too well clothed for their situation, with a record of the unlawful garments to be kept in the Counting House. Obviously some lords had been showing off by giving their servants more splendid liveries than the Queen thought proper, but this was to be a common failure.[15]

In the 1300s checked clothes and garments in two contrasting colours (*mi-parti*) were the height of fashion, but by the end of that century were going out of vogue, so people started to allow their servants to wear such clothing. *Mi-parti* became a tradition for servants throughout the fifteenth century down to the reign of Elizabeth I, as the accounts for Eton College in 1571–2 show, when it had some servants' clothing made for its dramatic productions:

ij servantes cotes of black cotten welted with yelowe
a servantes cote of whyte & black cotten/checker wourke
a servantes cote of redde & whyte cotten/checker wourke

ij servantes cotes for children which hathe one quarters of redd silke & and an other of blew silke.[16]

Not all servants were humbly born. At court, pages could be the children of gentlemen or noblemen, and a ducal establishment could have minor lords serving in the top posts, while the mediaeval custom was for peers to send their sons to the homes of other peers or bishops to be educated and trained as squires. When Frederick Duke of Wirtemberg visited London in 1592 he classified the pages with the lords, saying that they both kept servants:

They keep many retainers, for the most part portly and good-looking men who go without cloaks, but have only jerkins, of their lord's colour and bearing his arms rolled up and buckled behind; they likewise have the same arms upon their sleeves, so that they may be distinguished.

This was for the men who accompanied their masters as both bodyguard and escort. The women servants received only plain dresses and aprons. In 1598 the anonymous IM complained that a fashionable lady wanted too many men servants:

yf their Mistress ryde abrode, she must have vi or viii Serving-men to attende her, she must have one to carrie her Cloake and Hood, least it raine, another her Fanne, if she use it not herselfe, another her Box with Ruffes and other necessaries, another behinde whom her Mayde or Gentlewoman must ryde [with], and some must be loose to open Gates, and supply other Services.[17]

He also maintained that because of inflation the £100 that would be enough to maintain a gentleman's establishment in the past was now insufficient, and over £300 would be necessary. An aristocratic establishment obviously cost much more, but a drop in the size took place over the centuries. In the 1400s earls and bishops would have had households of 500–600 persons, but in the 1500s 100–200 persons became more common as the nobility started to reside in houses instead of castles, which needed less staff. Everybody who served in a household was regarded as part of that family, and in many country villages generations of servants came from the same families to serve in the family of the lord or lady, children of the one serving the children of the other.

TWO

The Seventeenth Century

Agriculture

This was the age, complained John Aubrey, when English shepherds in his native Wiltshire stopped wearing sheepskins:

Their Habit (I believe) is that of the Roman or Arcadian Shepherds too, sc. a long white Cloake with a very deep cape, which comes downe half way their backs, made of the locks of the Sheep; their Armature was a Sheep Crooke, a Sling, a Scrip, their Tar-box, a Pipe (or Flute), and their Dog. But since 1671 they are growne so luxurious as to neglect their ancient warme and usefull fashion and goe à la mode.[1]

He blamed the Civil War for destroying many local traditions, but one which survived into this century was nailed boots, which date back to the Roman army. Pepys was delighted by an old shepherd near Epsom Springs in 1667:

We took notice of his woolen knit stockings of two colours mixed, and of his shoes shod with Iron shoes, both at the toe and heel, and with great nails in the soles of his feet, which was mighty pretty.[2]

Nail patterns in the boots became a country tradition which entered town. Forde's play *Love's Labrynth; or, The Royal Shepherdess*, of 1660, speaks of shepherds playing bagpipes, which, coupled with Aubrey's reference to pipes and flutes, shows that they played to themselves out on the Downs. Knitting was also a common activity for men and women while watching sheep; Welsh shepherdesses in particular were regarded as wizards with the needles, making Monmouth caps.

Shepherdesses were too beloved of poets for the reality to come through very often, but the verses about the Jacobean beauty Mrs Overall seem accurate:

With her Mantle tuck'd up high,
She foddered her flock,
So bucksome and alluringly
Her knee upheld her smock.

Just a mantle and smock or shift would be the clothing of poorer working women along with woollen stockings, shoes and a straw hat. Poets waxed lyrical about shepherds wearing green on May Day, but since they were too poor to buy new clothes, this meant simply that they wore green branches and garlands. Foreign accounts of the Englishwomen not wearing mantles are shown to be inaccurate outside the London region, as the lawyer Roger North found on his legal circuits in 1680:

The counties near London, as Hampshire and parts of Wiltshire have little singular to be noted, either of strangeness of situation, or character of the people, more than ordinary; but on coming into Dorsetshire, the country grows new, and things looked a little strange; the people spoke oddly, and the women wore white mantles which they call whitells.[3]

This shows how Edward III's statute decreeing undyed blanket cloth for the lower orders had become a firm tradition in the West Country. Celia Fiennes, the first woman to undertake a survey of England, found russet tones too in Taunton in 1698:

. . . you meete all sorts of country women wrapp'd up in manteles called West Country rockets, a large mantle doubled together of a sort of serge, some are linseywolsey, and a deep fringe or fag at the lower end; these hang downe some to their feete some only just below the wast, in the summer they are in white garments of this sort, in the winter they are in red ones; I call them garments because they never go out without

them and this is the universal fashion in Somerset and Devonshire and Cornwall.[4]

She did not venture nearer to Wales than Holly Well where they spoke Welsh, and found 'the inhabitants go barefoote and bare leg'd, a nasty sort of people'. As a fine lady she was shocked by naked limbs, but it is possible that some kind of mantle was worn over the bare legs. They certainly were on the Scottish borders, only there they were called plaids. Celia Fiennes only crossed into Border country north of Carlisle, where the locals lived by fishing and digging peat for fuel, with bare-legged women and girls leading wide-wheeled carts:

these people tho' with naked leggs are yet wrapp'd up in plodds a piece of woollen like a blanket or else rideing hoods, and this when they are in their houses.

She thought them idle, and did not go any further; crossing back to England at the river Essex, she found plaids there too. Given the shortage of bridges, people had to wade across rivers, with their clothes held up and their shoes and stockings in their hands. She thought some of the people so doing seemed superior to ordinary folk, but they too wore plaids. Fynes Moryson found Irish country folk also wearing mantles. In Dublin, Waterford and Galway, the population were mostly dressed cleanly in English urban styles, but in the wilds it was barbaric nudity with only a linen rag over the organs and a mantle on top. The Irish gentry were still wearing fifteenth-century tight hose and breeches in one, as tights (which allowed the outline of the sexual organs to be seen), a loose coat and a three-cornered mantle. Their shirts, dyed with saffron, were worn until they fell to pieces; the saffron was supposed to keep off lice. The ladies had a gown laced at the breast, and the mantle, with layers of linen on the head reminding Moryson of Turkish turbans. Thus from Somerset to Scotland to Ireland, the most common covering was the mantle.[5]

Closer to London, country girls tried to follow the fashion. Comte Gramont was impressed in 1665 by the market girls at Tunbridge Wells: 'young, fair, fresh-coloured country girls, with clean linen, small straw hats, and neat shoes and stockings', selling produce. No doubt when nobility visited the town scruffy girls would have been driven off! Red, as a form of traditional russet, could be seen in another place near London, Audley End, which Charles II's Queen, Catherine of Braganza, the Duchess of Richmond and the Duchess of Buckingham decided to visit in 1670: 'it was a frolick to disguise themselves like country lasses, in red petticoats, wastcoats, etc. and so goe to see the faire . . .'. They attracted a crowd, however, because 'they had all so overdone it in their disguise, and look'd so much like Antiques than country volk', and their courtly accents also betrayed them. The wearing of petticoats and sleeveless waistcoats shows the presence of the common European peasant dress in England, slightly more fashionable than smocks and mantles, but shorter in the skirt than ladies wore, and often covered with linen aprons. White linen caps or coifs remained standard for married women, and were usually covered by straw hats out of doors. Pepys visited Hatfield in August 1667: 'there the women had pleasure in putting on some straw hats, which are much worn in this country'.

The hats were mostly made there, too. A lot of unmarried girls wore linen caps as well, in total contrast to the court where the ladies had ceased to do so. Proximity to the fashion centre was the dominant factor for working dress in southern England, for the court launched styles, as Fynes Moryson explained in 1617: 'All manner of attire came first into the City and the Countrey from the Court which once received by the common people, and by the very Stage Players themselves, the Courtiers justly cast off and take new fashions

6. Anon., 'Pontefract Castle, Yorkshire', c.1635. Reproduced by Gracious Permission of Her Majesty The Queen. The shepherd in the foreground, with his pipe and scrip, wears a sleeveless jerkin of sheepskin tied on with a belt. After the Civil War such traditional dress for shepherds began to disappear in England, although it survived in Europe. A train pack of pack horses sets off, probably laden with Yorkshire kersey cloth. Travellers arrive at the inn.

(though somewhat too curiously).' James I did consider passing some laws about clothes, but dropped the idea as too difficult to police. Moryson recognized that there was a problem over enforcement: 'In the generall pride of *England* there is no fit difference made of degrees for many Bankrouts, Players and Cutpurses, goe apparelled like Gentlemen. Many good Laws have been made against this Babylonian confusion, but either Merchants buying out the penaltie, or the Magistrates not inflicting punishments, have made the multitude of Lawes hitherto unprofitable.'[7] The last sumptuary law in England was issued by Charles I in 1643 to restrict the wearing of gold and silver, which hardly applied to the masses, and when Parliament cut his head off in 1649 they declared his laws invalid.

A country which had decapitated her king was not going to be afraid of copying court fashion, even if only in second-hand clothes, after the higher sections of society had finished with them. This democratic trend puzzled many foreign visitors. Why did the English worker around London imitate his betters by wearing his old clothes, instead of maintaining his own traditional styles? On the Continent, however, sumptuary laws continued to be enforced, and England was unique in the seventeenth century for dispensing with them in 1643. Charles II was asked to revive such laws but the only one he proceeded with was one obliging people to be buried in woollen shrouds. Thus the population was free to imitate upper-class fashion if it could, and this could be seen most clearly in men's suits. The fashion for the 'underwear' doublet and hose of the fifteenth century continued to be worn by some peasant men into the 1620s, ignoring the kneebreeches the Elizabethan nobility introduced, but under Charles I court fashion became increasingly simple in silhouette, gradually eliminating the slashes, panes and padded sleeves for a plain doublet and narrow kneebreeches. Of course Charles I's suits were in satin, not cloth, and the fashionable lace collars were fabulously expensive, so the mode was not intended for the masses. Given its simplicity, however, it could be copied in cloth with plain

7. Isaac Fuller, 'Charles II changing at Whiteladies', *c.*1661. After the Restoration Charles II had this record of his escape in 1651 made. Assuming a disguise he encountered the coarse home-made country suit and the tough boots, to his discomfort, but it was of course what the majority had to endure. This simple combination of doublet/jacket and kneebreeches became the standard costume for working men, and is still worn by gamekeepers, with slimmer kneebreeches.

linen collars, and copied it was. In fact, the hip-length doublet and the kneebreeches became a traditional working suit which survived into the Victorian period, and still persists in the clothing of contemporary gamekeepers in the country.

Charles II had to wear a country suit in 1651 when escaping after his defeat at Worcester, and very uncomfortable he found the experience: 'his travelling four days and three night on foot, every step up to his knees in dirt, with nothing but a green coat, and a pair of country shoes, that made him so sore all over his feet that he could hardly stir.'[8]

When Aubrey criticized shepherds for following the mode, he meant that they had started wearing suits, although in very rough wool. The roughness was stressed by Moryson: 'Husbandmen weare garments of coarse cloth, made at home, and their wives weare gownes of the same cloth, kirtles of light stuffe, with linnen aprons, and cover their heads with a linnen coyfe, and a high felt hat, and in generall their linnen is course, and made at home.'[9] The husbandman's duty was to rear the sheep and shear them; the wife then had to turn the fleece into wool. Gervase Markham's *The English Hus-wife* of 1615 gives a lot of detail here. The wife, he said, should sort the wool into coarse and fine piles, and then decide which she wanted to have dyed and which left white. He said the perfect wife should be able to do her own dyeing, but there were professionals to help those less talented. The wife should comb and card the wool to remove any knots, then at her spinning wheel turn it into yarn. It was best to spin yarn for the warp tighter than the yarn for the weft, but Markham had to admit that many wives did not bother to distinguish the two. Once spun, the yarn was to be taken to market to be sold to weavers, if there was more wool than the family needed, or taken straight to a weaver to be woven into cloth, from which the wife should then make all the family's clothes such as doublets, breeches, kirtles and cloaks, as well as having made their linen wear. The wives were also responsible for marketing the produce. This was in addition to all her other household duties.

Markham insisted that she should also dress modestly: 'Let therefore the Hus-wifes garments bee comely, clean and strong, made as well to preserve the health, as to adorne the person, altogether without toiish garnishes, or the glosse of light colours, and as farre from the vanity of new and fantastique fashions, as neere to the comely imitations of modest Matrons.'[10] When the country housewife found any time for vanity, he did not say.

The Protestant clothing ethic, dating from the sixteenth century, stressed sobriety of attire with dark colours, but the majority of country folk were too poor to dress in any other way. John Evelyn got very annoyed with his local parson at Wotton in Surrey who twice denounced luxury and pride in dress when the congregation consisted entirely of poor country folk, not ostentatious courtiers. The dress of the country wife changed little in its basic components of a bodice, sleeves and skirt, with the hem to calf- or ankle-length, between 1400 and 1600. During the 1640s a fashion for hitching up the gown skirt to show the petticoat was imported from the Netherlands, and very gradually percolated downwards through society, imitated firstly by milkmaids, shopgirls and servant girls in London, then over the next fifty years finding its way out round the counties.

Wooden-soled shoes, or clogs, were worn widely, especially in the western side of the kingdom which receives the most rain from the Atlantic. The English refused to wear the French all-wood sabots, and preferred the leather-topped, wooden-soled clog. In January the Shuttleworths of Gawthorpe Hall, Lancashire, ordered 'a pre of clogges for the cow boy *vjd*.', and in 1602 paid *iijd*. for having shoes clogged for another boy. In 1688 Randle Holme called clogs 'a Countryman's shoe', and not until the nineteenth century did they become associated with industry.[11]

The idea of the unemployed attending statute fairs had still not become established north of London. The gentleman farmer, Henry Best of Elmswell in the East Riding, in 1641 makes no mention of fairs or markets. Hiring of staff took place at a sitting, when the chief constable sat in the inn:

About a fortnight or tenne dayes afore Martynmasse the cheife constable of every division sendeth abroad his recepts to all pettie constables, willinge them to give notice to all masters and servants within their several constableries howe he intendeth to sitte att such a place on such a day, commanding everie of them to bringe in a bill of the names of all masters and servants within theire severall constableries.

Once arrived at a town, the chief constable would require all masters to pay him a penny a head if they wanted to keep staff. If a servant was allowed to leave, the servant had to pay the constable twopence, and be given a ticket of permission to change jobs. Some farmworkers would bargain for clothes: 'Some servants will (at their hyringe) condition to have an old suit, a payre of breeches, an olde hatt, or a payre of shoes; and mayde servants to have an apron, or smocke, or both.' Best also said they would try to make a good impression:'When servants goe to the sittings, they putte on their best apparell, that theire master may see them well cladde.'[12]

The check on pay was honouring Edward III's statute, and Elizabeth I's ruling that workers had to remain at a post for one year before they could change. All workers were called 'servants' into this century. The requests for old clothes illustrates how labourers' clothing was usually second-hand.

Smock frocks were spreading from the Netherlands, either as a loose coat of linen, or else going over the head as a closed garment. In both cases the smock frock was plain, without smocking. It could be any length the individual wearer liked, to the knee or below. While no examples survive from this period, later smock frocks were waxed and oiled for waterproofing, so it is quite likely that earlier smock frocks were also treated in this traditional manner. Grease, linseed oil, and tar were all painted on to textiles. Greatcoats existed for the better-off, and the overall appeared in the 1670s, then meaning an overcoat. This was eagerly adopted by travellers and coachdrivers, but poor labourers had to wait for an old one to come on to the market. When working in the wet, the labourer had to employ smock frocks or mantles, or even straw capes, with clogs or nailed boots to keep his

8. W. Hollar, 'Mulier Anglica habitans in Pago', 1643. This well-dressed country wife comes from the London area and follows the fashionable line, albeit simply. The linen coif was worn at all times, with a straw or felt hat outdoors. Her linen neckerchief and apron would be home-made, but the well-tailored bodice could be bought from a professional, while the braid on the skirt shows an acquaintance with court styles. In the London region everyone tried to copy the court, even if at fifth hand.

9. Set of clothes from a grave at Barrock, Caithness, c.1700. Away from London, in the West Country, Wales, Cumberland, Ireland and Scotland, mantles, rockets and plaids were worn as protection for both sexes, a custom which dates back to antiquity. The jacket, vest, kneebreeches, hat, stockings and plaid are all in home-spun cloth. The plaid was brightly striped but the peat has turned all the garments brownish. Poorer Scots would have discarded the kneebreeches as a feminine weakness and wrapped the plaid around their middles.

feet dry, both well applied with goose fat. The countryside was known for its smells.

Trousers continued down at that level in society, but as they also appear in a couple of clothing accounts in the century, they were evidently worn by the aristocracy, too, on occasion. In 1664 James Cecil, third Earl of Salisbury, bought a pair of worsted trousers from his tailor Mr Templar for £1.10s., and in 1672 Charles Stuart, Duke of Richmond, took worsted trousers with him on his embassy to Denmark, along with worsted drawers and waistcoats, as he rightly expected it to be cold. Similarly, ploughmen out in the fields in the cold could wear trousers.[13] They were not fashionable garments so they did not appear in portraits, but this does not mean that they did not exist outside fashion, as a form of functional dress.

Enclosures continued to gather pace, with more land being monopolized for sheep, so the drift of farm labourers townwards carried on, as the number of jobs in the countryside gradually diminished. While the whole village was called out for harvest time, this was temporary work insufficient to maintain a family. Alternative work was needed, so they travelled to town, and some turned to crime.

With good-quality clothes so expensive, and since the yearly income of members of the nobility exceeded what peasants could earn in a lifetime, the garments of the upper classes were desirable objects as far as robbers and highwaymen were concerned. These characters often dressed in what they stole, if it was not too rich, and when Fynes Moryson encountered some French highwaymen they told him it was not a robbery but a clothes exchange, whipping off his fine English hat and slapping on one of their old greasy French ones. They took his shirt, his cloak, his sword, and, unfortunately, his doublet, where Moryson had hidden money in the quilting in the vain hope of outwitting any robbers. They left him his jerkin and his hose inlaid with gold lace, which had obviously attracted their attention in the first place, although Moryson had worn a shabby cloak over all. The important object they did not take was his medicine box, in which he had hidden more money underneath some foul-smelling ointment, so with that the unfortunate traveller was able to get home to England, but when he reached his sister's house her new manservant chased after him thinking that such a shabby-looking wretch had no right to set foot in a lady's residence.[14] The long-drawn-out wars for Dutch independence and the battles of the Protestant north against Catholic imperialism were another source of clothing for thieves and scavengers, who after a battle would strip the dead bodies of everything they wore, to sell at markets and fairs; thus one could find poor girls sporting items of military splendour that had known braver days.

Behind an army trudged its womenfolk and babies, often clad in rags, for the wife who lost contact with a soldier husband could end up destitute. Such women acted as cooks and nurses, sometimes carrying wounded men on their backs. If they started out in respectable plain dress, by the end of the campaign their clothes could be quite a mixture of patched and acquired articles from both sexes, such as a dead man's boots, an enemy cloak, and an ex-officer's hat decorated with gunshot holes. History books ignore their existence, but before there was an army medical corps their presence was essential.

Artisans, trades, professions

The Protestant ethic changed the clothes worn by professionals from colour to black sobriety, which was further reinforced by the Puritan regime during the Civil War. Lawyers, university dons in holy orders, teachers, doctors of medicine, and apothecaries were all wearing black suits or else dark grey, on an increasing scale. Even the Parliamentary Secretary of State for Foreign Affairs, John Thurloe, in 1652 dressed entirely in a black suit and cloak with only a white collar and cuffs, and so did the Royalist Secretary of State Sir Edward Nicholas, whose black skull cap, black gown, and black suit made him look rather like a bishop. Sobriety of dress was very much a middle-class development, and it was another two hundred years before the aristocracy and the workers started to wear black in any numbers, but it all started with the establishment of Protestantism. Modesty was also expected of civil servants, and when Samuel Pepys, Clerk of the Acts at the Navy Office, tried to do otherwise, he was reprimanded. Lord Sandwich's servant, Creed, told him that gold-laced sleeves were too singular for a government servant, and Pepys had to have the gold lace taken off. There might no longer be a law against sporting gold lace, but the social attitude took longer to relax. Modesty of dress for the king's servants spread across religious divisions, for in France ministers were expected not to challenge the monarch with their clothes. Louis XIV's Controller General of Finances, Colbert, wore black relieved only by the order of the Saint Esprit, and the king's secretary, Rose, always wore a black suit, a black skull cap, a short black cloak and white bands. Nevertheless, by the end of the reign the Duke of Saint Simon Vermandois was accusing the king of allowing his ministers too much freedom by treating them as extensions of himself, so that they stopped wearing black and started wearing periwigs and velvet coats like noblemen of quality. In Britain, however, black became firmly established among the professionals.

Women were not allowed to attend grammar schools or universities, so their education varied greatly from family to family. Some girls had good governesses, others none, and a lot of letters show that women had problems with spelling as they were rarely trained; even the queens regnant Mary and Anne were not educated for the job. The governess Hannah Woolley had no doubt that it was a male conspiracy: 'I am induced to believe we are debarred from the knowledge of humane learning, lest our pregnant wits should rival the towring conceits of our insulting Lords and Masters', she wrote in 1675, in her *Gentlewoman's Companion*. Women could be humble mistresses in village schools, or private governesses, but all higher education was barred to them. Poor and plainly dressed, with caps and aprons, they were kept at the bottom rung of the educational ladder.

This was particularly obvious in the area of

10. Nicholas Maes, 'The Milkwoman', *c*.1660. This Dutch costume is the basis of later European women's peasant dress, with its linen shift, front-fastened bodice to which sleeves can be attached, plain skirt and straw hat. The bodice could be boned and in England was called a corset or waistcoat. The copper milk vessels and the yoke were common on both sides of the Channel.

midwifery where doctors denied women knowledge of their own anatomy. A midwife of 30 years' experience, Jane Sharp, argued in 1671 that the Bible did not mention male midwives, so why could only men study anatomy at university, when it was a female occupation hallowed by the scriptures? In 1687 Elizabeth Cellier proposed that there ought to be a royal hospital to train midwives because the lack of proper training was responsible for the high rate of mortality:

within the Space of twenty years last past, above six thousand women have died in child-bed, more than thirteen thousand children have been born abortive, and above five thousand chrysome (christened) infants have been buried, within the weekly bills of mortality: above two thirds of which, amounting to sixteen thousand souls, have in all probability perished, for want of due skill and care, in those women who practise the art of midwifery.[15]

James II agreed to establish the hospital under royal charter, but he was driven into exile in 1688, and the proposal was forgotten. The French had a school for midwives at the Hotêl Dieu in Paris, which meant of course that the rich would send to France for a midwife, but the less wealthy English were left to the mercy of native midwives who had to pick the subject up as they went along. Midwives were distinguished by their extremely long aprons right down to the ground, as they could get covered in blood and water, but otherwise they dressed like a housewife in a plain dress, with a cap, a neckpiece, and possibly working sleeves, as other trades had them by now. Doctors were expensive, so many people resorted to the village wise woman or 'doctress' cum midwife for herbal cures. Jane Sharp recommended the boiled leaves of lupins, pines and cypresses to deal with lice, frankincense and rose leaves for baby's dusting powder, and brimstone and wormwood for pests. These were certainly less dangerous than the blood-letting that the doctors believed in. Thomas Hobbes, the philosopher, said he 'would rather have the advice, or take Physique from an experienced old woman, that had been at many sick People's Bed-sides, than from the learnedst but unexperienced Physitian'. However, there was no training for nurses, and women were expected to be able to nurse by instinct.[16]

For doctresses (as they were then called) to have their own cures was seen as a threat by the male medical establishment, and the campaign against witches was sometimes no more than an attempt to kill the competition. There was never, however, a special working costume for 'witches' because that would have been suicide. Witches or wise women dressed in exactly the same way as other village women, with a homespun linen cap and apron, and the simple woollen dress, donning

a mantle in winter, and with a straw or felt hat depending on the season.

As there were no longer laws about the colours people could wear, traditional russet and undyed cloth were now challenged by native woad. In about 1694 Celia Fiennes passed a woad works at Hailes Abbey, but the smell was so strong her horse refused to go nearer. Blue began to be associated with certain trades, as can be seen in Pepys' description of the fight at Moorfields in July 1664 when it was election day for the Weavers' Company and the apprentices ran wild: 'At first all the butchers knock down all the weavers that had green or blue aprons, till they were fain to pull them off and put them in their breeches. At last, the butchers were fain to pull off their sleeves that they might not be known, and were soundly beaten.'[17] Thus the weavers had blue or green aprons, and the butchers oversleeves. The journalist Ned Ward described 'a *Butcher* with his *Blew Sleeves*, and *Wooll-Apron*,' and also wrote that blue smock frocks were typical of butchers and tallow chandlers, so blue was becoming established in those trades.

Aprons and oversleeves were also worn by the public executioners, as two plays make clear. In Samuel Pordage's *Herod and Mariamne* of 1673, V.iii, we see enter 'the Executioner with an Axe in his hand, dressed with Linnen Sleeves and Apron, and in his other hand a black Cypress Scarf' to bind the victim's eyes. In John Wilson's *Belphegor* of c.1675, V.i, 'Enter Picaro (common Executioner) in a white Cap, Sleeves, Apron, tuck'd round his waste, and a large Knife stuck in it.' Oversleeves and aprons were used to protect the men's clothes from blood.

Ben Jonson, the Poet Laureate, began his career as a bricklayer, and continued to dress with working-class simplicity even when famous. Aubrey wrote 'his habit very plaine. I have heard Mr. Lacy, the Player, say that he was wont to weare a coat like a coachman's coate, with slitts under the armpitts.'[18]

This interesting detail shows that coachmen's sleeves were left open underneath to place less stress on the fabric when wielding the whip.

11. M. Laroon, engr. Tempest, 'A London Chimney Sweep', drawn c.1690, pub. 1711. The sweep's boy is still mediaeval in doublet and hose, but his master wears kneebreeches. Many workers still laced their clothes, as buttons and holes required some skill of the maker. The master has a coif underneath his hat to keep the soot out of his hair, and a pair of gaiters to keep it out of his shoes.

William Shakespeare is said to have been the son of a butcher, so he would have been very familiar with blue aprons and working oversleeves, before he turned actor. Oversleeves became traditional for writers and printers, given the dirty nature of ink. The Restoration saw the introduction of actresses and the rise of women playwrights, possibly the first professional women since the abbesses who had run monasteries, but the dress of the former was theatrical, and of the latter professional. Under Charles II actresses were classified with actors as the King's servants and received the same livery as the men: a scarlet cloak with a crimson velvet cape, a unique privilege at the time, as women servants did not wear family colours elsewhere.[19]

Cosmo III, Grand Duke of Tuscany, visited the Old Royal Exchange in 1669: 'four spacious galleries, in which are shops of different kinds, abounding with merchandise of every description, not only equalling but surpassing those of the New Exchange'.

This rival establishment had opened in the Strand, on land bought by the Earl of Salisbury in 1608, where Simon Basil erected Britain's Bourse, but the people called it the New Exchange. The Grand Duke described it, too:

It contains two long and double galleries, one above the over, in which are distributed, in several rows, great numbers of very rich shops of drapers and mercers, filled with goods of every kind, and with manufactures of the most beautiful description. These are, for the most part, under the care of well-dressed women, who are busily employed in work; although many are served by young men, called apprentices.[20]

The well-dressed women were probably the wives and daughters of the shop renters, who could afford to look smart, for the exchanges supplied the court and nobility. Their caps, kerchiefs and aprons would be in the finest linen, and the cloth of their dresses not home-made either. They evidently used sex appeal to sell the goods, for Ned Ward commented that they exuded so much charm that he wondered whether they were selling the goods or themselves. Lace was the most expensive fabric, and could be made from gold and silver; and the richest silks, satins and velvets, the finest gloves, the softest shirts, English silk stockings which were famous, taffeta ribbons, cambric handkerchieves, laced nightshirts, laced stocking tops, laced bands and ruffles, gauze scarves, French hoods, and embroidered hatbands formed the luxurious merchandise, for the exchanges represented the quality trade.

Regular trade with the Orient resulted in shops selling exotic items. Evelyn found a shop called 'Noah's Ark' in Paris in February 1644 which sold Indian cabinets, shells, ivories, porcelain, dried fishes, exotic birds, insects, prints and 'all the

Curiosities naturall or artificial imaginable'. The term 'Indian' was used to describe anything imported by the East India Company, so it could include Chinese and Japanese artefacts as well. Evelyn saw his first examples of lacquer work when Catherine of Braganza brought some as part of her dowry from Portugal when she married Charles II at Portsmouth. These trunkloads of lacquer and the Indian cabinets were placed in Hampton Court Palace in 1662, and made collecting exotic wares very fashionable. An Indian shop was opened at Temple Bar, while Henry Kirk at St Clement Danes and the royal featherman Robert Crofts both started selling Indian gowns as well as *objets d'art*. These were actually Japanese silk kimonos, more accurately called by the Dutch *japonrocker*: Japanese coats, but the oriental craze made them very fashionable for undress. An aristocratic lord or lady could wear an Indian gown to relax in when not in full dress, removing the formal coat and waistcoat or the dress, to sit in comfort. Of course, nobody else could enter their presence in just a nightgown over shirt and kneebreeches, or petticoat and stays, and all lower ranks had to be fully dressed before their superiors, but at home the inferior ranks could imitate them, and they did. Indian gowns, being very simple in shape, made their way down through society, and by 1700 some shopkeepers were wearing them, as were fashionable tailors. Their grandparents would never have dared to dress so informally before customers, but Cosimo III thought Charles II had made the English court the most informal in Europe, and this attitude evidently affected fashionable shopkeepers.

Indeed, the fashionable city shop was the place to see the latest styles and once periwigs came into vogue in 1663–4, even some apprentices copied the look:

a parcel of cleanly Beau Prentices, who walking in their Masters Shops with their Periwigs just Comb'd out of Buckle, well drudg'd with the Barbers Powdering Puff, the extravagant use of which made them appear so Party-Colour'd, that their upper Parts look'd like Millers; and their Coats, from the Waste downwards, hanging in as many folds as a Watermans-Doublet; to show they had more Cloth in the Skirts of one Tunica,

than any of their Ancestors wore in a whole Suit. But this much may be said in Excuse of 'em, that they might the better afford it, because they were Woollen-Drapers.'[21]

Ned Ward's insults are very informative. Millers and bakers were often white with flour, so they wore white aprons and white caps. The loose folds in a waterman's doublet were obviously to make it easier to row in. It often happens that only when people see something to criticize in a costume do they bother to describe it. Anything taken for granted as normal was rarely written about, so what most workers wore was not commented on unless it was unusual.

There was no division between town and country wear, because the country came to town. Drovers brought cattle, sheep, pigs and geese to town; a lot of animals were kept in town awaiting slaughter; dairy cows lived in backyards, along with chickens and the Christmas goose; and huge numbers of horses, to pull all the vehicles, occupied the mews. Smock frocks on drovers, shepherds, ostlers, grooms and cowmen were common urban sights, and were also worn by bricklayers. The Great Fire of London in 1666 resulted in a large number of jobs in the building trades, with kilns at Whitechapel and a non-stop stream of horses and carts bringing bricks into London. Men and women mixed the clay, straw and ashes, usually in bare feet and wearing rough aprons like sacking, since it was dirty and wet. The new metropolis needed to improve its communications. Charles I had opened the royal long-distance post to the public in 1635, but the London penny post was not established until 1683 by William Dockwray. He offered eight deliveries a day inside the city, and four a day to the villages of Kensington, Hammersmith, Newington, Hampstead, Stepney, Bow, Deptford and Greenwich. The first postmen had no uniforms, so they probably identified themselves by a badge on the arm similar to that on the arms of watermen. In 1663 the first turnpike was set up by a private trust in Hertfordshire, with powers to charge travellers for the upkeep of the roads. Previously this charge had been put upon the parishes, and the 1555 Act required all fit males in a parish to repair the roads, which they did with great reluctance. The turnpike system improved on this with gravel roads maintained regularly by their roadmenders, who wore the same hip-length jacket and kneebreeches that became the standard uniform for male workers from the 1630s onwards. In summer most stripped down to the shirt, a common sight among men working outdoors. When a stage coach travelled from Manchester to London in one day in 1669 it caused consternation. Ostlers, postillions, lorimers, and watermen all protested that faster communications would reduce the work available – a common reaction to new transport systems.

The Restoration court made knee-length coats a component of the male suit, and periwigs the mark of the gentlemen, but neither were followed by workers outside the fashion trade. Long-skirted coats were too dangerous for blacksmiths, iron foundries and cannon makers, and so were periwigs. It became the visual distinction between the workers and the men of leisure that the former wore their own hair and jackets to the hip, and the latter periwigs and knee-length suits.

A garish style of dress was usually the mark of a prostitute in town, where they would haunt alehouse doors and hairdressers:

. . . a Shop, wherein sat three or four most provoking Damsels, with as much *Velvet* on their Backs as would have made a *Burying-Pall* for a Country Parish, or a *Holiday Coat* for a Physician, being glorified at bottom with Gold Fringes that I thought at first they might be Parsons daughters who had borrow'd their Fathers Pulpit Cloths, to use as Scarfs to go visiting in; each with as many Patches in her *Market-place* as are Spots in a Leopards *Skin*, or Freckles in the Face of a Scotchman.
I ask'd my Friend, what he took them for? Who answer'd, They were a kind of first rate Punks by their rigging, of about a Guinea purchase. I further queried, what reason he had to believe them to be Leachery-Lawyers? He reply'd, because they were sitting in a Head-Dressers-Shop.

'Punk' was slang for prostitute, and Ward was also using an early example of London rhyming slang, with 'market-place' meaning face.[22] A lot of this finery was probably the result of robbing their clients, for many whores operated as the bait to inveigle their victims into the grip of a gang, or else

12. M. Laroon, engr. Tempest, 'A Basket Seller'. The straw hats attached to the basket seller's hip were essential headgear for women in summer. As this is a London street seller she wears a dress of approximately fashionable type, with an apron and neckerchief, and up-to-date shoes. Baskets were very widely used containers, and the workers who made them lived along the banks of the Thames.

robbed them themselves when asleep after the cold-blooded performance.

The masculine monopoly of professional clothes making saw a challenge coming from France, where in 1675 the law was changed to allow women to take apprenticeships in dress-making and to go into business as seamstresses/couturières (literally 'cutters') in the special areas of women's clothing, children's clothes, linen underwear for both sexes, and garniture, the trimmings and accessories department. Male tailors continued to make men's suits and coats, and tailored garments for women like riding habits. They also retained the business of stay making, for it was felt that the sewing of canvas, and boning corsets required stronger fingers than women were believed to possess – a belief that women miners would have laughed at. Gradually the French system came to be followed in England, and by 1686 Lady Margaret Cecil's dressmaker was a Madame Bourchier, while the Duchess of Somerset went to Mrs Groves.

However, some women had begun to be professional linenmakers before 1675, for the accounts of Algernon Percy, Earl of Northumberland, in 1662–6, show regular payments to Widow Sebbage and Widow Mary Bullocke for mending and altering linen, and making shifts, cuffs, lace cravats and pocket handkerchieves, while Widow Penfold made caps and night bands as well as doing alterations. Obviously there was some charity involved here in helping the widows of local villagers to earn a living if they could sew neatly. At the time of the coronation of Mary II and William III the shirts came from Edith Colledge, and Judith Radcliffe, while Mary Sanderson supplied 21 half-shirts – these were left open at the sides, probably to make it easier to wear two or three at a time, as there was no underwear like modern vests. Thus male shirts, like the rest of underwear, became a female industry. The dress of the linen makers would have been that of an ordinary housewife: a simple gown laced in front, with a coif or cap, an apron, and a kerchief draped round the shoulders. An important French house near Covent Garden was that of Marie Cheret who supplied Mary II,

the Duchess of Lauderdale, the Earl of Northumberland, and Samuel Pepys with such fashionable items as lace collars, lace cuffs, ribbons, hatbands, hoods, lace, and gauze scarves, as well as gloves scented with orange or jasmine, and masks. Some of the goods were imported, but some of the fitting and making would have to be done on the premises, so she was an example of the seamstress specializing in trimmings.[23]

Industry and the sea

The Derbyshire hills were full of coal, lead, copper and stone. When Celia Fiennes visited Buxton she observed 'they digg down their mines like a well, for one man to be let down with a rope and pulley'. She thought the miners looked very pale and yellow, which was caused by the lead poisoning. Women and children still worked underground, stripped to their shifts and shirts in the heat, more often covered with rags than anything else. Celia Fiennes was shocked to see the tin-mine women at Austell in Cornwall smoking pipes: 'as comely sort of women as I have seen any where tho' in ordinary dress, good black eyes and crafty enough, and very neate'. Presumably they had taken a wash before sitting down for a smoke. The international European miner's costume (see fig. 3) began to face competition from kneebreeches which, with the shirt, were a simpler costume to don. The attached hood underground would grow too hot, so a preference for sweat bands probably came to the fore, and the sixteenth-century uniform went into decline. On the surface the women and children hammering the coal and iron rock into lumps wore stout linens, if they were female, over rough dresses, and the males increasingly shirts and kneebreeches. Inadequacy of covering was a common feature of most workers, and children in only shirts in mid-winter were not unusual. Wooden railways with wagons pulled by horses were at Broseley mine near the Severn by 1608, and Roger North noticed them at Newcastle-upon-Tyne in the 1680s. Celia Fiennes said one could smell Newcastle from a distance because of the sulphur in the air, as pits spread for two miles around. The coal was taken down to the Tyne to the barges which carried it out to the colliers at sea, where the keelmen transferred it from barge to ship. Both these early railway workers and keelmen gradually converted to kneebreeches, and the possibility of smock frocks for the drivers cannot be exluded. So many forests had been cut down for firewood that coal production increased fourteen-fold between 1600 and 1700, and colliers and coal barges were one-third of all British shipping.

In 1675 John Evelyn wrote to John Aubrey that it was amazing how many watermills had been driven by his local brook in Surrey: 'There was likewise a Fulling-Mill upon the same Stream, now demolish'd, but the Hammer for the Iron remains. These I mention because I do not remember to have seen such a Variety of Mills and Works upon so narrow a Brook, and in so little Compass, there being Mills for *Corn, Cloth, Brass, Iron, Powder* &C.'[24]

Water continued to be an important source of power, but in 1698 Thomas Savery from Cornwall showed William III his steam pump and was granted a patent. This was the first pump not powered by muscles, water or wind, and many mines adopted it, since it could lift water 60 to 80 feet from one cistern to another in tiers underground, instead of the 20 feet on hand-operated pumps. The Savery pulsometer was not efficient but it was the first, and it was fuelled by coal. Captain Savery was an officer, so this inventor wore a uniform, and when in mufti dressed as gentleman in three-piece English suit to the knee, a periwig and the new mathematical tricorne hat. The operatives who had to shovel the coal into the furnaces and pull the levers, stripped to the shirt and kneebreeches.[25]

The biggest industry was still wool, and Guy Miège wrote:

Now for *Rayment*, English *Wool* is famous all the World, both for its fineness and goodness. But that of the *Cotswolds* in Glocestershire, of *Lemster* in Herefordshire, and the Isle of *White*, has the pre-eminency. Of this wool are made excellent broad Cloths, dispersed not only all over England, but all over the World, especially high Germany, Poland, Muscovy, Turky and Persia.[26]

The excellence was due to English long-haired sheep. Fynes Moryson said continental sheep were much inferior:

Their sheepe are very little, bearing a course wool and commonly black, which they export not, but make course cloath thereof for the poorer sort, the Gentlemen and for the most part the Citizens, wearing English Cloath.[27]

Celia Fiennes observed that Devizes specialized in drugget/broadcloth, while for twenty miles round Exeter people made serge. That city saw a weekly turnover of £10,000–15,000, the biggest in the country, as weavers bought yarn from the spinsters, and sold cloth. Most West Country cloth was not dyed and formed the 'whitells' worn by women. For dyeing most of the cloth was sent to London. Colchester produced and dyed its baize, large quantities of which were exported to Spain; as Pepys observed, the Spanish court wore Colchester baize cloaks in winter, the women white flannel mantles. Norwich made calico and damask. Leeds was the centre for Yorkshire cloth, a kersey cheaper and narrower than broadcloth, which pedlars sold all over the kingdom and in the Netherlands and Germany. Canterbury, being close to France, received an intake of refugee Huguenot silk weavers from 1685, which helped the English silk industry. Celia Fiennes saw as many as 20 silk looms in a house making flowered silks. Gloucester, she said, produced cotton stockings, gloves, waistcoats, petticoats, sleeves, knitted goods, and cotton yarn, showing how many readymade garments were available. Nottingham she called the neatest town, and it made stockings, as well as bricks and tiles. Cumberland produced its green cloth called Kendal cotton, 'used for blanckets, and the Scotts use them for their plodds, and there is much made here, and also linsiwolseys and a great deale of leather'.[28] Hampshire produced blue kersey cloth.

Linen was called 'housewife's cloth' because many of them made it. Cleveland and New Malton specialized in a fine linen, but Henry Best wrote in 1641 that lengths and quality varied greatly. Maids bought cheap linen at 14 or 15 pence a yard for their holiday aprons, and for their neckcloths and

berthas. Fine linen at two shillings a yard was used for gentlemen's shirts. Holland linen was made by nuns in the Low Countries and was fine, used for kerchiefs, collars and half-shirts. Scottish linen was rougher and was sold at 18 pence a yard for handkerchiefs. Cambricke fine linen was eight shillings and cambricke lawn ten shillings a yard, and ladies used it for ruffs early in the century. Tiffany at four shillings was a cheaper lawn, much used for neckcloths, sometimes over a Holland linen as starching was being used so much. Best may mean that something soft between the starch and skin was necessary. All the cloth and linen industries were supplied with yarn by women

13. Joost de Momper, 'A Market and Laundry in Flanders'. Linen was easier to wash than dyed cloth, so it was shirts, shifts, drawers, sheets, neckerchieves and baby clothes which were washed most often and then laid on the grass to bleach in the sun. The washerwomen's plain dresses or jacket and skirt are without the fullness of fashionable petticoats. The hems were always a foot shorter than those worn by middle-class or upper-class ladies.

working at home, so housewife's dress was the dominant working costume with its coifs, aprons, plain dresses and kerchiefs. The weavers could be either sex: housewives, or men in shirts, waistcoats

36

and kneebreeches. Whether they worked barefoot or in stockings would depend on the temperature; a lot of workers did not wear shoes indoors to make them last. The pedlars who sold the various cloths could also be men or women, and their dress would depend upon the state of sales. If low, then rags and tatters were their fate, if high then a good second-hand suit and dress would follow. Straw hats and felt hats would do for either, but hoods were female, apart from monks and miners.

Women brewsters dominated brewing until 1620 as most farmers' wives made beer for the labourers, and so did innkeepers' wives. That year, however, some male brewers told the government that if it gave them a monopoly on brewing and closed down all the brewsters, it would make it easier to collect the tax. The government agreed despite huge protests. As Alice Clark has shown, many brewsters were taken to court, but brewing was their livelihood. Many a widow, alehouse keeper and inn made their own beer. As it had been a feminine industry, brewing saw the housewife's apron much in evidence, and brewers had to adopt aprons too. The drivers of the drays from the new centralized male breweries wore smock frocks for working with horses. Henceforth women could not sell their beer for consumption on the premises, and had to be beer retailers. Some women were still working as beer makers/retailers in the nineteenth century, the local men preferring home-brewed beer to the tied inns.[29]

Celia Fiennes discovered that the whole of Southampton-Portsmouth area was involved in shipbuilding, backed as it was by forests inland, but fishing boats were built all round the coast. Teams of oxen would haul the logs out of the forest once the gangs of wood cutters had chopped them down, and enormous carts carried the wood down to the ports, with thousands of oaks needed for one man-o'-war. Activity soared or declined according to the state of peace or war, but leather aprons, rough sacking aprons, and linen aprons were common among wood cutters, shipwrights, carpenters, joiners and figurehead sculptors.

In 1628 the Admiralty at last decided that when it press-ganged men in just what they stood up in, it

14. M. Laroon, engr. Tempest, 'The Old Cloaths Man'. Foreigners were puzzled that in London the workers preferred old fashionable clothes to their own type. This street seller offers a coat of 1670s type, three felt hats, two skull caps, and a few cravats, as well as two gentleman's swords. Old clothing is a very ancient trade.

ought to make available a change of clothes for health reasons. Ready-made clothes were called 'slops', and the men were offered slops suits of canvas with a doublet and kneebreeches, Monmouth caps, cotton waistcoats and drawers, stockings, linen shirts, and shoes. Five thousand suits were ordered, but only 500 were sold because the

clerks and pursers charged so much 'the poor men had rather starve than buy them'. Eventually in 1663 the Admiralty decided to set a fixed price for slops. They had to be sold before the mainmast once a week in the captain's presence. Monmouth caps should be 2/6, red caps 1/1, blue shirts 3/6, yarn stockings 3d., Irish stockings 1½d., cotton waistcoats 3/–, cotton drawers 3/–, neat's leather shoes 3/6, blue neckcloths 5d., canvas suits 5/–, blue suits 5/–, by order of the Lord High Admiral the Duke of York. Canvas was not dyed, but the blue suits were a coloured alternative in the traditional tones.[30]

Matters were less organized in the Merchant Navy, where membership was voluntary. Even so, they could be press-ganged. The shipwright George Everett complained that it was the height of injustice to take sailors off a merchant ship when she sailed into port, for naval service. As there was no slops system for merchant seamen they were deprived of the opportunity of buying new clothes for themselves or their families. The boom-boat women charged inflated prices, and how could a sailor pay for naval slops when press-ganged from his merchant ship before he had been paid? Everett argued that there ought to be a register of suitable men, instead of the haphazard rounding-up of merchant sailors, fishermen, farm labourers, blacksmiths, quarrymen and pedlars. Pepys admitted that it was a rotten system, after seeing how hysterical the wives became with grief and worry when their menfolk were taken away without their knowing to which ship, or what destination. Since more men died at sea from disease than from war they might well never return home. Rags for the family was the result.[31]

Fishermen were often conscripted into the navy, so a similarity in dress was quite common, for both shared the feeling that they were tougher than landlubbers. Leather, greased canvas or tarred garments were equally important for keeping out the wet in fishing boat or man-o'-war. Evelyn noticed a similar use of skins or leather on the French side of the Channel in March 1644 at Honfleur: 'a poore fisher-towne, observable for nothing so much as the old, yet usefull habites

15. M. Laroon, engr. Tempest, 'A Mackerel Fishwife'. The poor wore the clothes of both sexes, so this fishwife has a man's coat and long-sleeved vest of about 1688, over which go her apron and money bag. She wears a woman's hood, neckerchief and skirt, and a man's hat. Her shoes she may only have donned for the city.

which the good-Women weare, of beares & other skinns, as of ruggs &C at Diepe and all along these maritime coasts'. The men caught the fish at sea; the women waded out to the boats to bring the baskets ashore, then cleaned and gutted the fish, hoisted the baskets on to their backs and went all round the area to sell it, so that skins were important as waterproofs for English, Scottish, French and Dutch fisherfolk alike. The rugs John Florio defined in 1598, as 'An Irish rugge, or mantle, a rug such as seamen weare', and he also called it a 'gabardine'. This very rough woollen hairy cloak or plaid was also used as a bedcover, and was worn by soldiers too. Canvas clothes were not warm, so some kind of thick wrapping was essential. The rough Irish rug was relatively cheap, so many low-paid workers wore it in winter, as they could not afford tailored overalls (overcoats).

Many seamen fell victims in the Mediterranean to pirates and Arab corsairs who used them as galley slaves. The French also sent criminals to the galleys, and Evelyn saw the slaves' costume at Marseilles in October 1644: 'hundreds of miserab[l]y naked Persons, having their heads shaven close, & onely red high bonnets, a payre of Course canvas drawers, their whole backs & leggs starke naked, doubly chayned about their middle, & leggs, in Cupples, & made fast to their seates.'[32]

The evolution of a special costume for fishwives probably began after the Restoration. Before then, skirts had to be hitched up and pinned underneath, 'breeching' their dresses, as it was called, like a farmer's wife when riding a horse, in order to wade through the sea. The Restoration theatre liked its new actresses to show their legs in green silk stockings, so dressed them in 'breeches roles', wearing kneebreeches or trunkhose. This style was copied by other female entertainers like rope dancers and acrobats, who took the costume into touring theatrical companies and to fairs. Ned Ward saw at St Bartholomew's Fair 'a couple of *Plump-Buttock Lasses*, who to show their Affection to the *Breeches*, wore 'em under their Petti-coats; which, for decency sake, they first Danc'd in'. When things warmed up, however, they took off the petticoats and danced in only the breeches.

16. M. Laroon, engr. Tempest, 'The Fishseller'. The lacing of the doublet is clear. Buttons were banned for workers in the Middle Ages, so lacing was the tradition among the lower classes long after the law had passed into history. To let the lining of the kneebreeches show had been the fashion in 1666, but here it is still being worn in the 1690s. A few buttons on the sleeve, however, show a slight trend towards aping the aristocracy.

Consequently, fisherfolk who went to the fairs could have seen this outfit of kneebreeches worn under the skirt and adapted it for their fishwives where it became an institution. However it arose, it meant that the skirts could be shockingly short to the knee, but that the girl was still decent underneath, as she waded through the water where long skirts would have been a terrible impediment.

Away from London mantles or plaids were common from Wiltshire to Scotland and Ireland, as a very ancient method of protecting the wearer against cold and wet. Garments like cloaks and capes or overalls (overcoats) cost money, so the poor kept to their ancient style. In the London region, however, the workers would look like a jumble of fashions from the last hundred years in their second- or third-hand relics from higher up the social scale. Ward described the women of Deptford as being 'Accouter'd most commonly like the meanest of our Oyster-Women in Ragged Gowns, Daggled Petticoats, Blue Aprons, Speckled Handkerchiefs about their Necks, and their Heads adorn'd with Flat-Caps.'[33] The flat caps doubtless went back to the Tudor period in style, and the gowns, a very courtly word for a dress, had probably come from a better wardrobe twenty or thirty years before. So close to the capital, people would be influenced by fashion even if they could only obtain the clothes when the fashionable world had finished with them. The class which was accused of taking fashion out to the provinces was the servants.

To the Lowland Scots, the Highlanders were barbaric. They themselves wore English-type dresses and doublets and breeches, with some local style on top, as John Ray discovered in 1662:

The Scots generally (that is, the poorer sort) wear, the men blue bonnets on their heads, and some russet; the women only white linnen, which hangs down their backs as if a napkin were pinned about them. When they go abroad none of them wear hats, but a partly coloured blanket which they call a plad, over their heads and shoulders.

He was puzzled how the men managed to plough with a plaid on, but one saw them doing so frequently. The Reverend Thomas Morer, chaplain to a Scottish regiment in 1689, agreed, and thought plaids good for undress. He said of the Lowlanders:

Their Habit is mostly English, saving the meaner sort of Men wear *Bonnets* instead of *Hats*, and *Pladds* instead of *Cloaks*: and these Pladds the Women use in their ordinary Dress when they go abroad, either to Market or Church. They cover Head and Body with 'em, and are so contrived to be at once Scarf and Hood. The Quality go thus Attired when they would be disguised, and is a Morning Dress good when some hasty business calls them forth, or when the Weather disheartens 'em to Trick themselves better.

The Highlanders, however, were regarded as a lot of thieves, who lived by fighting, hunting, and raiding the Lowlanders. The chaplain wondered how they managed to fight wearing plaids, so he asked:

They are constant in their Habit or way of Clothing; *Pladds* are most in use with 'em, which tho' we English thought inconvenient, especially for Swords Men in times of Action, and in heat of Summer, as when we saw 'em; yet they excused themselves on these accounts. That they not only served for Cloaths by *Day* in case of necessity, but were Pallats or Beds in the *Night* at such times as they travelled. These Pladds are about seven or eight yeards, differing in fineness according to the Abilities or Fancy of the Weavers, They cover the whole Body with 'em from the Neck to the Knees, excepting the Right Arm, which they mostly keep at liberty. Many of 'em have nothing under these Garments besides Wastcots and Shirts, which descend no lower than the Knees, and they so gird 'em about the Middle as to give 'em the same length as the Linen under 'em, and thereby supply the defect of *Drawers* and *Breeches*.

According to the Lowlanders, the Highlanders only used plaids to cover their barbaric nudity, and in order to conceal stolen goods inside, for once or twice a year the clans got together for a mammoth raid on the southern Scots. The absence of any reference to clan tartans will be noted. To identify one's clan during the warring period would have been death.

Morer noted that the Highlanders did not knit stockings, but cut and sewed them from the same material as the plaid. They were tied at the knee with tufted garters. Their shoes, called 'brocks', had no heels and were thin-soled like pumps. They were worn only by men, in the main: 'Their Ordinary Women goe bare-foot, especially in the Summer, yet the Husbands have Shooes, and therein seem unkind in letting their Wives bear those hardships without partaking themselves.'[34] Morer was told that by an ancient Scottish law, males could not wear shoes until they were 14 in order to toughen their feet ready for the king's wars. No explanation was offered as to why the Scottish women were expected to be even tougher-footed than the troops, but they were used as beasts of burden, even having to carry their 'shooed' husbands out to boats. The Highlanders themselves thought civilized luxuries like soft sheets and beds a barbarous effeminacy compared to plaids and sleeping out on heather: and kneebreeches were for weaklings. They were called 'redshanks' because of their bare thighs in the coldest weather.

Servants

A major change in tradition took place after 1600 when the nobility began to allow its servants to follow the fashion more closely. Moryson complained:

Servants of Gentlemen were wont to wear blue Coates, and their Masters badge of silver on the left sleeve: but now they most commonly weare cloakes garded with laces, all the servants of one family wearing the same liverie for colour and ornament, and for the rest are apparelled with no less pride and inconstancie of fashions than other degrees.

This criticism continued down to this century, that if servants were allowed to look fashionable it became impossible to tell who was the mistress and who was the maid. The trend was further encouraged by the fact that servants had a right to the master's or mistress's clothes when they died or had finished with them. This meant that fine linen shirts and smocks, silk gowns, and velvet coats could be sported by domestics, and nothing annoyed a visitor more than having the front door opened to him by a footman dressed more finely than the visitor him or herself. Trying to impress people by

maintaining huge staffs gave way to impressing by way of fewer servants in even richer clothes.

Elizabeth I regularly gave away clothes to friends and servants alike. In 1562 she presented one sewer with:

Item gevon by her Majestie the said Daye and yere to Sir Robert Riche knight sewer to her highness One Cloake of blak vellat weltid with thre weltes of the same cutt & ravelyd lyned with sarceonett.

In 1568 a woman servant received:

Item gevon by her Majesties commandement to Mrs Elizabeth Stafforde one of the Chamberers the xxvj[th] of October Anno x[mo] predicto One streight bodied Gowne of blak Satten cutt and raste allover garded with blak vellat cutt upon white sarceonet powderid with white and blak silke.[35]

By the time of Charles II this donation was regarded as an established right, to the extent that servants would help themselves to the clothes, which caused an enormous row between the Senior Clerk of the Great Wardrobe, Thomas Towns-hend, and one of the royal grooms in 1667, as recorded by Samuel Pepys:

a horrid rateing, which Mr. Ashburnham, as one of the Grooms of the King's Bedchamber, did give him for want of linen for the King's person; which he swore was not to be endured, and that the King would not endure it, and that the King his father would have hanged his wardrobe-man should he have been served so; the King having at this day no handkerchers and but three bands to his neck, he swore. Mr. Townshend answered want of money and the owing of the linen draper 5000£; and that he hath of late got many rich things made, beds, and sheets, and saddles, all without money, and that he can go no further; but still this old man (endeed, like an old loving servant) did cry out for the King's person to be neglected. But when he was gone, Townshend told me that it is the grooms taking away the King's linen at the Quarter's end, as their Fees, which makes this great want: for whether the King can get it or no, they will run away at the Quarter's end with what he hath had, let the King get more as he can.[36]

The 'servant problem' meant different things in different times. The debt to the royal linen draper will be noted as an example of how suppliers to the crown and aristocracy were often expected to be satisfied with the honour of serving the upper classes, rather than the payment of bills.

Some traditional dress survived the Civil War. The tabard worn by heralds from the time of Henry V was revived in 1660, but others were invented on historical principles. Before the interregnum pages had been dressed like small adults in the same fashions as their masters, but when the court was re-established it chose some old styles to suggest the continuance of the Crown. Pageboys were put into trunkhose now that most men were wearing kneebreeches, except for sailors and some peasants. Trunkhose were also revived for coronation dress and for the costume of orders like the Garter and the Saint Esprit. Pages in trunkhose were decorated with ribbons, points and laces to create a fanciful figure. Footmen were also ornamented to suit Baroque taste by being dressed in a combination of kneebreeches and trunkhose with much pleating below the waistline and trimmed with points and ribbons. The use of braid on a livery was also introduced at this time, being applied down the seams of doublets and breeches, often in a gold or silver lace. This style is still in existence today, with the braid on coats more often a dark ribbon.

Even a philosopher could start as a page, for Thomas Hobbes, who went to Oxford University when he was 14 in 1602, when he had won his BA, was engaged by the Earl of Devonshire, who felt he would learn more from an educated page than from a dry doctor. Aubrey said:

He was his Lordships page, and rode a hunting and hawking with him, and kept his privy-purse. By this way of life he had forgott his Latin. He therefore bought him bookes of an Amsterdam print that he might carry in his pocket (particularly Caesar's *Commentarys*) which he did read in the Lobbey, or Ante-Chamber, whilest his Lord was making his Visits.[37]

17. Michael Sweerts, 'Playing Checkers', 1652. Footmen and pageboys were often the most richly dressed of servants. The footman on the left has the combination trunkhose and kneebreeches that such servants were given in the seventeenth century, but the pageboys retain the trunkhose alone. Gold and silver braid on the seams, coloured ribbons, clean linen and plenty of colour characterized the male servant.

One must doubt if many pages employed their waiting time so wisely. The principal clothing problem with pageboys was that they grew, which is reflected in the first Duke of Lauderdale's accounts for 1673 by a livery bill from the tailor Jo. Hay.

Altering and Scouring y^r Graces two pages Cloth Sutes & Silke to them at 6^s 6^d to both . . . . . . 13^s
Altering yor pages breeches & trimming y^m round with Ribbond at 3^s for both . . . . 6^s

A new kind of footman also appears in these accounts, the running footman who had to carry messages or despatches, and run ahead of his master's coach to tell an inn to make suitable accommodation available. Fleetness of foot was an essential qualification, and, in 1673, a simple costume. The Duke's running clothes for the footman were serge breeches and waistcoat, lined with calico, and decorated with three dozen buttons. A pair of drawers was also supplied, although a shirt must have been worn as well given the absence of a coat or doublet. The total came to 17 shillings.[38]

Sometimes a livery would reflect the wearer's job, as happens with Charles II's ratcatcher:

A Warrant to provide and deliver unto Randolph Holden his Maties Ratt Killer in ordinary, two yards and a quarter of Bastard Scarlett at twelve shillings the yard and also one yard and three quarters of velvett, for his Livery to be made after the fashion of his Maties Messengers, and also to be embroidered with C:R: before and behind and six Ratts eating a wheat Sheaffe before and behind on the sayd Coate. 10 November 1662.

This suggests a tabard in a mi-parti contrast of velvet and cloth, with the King's initials for Carolus Rex and the special illustration of the occupation embroidered on top.[39]

Scarlet was the English royal livery colour, being an extremely expensive dye, and was used for the beefeaters, musicians, and watermen. The Master of the Queen's Barge had a scarlet coat in fine cloth, the watermen who did the rowing cheaper wool but still red. In 1671–2 there were 27 of them including three pensioners who still got livery coats. The watermen of the King's barges dressed similarly and had black velvet caps. The trumpeters and kettle drummer also wore royal scarlet, as did the children of the Chapel Royal when not in ecclesiastical dress, and so on throughout the household. When the heir to the throne had his own household he chose a different livery, and in 1620 Charles, Prince of Wales, instructed his tailor Patrick Black to dress his grooms of the privy chamber, footmen and pages in green satin and green velvet decorated with gold and silver lace. His livery bill that year, including some garments for himself, cost the prince £6,467.16.5½d. To give an idea of what that sum represented one could have built ten warships at £600 each in those days.[40] Green was often chosen as a hunting colour; Evelyn's father selected green when he was appointed Sheriff of Surrey and Sussex in 1633, and had 116 servants in green satin doublets. The gentlemen and quality who came to congratulate him wore the same livery in his honour. This was a common gesture in that era; wearing somebody's livery colour showed one's loyalty and support on a public occasion, without actually being a servant of that household.

Thomas Tyndale, born in 1588, was disgusted at the behaviour of masters and servants in the next century. No Elizabethan lord would have travelled in a coach for fear of being thought effeminate. He walked to Parliament or rode on horseback with his six or ten servants in their blue coats and badges and long basket-hilt swords. But now it was coaches and lackeys and pages and general softness. In Tyndale's day the gentry had lived hard, hunting and hawking, and so were good for wartime, but the gentry of the Restoration spent their time getting drunk, and their servants copied them. 'Their servants like clowns too, drunkards too; breeches of one sort, Doublet of another, drabled with the teares of the Tankard and greasie. Dick Pawlet built an alehouse for his Servants, withouth the Gate, because Servants should be within call.'[41]

Imitating their masters in dress and manners was a constant accusation levelled at servants, but it was also the way by which ideas about cleanliness, neatness, polite manners, and good

44

18. G. van Tilborgh, 'The Tichborne Dole', 1670. The male servants are distinguished by bunches of ribbon on the shoulder of their fashionable suits. The housekeeper and maids, at the back, are not so honoured, but have plain dresses, coifs, neckerchiefs and aprons. On the right, the peasants of both sexes wear sugar loaf hats, the women coifs, and some men tall caps. Their overall tone is russet. The woman with the baby has the same sleeveless bodice as across the Channel (see fig. 10). The lighter tones of the family stand out considerably.

45

taste were passed down society, when servants told their relations all about the behaviour up at the big house. To the peasant, who never saw any new clothes in his life, the servant with his new clothes twice a year and as much meat in a week as the peasant ate in twelve months, was a figure greatly to be envied. Entry into the system, however, was not so simple because servants would always tell their own relations about any vacancies. Trying to hand a job on to one's own family was a tradition in the working class.

Compared to the finery of the male peacock, the women servants looked drab and domestic like their jobs. No tabards and heraldry for them, but white coifs or caps, a white kerchief, a plain dress and an apron, no different from what was worn by ordinary housewives. The lucky lady's maid might receive her mistress's old silk gown and wear that indoors and on Sundays as her best, and this wearing of imported silks and satins instead of native woollen cloth annoyed many critics, who claimed that it was unpatriotic as well as dressing above one's station.

It was a status symbol to have a foreign servant, but they could prove difficult, especially if they were French. When Evelyn fell sick in Paris in 1647, 'My *Valet* de Chambre *Herbert* robbed me of the value of threescore pounds in *Clothes* and *Plate*.' Fortunately, through the agency of his future father-in-law, Sir Richard Browne, the king's resident at the French court, he got most of it back. Even the French Comte de Gramont, a familiar figure at the English court in the 1660s, was robbed by his French valet-de-chambre Termes whom he had sent back to Paris to get a richly embroidered coat to wear at the queen's masquerade in 1664. Termes returned without the coat, saying that he had lost it. The Comte later found out that Termes had sold it to a gentleman near Abbeville for 150 louis, but forgave him for his cheek. The foundation of the East India Company saw some servants being imported from India, and subsequently from Africa. Black pages in particular, it was felt, would help to emphasize the purity of the mistress's complexion by contrast, and they became popular from the 1680s. It became the tradition to dress such pages as Turks with turbans, regardless of where they came from. There was no attempt to reproduce all aspects of Turkish dress; a few details would suffice. The decorative servant had arrived.

THREE

1700–1795

Agriculture

There was no major change in agricultural working dress in this period. The basic male suit of hip-length jacket and kneebreeches established under Charles I continued as the most common form of clothes for working men, with the only difference that the breeches were narrower in the eighteenth century than they had been in the middle of the previous one. Russet brown remained the dominant colour for dyed clothes, which were still made at home along with the home-made shirts, drawers and neckerchiefs in home-grown linen. Women still wore linen shifts or smocks, sometimes drawers but not necessarily, linen caps and kerchiefs, and aprons, with plain dresses in rough wool. Outdoors, felt or straw hats were worn on top of the caps as in the Elizabethan era. The only impact of courtly fashion concerned the display of the petticoats. In the 1640s fine ladies had begun to hitch up the skirt of the gown to show part of the petticoat, and this led to the opening up of the front of the gown skirt to show the petticoat beneath, which of course then began to be elaborately decorated. Peasant women could not afford this decoration, but they could leave the gown skirt open in front to show a red or blue petticoat, which they started to do during the Restoration period and now continued into the new century. The petticoats also grew much wider at court, when Queen Anne's ladies launched the hoops in 1708, so those working women within reach of London tried to imitate the fashion by adding to the number of their petticoats to give some impression of width, even if they could not copy the full width

to which paniers stretched by the 1740s. Such skirts were impractical for milking cows or carting manure; indeed the whole point of the fashion was to discriminate between the idle rich and the labouring classes.

Smock frocks were an institution by now, but the length, to calf or knee, was a matter of personal choice. Farmworkers on estates were given frocks/smocks by their employers, as were stable staff. Thus in 1746 Henry Purefoy wrote twice from Shalstone Manor to the tailor Edward Fell at Chipping Norton, 'Bring the Coachman a linen frock to put over his cloaths when he rubs the horses down,' and, 'My Mother desires you will bring 3 Linnen washing frocks for the 3 men servants such as you used to bring; let them be big enough, the last were too tite upon 'em.'[1] Where the term smock frock was abbreviated to 'frock' one has to deduce from the fabric and the context whether a smock or a frock coat is intended. The latter were a new simple form of knee-length coat worn as part of the suit, with a turndown collar and narrow skirts, which became very popular among the merchant classes as a form of undress easier to wear in town than full dress. Some footmen were given such frock coats, so care must be exercised when reading accounts.

Smock frocks were worn very widely by both the farmer and the labourers he employed. While artists depicted only men in smocks, one cannot conclude that women never wore them for such activities as cleaning out the pigs or raking out the hens. Such tasks did not come under the gaze of the fine arts, which regarded landscapes as pictorial

subjects from which details of squalid labour were to be excluded.

Shepherds and drovers continued to sport the garment, and Daniel Defoe noted on his tour of Britain in 1724 how beneficial the new turnpike roads were to the movement of livestock. No longer did cattle and sheep have to be driven to London before September or October, when the rains set in and all traffic on the roads came to a halt. No longer did the animals have to be kept in compounds over winter, eating expensive hay until they were slaughtered nearer to Christmas. The new roads meant that the herds and flocks could stay out in the countryside eating grass for nothing, and only needed to be driven to town in January or February because the roads stayed open all year. The absence of potholes also meant horses could pull much bigger loads, while the value of the inns and properties near the turnpikes soared in the same way that proximity to a motorway affects values today.

Defoe examined the hire of workers, particularly the way in which they illustrated their occupations:

I have observed at some of these Fairs, that the poor Servants distinguish themselves by holding something in their Hands, to imitate what Labour they are particularly qualifyed to undertake; as the Carters a Whip, the Labourers a Shovel, the Woodmen a Bill, the Manufacturers a Wool-Comb, and the like. But since the Wages and Manners are advanc'd as we now find them, these Fairs are not so much frequented as formerly, tho' we have them at several towns near London; as at *Enfield*, *Waltham*, *Epping* &C.[2]

London, of course, was now big enough to have permanent employment offices open all the year round, so the idea of hiring fairs began to die out there, but out in the provinces the concept was only just beginning to spread and to become an institution. No law required the unemployed to attend fairs, so it was due to custom, which took time to reach Yorkshire and beyond.

The Swiss visitor César de Saussure was very impressed by English farmers and peasants but he visited only London and Kent. He observed that the peasants looked better off than continental ones, and did not eat the coarse black bread that was their lot across the Channel. Kentish farmers could afford to give their daughters dowries of £3,000–4,000, and owned their own riding horses, riding into London in riding coats, boots and spurs like gentry. Their families looked well dressed, their homes were neat, and some even owned silver spoons and mugs. Even the carters owned their own horses, and there was at least one woman carrier, Mrs Eagles, of Buckingham, who set out from the George Inn at Smithfield at 4 a.m. every Tuesday, according to the Purefoy accounts.[3]

The good impression on visitors continued, for when in 1784 François, Duc de La Rochefoucauld, landed at Dover, he recorded, 'I observed that all classes of people – peasants from the neighbouring country, servants even – were well clad and remarkably clean.'[4]

Even this late in the century the term 'hiring fair' had not reached Norfolk, for William Marshall wrote in 1787: 'At the public hiring of yearly servants, an excellent custom subsists in this District: The High Constable of the Hundred in which a statute is held holds at the same time and place, what is called a "petty session", at which the hiring and its attendant circumstances are, or may be, registered.'[5] Thus the constable had moved his sitting to the time of a statute fair, but did not take part in it. A similar development was noted by the American loyalist Judge Samuel Curwen, who went to the Waltham Abbey statute fair on 26 September 1783 and found that the hiring of servants took place the day after the fair, and not during the fair. It cannot be said that the hiring was part of the statute fair itself, as the law did not require it.

19. William Hamilton, 'Gleaners', 1796. The simple smock frock was widely established in the country, with a scarf or cloth around the neck. It could be long or short as the wearer wished, and this one has side slits. Leather kneebreeches and leather gaiters were durable items passed on from one generation to another. The woman wears a bedgown, the descendant of the seventeenth-century matinée undress jacket. Such jackets were worn from Russia to Italy as well as in Britain.

Curwen found nothing remarkable about the labourers waiting for hire, but the women had evolved a sophisticated system of differentiation: 'The males appear with the tool or insignia of their respective employments; the females of the domestic kind are distinguished by their aprons, viz., cooks in colored, nursery-maids in white linen, and the chamber and waiting-maids in lawn or cambric.'[6] The finer aprons displayed a finer post in the household.

When Madame du Bocage visited England in 1758 she had waxed lyrical on the rural nymphs and sylphs, stating that all Englishwomen looked like shepherdesses. When Sophie von La Roche came here in 1786 she expected to find such Arcadian goddesses in London and was sadly disappointed until she found one surviving example in Mrs Burch, who was about 60. She wore a straw hat like a shepherdess, decorated with real roses, and had painted trailing roses around the white skirt of her dress. Her bodice was of pink and white taffeta, decorated with pearls on the seams and the binding of the short sleeve. Clearly the nymphs were a middle class and

20. J. Ibbetson, 'A Ferry', c.1795. The problem of transport. The driver at the far right with the whip wears a traveller's overall for weather protection, not yet an industrial garment. The man pushing the wheel is clad in a short smock and trousers. As this is an estuary scene the men wear sailors' trousers on the ferry, and top them with coats or smock frocks. The horses appear to have been ferried over first.

aristocratic attempt to play at country maids, rather than the genuine article, to the confusion of foreigners.

When Sophie examined milkmaids in the London area she found that they had actually stopped wearing straw hats. 'The beautifully bright milk-cans hung so prettily against the frocks and white aprons of the country wenches, who wear black taffeta hats like the town maids.'[7] She was within that hundred-mile region where country folk did try to imitate the fashion of the capital, if they could. On the other hand, the smock frock frequently appeared in town, worn by drovers, ostlers, bricklayers, coopers, and carters, so the country look came the other way.

Getting drenched to the skin was a regular occurrence for all outdoor workers, so the garment they put over the smock frock, if any, would be a coarse mantle or shaped cloak. To protect the ankles in the mud various kinds of wrappings were employed, like straw, a piece of sheepskin, or some sacking. Despite the weather, Saussure said English country girls deserved their reputation for beauty, with complexions like roses and lilies – better than the ladies at court, who painted. Doubtless all those straw hats protected complexions from the sun, for to be tanned like an Ethiope was considered decidedly inferior. The Swiss also observed that Englishmen were not servile to fashion and disliked being troubled: 'There are some people who keep so apart from fashion that in any other country they would be considered singularly odd and perhaps something more; but in this country people are above caring what is thought of them, and do not trouble themselves about other people's opinions.'[8] Going one's own way was certainly quite a custom in the countryside where metropolitan niceties could be ignored, and wearing clothes that were thirty years out of fashion did not bother many a farmer. Town wits might declare that farthingales were still being worn in the Hebrides, but who cared what they said? There was still a huge body of people to whom fashion was purely something that happened at court and in the capital, and did not concern them except every two hundred years or so.

Saussure witnessed a smock run at Kew Green, when girls and women stripped down to their scanties and raced each other to win a smock chemise, and such races were still being held in the Regency period.

A new industry in the country was devoted to sport, and employed a lot of countryfolk as it increased in importance. Racing at Newmarket began under James I, as an alternative to hunting and hawking, with the stables, riding house, lodgings, dog house and brewing house all designed by Inigo Jones. Those employed: grooms and stable lads, riding master, dog handlers, housekeepers and staff, and brewers, were on the King's staff, so it was a case of livery in royal scarlet for their clothes. The Civil War put a stop to the races, but Charles II revived them. The horses, however, were still compact riding horses, and the development of the streamlined racer did not happen until the eighteenth century when Arab blood was imported to improve the stock. Races became highly competitive, regular meets were spreading across the kingdom, and it became very fashionable for aristocrat or prince to maintain a famous stable. This resulted in a big demand for stable staff and trainers, and the majority of the owners were wealthy men who showed it by dressing their employees in livery. Many grooms were dressed in frock coats with collars and cuffs of contrasting colours, such as navy blue with red, or green with blue, and the horses' sweatcovers were to match. In 1727 Saussure described the jockeys at Newmarket: 'they wear little shirts, and tight breeches of red, blue, green and yellow cloth, and little caps of the same colour, or black velvet'.[9]

The tight cloth kneebreeches were not so durable as buckskin, so gradually the latter became more common, as well as leather patches on the seat and on the inside leg, which characterized many breeches worn by riding workers and were copied from postillions. The little peaked caps also were borrowed from postillions in the previous century, the peak being a means of keeping the rain out of the face when guiding the horse team and carriage through bad weather. Black was the most common form, and was worn by hunting parties, as well as by jockeys, ostlers, grooms, and postillions. Riding boots were worn by the aristocracy in the Middle Ages, while ordinary workers could not afford them, but once sporting became a craze employers supplied jockeys and grooms with such boots as part of the livery. The most famous shine was that created by the Melton hunt, which mixed champagne with the blacking, but that did not occur until the Regency period, and earlier efforts had to use elbow grease to produce a gleaming boot. The plain colours for jockeys' shirts were joined by the 1760s by striped versions as the number of owners multiplied and simple liveries could no longer suffice. The shirts worn during the race were of silk, but during the training sessions it is possible that knitted shirts were worn as an early form of jumper, since many of the shirts in paintings fit very closely.

Defoe stated that the biggest horses were bred in Leicestershire, huge black creatures which were taken to London for use as coach and dray horses – the working opposite to the sporting thoroughbred. The sheep in that county were also large, with long-staple wool like the sheep on the Sussex and Hampshire Downs and in the West Country. As a result the graziers could afford to rent farms at £500–£2,000 a year, as well as keeping several shepherds in their employ. The French still wanted to get their hands on English raw wool while prohibiting English cloth, and Romney Marsh continued to be the centre of the smuggling. The dragoons told Defoe that their patrols were often outnumbered by the size of the smuggler gangs! There was also so much corruption among local magistrates and gentry that the laws were not enforced. When the wool factor Jo Haynes was made a commissioner in 1698 he found that even a royal yacht, *Isabella*, had raw wool under the cabin beds, so the corruption went a long way up the chain of command. The Attorney General claimed the yacht so that no prosecution followed. Haynes told George I that there ought to be a government department with wool inspectors and its own patrol ships, but his appeal met the same lack of action in 1715 that had greeted it in 1706.[10]

The wearing of wigs continued to be an immediate indicator of social position. The enormous periwigs of 1700 were too large to allow any labourer to see what he was doing, and even army officers found them a nuisance, so they answered the problem by tying back the periwig in a bag. After 1715 these bag wigs gained in popularity, and were constructed with much less hair, so the price came down. A full periwig had cost a year's income in the 1660s, but by 1748 when the Swedish horticulturalist Pehr Kalm visited London he was surprised to see some labourers wearing cheap wigs costing one guinea. Better wigs cost from two guineas upwards, and the full-bottomed wigs were still worn by officials and some of the aristocracy.

Even the cheap ones represented about two months' pay, but even so that was a reduction compared to the first periwigs. Farmers who had found perruques too impractical started to wear bag wigs, and slowly the style appeared all over the country, but for the mass of working men one guinea was still a lot of money and they exhibited their poverty by wearing their own hair.

Aprons continued to be worn very widely by housewives and by blacksmiths, ironmongers and cart builders, always of linen in the home, but of leather for those working at a forge. A lot of men wore the apron fastened to a button on the jacket, a style which seems to have started with hairdressers in the previous century and now spread more widely. The women, of course, tied theirs round the waist, as they did not have buttons on their dresses. For such women fashion was restricted to the amount of hair they showed or the size of their linen caps. Hair, of course, was free, and they made their own caps, so a little modification could creep in among those who had had a chance to see what the upper classes were wearing. If they were lucky they might have a sister or cousin who was a lady's maid and could show them just how the latest look in caps was achieved, for it was the servant class which spread information on style among the lower orders. The principal trend was for caps to grow smaller, without the long lappets of 1700, so all the country girl had to do was to make her own cap smaller to echo the metropolitan mode. Such modifications became a tradition into this century, with working women reflecting fashion in their hairstyles and caps, but, being unable to obtain a whole new wardrobe in the latest silhouette, remaining fairly constant in their basic clothes. Previously the aristocracy had had to obtain information on court fashion through their letters to each other, but now magazines began to be published. *Le Nouveau Mercure Galant* of 1678 had some engravings of dress and long written descriptions of courtly splendour in France, as propaganda on French style. The first magazines for women in England were not illustrated, but by the 1750s annual ladies' pocket books started to appear, with a frontispiece illustrating the latest fashion, like *The Ladies Complete Pocket Book* of 1758, published by John Newbery. While most servants could not read English or French, they could look at the engravings, so once the mistress had finished with the latest edition it could be taken home for mother, sisters and cousins in the country to gaze at in wonder. It was a tiny step in making the country fashion-conscious, and most of the styles illustrated were too extravagant for working women, but a trickle of information had started that was not available before.[11]

Accordingly, when the German Carl Philip Moritz visited Windsor and Henley-on-Thames in 1782, he was surprised how metropolitan farming dress now looked: 'All the farmers whom I saw here were dressed not as ours, in coarse frocks, but with some taste, in fine, good cloth; and are to be distinguished from the people of the town, not so much by their dress, as by the greater simplicity and modesty of their behaviour.'[12] On his way from Harwich to London Count Kielmansegge described the whole of the country as looking like a well-kept garden, and foreigners got the impression that England was the best-dressed and managed country in Europe, with no barefooted peasants. But the Jesuit Battista Angeloni, who lived in England for 20 years, saw how they could be taken in: 'The peasants wear no shoes about their houses, and in their common travelling the roads they carry them in their hands, and wash their feet near the towns they are travelling to, when they put them on, and their stockings, many of them however have none.'[13]

English peasants refused to wear wooden sabots because they were French. Angeloni found another important distinction between peasants and artisans in England and Naples. According to him, as the Neapolitans were not free, they strove to dress richly with even the smith wearing crimson velvet kneebreeches decked with gold lace, and a laced waistcoat. The peasant wives went to market in cloth-of-gold jackets, and scarlet petticoats double-laced with gold, and their asses were also decorated. To some extent this still applies, with the peasant farmer in southern Italy willing to bankrupt himself or at least place himself deeply in

21. David Allan, 'Edinburgh Sedan Chairmen', *c.*1788. Apart from a Scottish bonnet, usually blue, and the patterned stockings, these chairmen wisely sport the 'overall' or overcoat against the weather that was common on both sides of the Channel. All male workers were wearing kneebreeches inland.

debt in order to put on a splendid show at a wedding or funeral. The English peasantry, on the other hand, felt that England was the land of the free, so why should they bother to impress anybody? The Jesuit padre should also have observed that England was the country of Protestantism, which preached modesty in dress and demeanour, the country where Quakerism began, and where even the aristocracy dressed plainly unless attending a gala occasion at court. When princes dressed simply, why should anyone wish to outshine them? – unlike Italy, where everyone wished to be taken for a member of a princely house, and the aristocracy dressed grandly all the time. Moreover,

22. David Allan, 'The Edinburgh Lace Woman', 1784. Laces for corsets are here sold in the street. The woman's black satin bonnet predates the fashion and became established across the United Kingdom. She wears a shawl and a check apron over a check pattern petticoat, with the overpetticoat pulled back.

England had a softer light, where garish garments appeared too bright, and lots of rain in winter, which would soon have ruined gold lace. The matter had more than one strand, but they all contributed to a national mood over dress.

Artisans and professionals

Professional black continued to dominate in medicine, the church and the law. A doctor wore a black suit, waistcoat, and kneebreeches, with a black three-cornered hat, and the only relief was the white bands, the white shirt, and the white powdered periwig. Lawyers still sported the black mourning gown, most commonly with a dark grey suit, and many still retained the formal periwig.

Sobriety was a national characteristic under the influence of Protestantism, as the Scot John Macky remarked in 1722:

The Dress of the *English* is like the *French* but not so gaudy; they generally go plain, but in the best Cloths and Stuffs, and wear the best Linnen of any Nation in the world; but they wear Embroideries and Lace on their Cloaths on solemn Days, but they do not make it their daily wear as the French do.[14]

Modesty was the basis of the Protestant Clothing Ethic, and finery was reserved for gala occasions. Even the aristocracy began to reflect this in their attire, and César de Saussure was surprised to see English dukes walking the street in simple frock coats in the morning, only having to dress up for court events and the season. Middle-class sobriety had already begun to spread upwards, but it did not reach the labourers until the nineteenth century. For them it was still russet brown for most suits, and a waistcoat if they were lucky.

Macky reported that London's Leadenhall Market near the Royal Exchange was the best daily market in the world, and Don Pedro de Rosquillo had told Charles II that more meat was sold in Leadenhall in one week than in a whole year in Spain. There must have been many blue aprons and blue oversleeves worn by butchers and their delivery boys, but the men and women selling vegetables would have had undyed linen aprons. Booksellers were centred on Paternoster Row, but legal, historical and dramatic tomes were sold mostly in Temple Bar near the theatres and legal inns-of-court. French bookshops were to be found in the Strand. This was a trade where a respectable suit in sober tones was *de rigueur* to give the impression of worthy scholarship. Similarly, respectability was important in Lombard Street, where many goldsmiths were now to be found; others were around Temple Bar. Silversmiths were in Silver Street, Gutter Lane, and a French one was located in St James's Street. Silk mercers clustered around Aldermanbury, Ludgate Hill, and Covent Garden. Woollen drapers were at the Royal Exchange, Covent Garden, and on the south side of St Paul's. Linen drapers were to be found mostly in Cheapside and Cornhill, but brasiers and pewterers were all over London. There were also reputed to be over 8,000 taverns and coffee houses, where men gathered to read the newspapers that the Civil War had started off, and to talk political gossip.

Tailors' and mercers' or woollen drapers' shops were still the places to see the undress of high society imitated, with the nightgown worn over the shirt, waistcoat and kneebreeches, and a turban or montero cap instead of a wig. For most other tradesmen, however, it was the apron worn with the suit, and the apron with a plain dress for their wives. Daniel Defoe had stressed in 1727 that the wise tradesmen trained their wives to run the business after them, for women generally lived longer.[15] He was very critical of apprentices. In the past they had cleaned the master's shoes, waited at table, collected water in long tankards from the public conduits, and attended the master to church on Sunday, but now all they condescended to do was to remove the shop shutters in the morning and sweep out. They got old women to clean the shoes, he maintained in 1724. William Hogarth took up this theme in his engravings on *The Industrious and Idle Apprentices* in 1747. Conduits were now only to be found in poorer areas, for oak pipes were being installed in classier streets from which lead pipes carried water direct to individual houses – to the astonishment of Saussure. Houses had also begun to display insurance plates, for fire companies had now begun. It had taken a major disaster like the Great Fire of London in 1666 to force people into setting up professional fire-fighting services. The property developer Nicholas Barbon set up his Fire Office in 1680 to insure buildings, and in 1696 the 'Hand in Hand' fire-fighting service was established, with six watermen on permanent call. The company chose a blue livery with jacket, waistcoat, kneebreeches, and a copper badge, which was to become the traditional colour for firemen. John Gay said that firemen in 1727 were wearing 'A leathern Casque', so that they had a leather helmet and probably leather boots too. They had to pump the engine to produce the flow of water into the pipes, but as the jet could not reach very high, they also had naval grappling irons to pull down blazing buildings. The Great Fire had involved calling out the army and blowing up houses with gunpowder, but now fire companies had arrived, each with its own badge such as the Sun, the Phoenix and so on. The journalists who reported on such disasters varied in their dress according to their status, from gentlemanly writers like Joseph Addison who founded *The Whig Examiner* in 1710, and Sir Richard Steele, founder of *The Tatler* and *The Spectator*, who both wore respectable suits and periwigs, to the scandal hacks who were notorious for their scruffiness and ink-stained clothes.

According to John Gay, walking through London was an art requiring special care in view of the number of artisans on the streets. Firstly, he stressed that only one kind of material offered protection against the weather:

Thy silken Drugget ill can fence the Cold;
The Frize's spongy Nap is soak'd with Rain,
And Show'rs soon drench the Camlet's cockled Grain;
True *Witney* Broad-cloath with it's Shag unshorn,
Unpierc'd is in the lasting Tempest worn . . .

Keeping the coat clean was another matter. Gay advised his readers to avoid the aprons of barbers, perfumiers and bakers, who would smother them either with powder or with flour, and to be careful in the throng:

The little *Chimney-Sweeper* sulks along,
And marks with sooty stains the heedless Throng;
When *Smaller-coal* murmurs in the hoarser Throat,
From Smutty Dangers guard thy threaten'd Coat.
The *Dustman's* Cart offends thy Cloaths and Eyes,
When through the Street a Cloud of Ashes flies;
But whether Black or lighter Days (dyes) are worn,
The *Chandler's* Basket on his Shoulder born,
With Tallow spots thy Coat; resign the Way,

dustbins, so the ashes had to be cold. It is possible that they had begun to wear a thick leather protective piece over the neck, because Hogarth showed a porter with such a piece buckled on to his hat in 1754, and both dustmen and coalmen did adopt this in time, as they all had to carry loads on their shoulders and necks. By the turn of the century someone had the idea of making the leather neckpiece and the hat in one, which became a traditional style throughout the nineteenth century, although the porters usually had the thickest neckpieces, as the more they could carry the more they could earn. Otherwise their clothes were the same as those of other workers; the hip-length jacket and kneebreeches in russet brown.

Of middle-class women Gay wrote that:

Good huswives all the Winter's Rage despise,
Defended by the Riding-hood's Disguise,
Or underneath th'Umbrella's oily shed,
Safe through the Wet on clinking Pattens tread.

This shows that the mediaeval patten was still being worn to protect the shoes in 1727, the clink being caused by the iron base, probably produced in Birmingham, which was now rising as an industrial town. The parasol or umbrella had been imported from the East from the 1670s, where, as its names show, it was used to ward off the sun and provide shade, but in wetter Europe the oiled version was invented. This was exclusive to the feminine wardrobe to begin with, and men were still expected to battle through downpours in cloaks or coats; when in 1756 Jonas Hanway started to carry an umbrella he was damned as effete.

Merchants' wives and prosperous tradeswomen were now wearing hoops of increasing width, with short-sleeved dresses, and little mantles in scarlet or black. The little straw hats Saussure considered most becoming, and found ladies of quality dressing in this bourgeois simplicity for walks and visits, like the men's unofficial undress. Of course, London was not England, and when Saussure speaks of Englishwomen wearing silk for winter, and Indian cotton for summer, with woollen cloth worn only by a few, he was not writing about the toiling masses. This dressing down for daytime

23. David Allan, 'The Edinburgh Fireman', c.1788. This fireman of the Sun company looks very maritime with his striped jacket and sailors' trousers, and could have been a seaman. A leather helmet protects his head. The fire-fighting insurance companies were among the first to give workers any protective wear.

To shun the surly *Butcher's* greasy Tray,
Butchers, whose hands are dy'ed with Blood's foul stain,
And always foremost in the Hangman's Train.[16]

Sending little boys up chimneys probably dates back to the introduction of chimneys. In England farmhouses in the fifteenth century still had an opening at the gable to let out smoke, and Celia Fiennes found such holes in cottages in Cumberland and in Scotland as late as 1700, but grander residences had begun to have chimneys throughout that period so the soot-covered boys probably started in the Middle Ages when a lord's great hall had a fireplace and so did his kitchen. Dustmen, previously called 'garbagers', carried wickerwork resulted in a reduction in the wearing of ribbons, flowers and feathers in the hair, in favour of plain caps in cambric or lace. The pride in neatly shod feet was centred in the south, where he saw no barefooted poor, but they existed in plenty elsewhere.

As the unprivileged had to do anything to earn a living Saussure came across some gladiatorial contests in London which surprised him. Two women fighters wore white linen bodices and short petticoats. One, a big Irishwoman had blue ribbons in her hair, at her waist and on her right arm; her short English opponent wore red ribbons in the same positions, to distinguish between the two. The linen clothes were cheap, and easy to wash the blood out of. The swords used were two-handed, three feet long and three inches wide at the blade. Action was stopped whenever a cut was made, and a surgeon would leap into the ring and sew up the wound on the spot without anaesthetic. This contest was won by the Englishwoman slashing the Irish one three times, twice on the head and once on the throat. He also saw male gladiators, who wore white linen jackets, kneebreeches and stockings, one with green ribbons and his opponent yellow. They shaved their heads, and their faces were ugly with scars and seams. This battle was more ferocious, resulting in one ear nearly off, and a scar cut from the left eye to the right cheek, which the surgeon sewed up. Saussure felt that cockfighting was more diverting than this sport, but the participants would have replied that it provided an income.[17]

At least the gladiators were not breaking the law, but Gay warned his readers to beware of those who did: the pickpocket boys in a crowd, who would lift watches and snuffboxes, or whisk off a wig, and vanish, or of the prostitutes who could be identified by the fact that they did not wear corsets:

'Tis She who nightly strowls with saunt'ring Pace,
No stubborn Stays her yielding Shape embrace,
Beneath the Lamp her tawdry Ribbons glare,
The new scower'd Manteau and the slattern air.
High-draggled Petticoats her Travels show,
And hollow Cheeks with artful Blushes glow;
With flatt'ring Sounds she sooths the cred'lous Ear,
My noble Captain! Charmer! Love! My Dear!

In particular, a man should watch out for prostitutes pretending to be respectable housewives, servants or pious persons:

In Riding-Hood near Tavern-Doors she plies,
Or muffled Pinners hide her livid Eyes,
With empty bandbox she delights to range,
And feigns a distant Errand from the *Change*,
Nay, she will oft the Quaker's Hood profane
And trudge demure the Rounds of *Drury Lane*,
She darts from Sarsnet Ambush wily leers,
Twitches thy Sleeve, or with familiar Airs,
Her Fan will pat thy Cheek: these snares disdain,
Nor gaze behind, when she turns again.

Pinners were caps with long side pieces which were now going out of fashion but could be seen on elderly conservative women. The high-pulled petticoats, not necessitated by working on a beach or muddy field, were another mark of the prostitute in town. The fan was an attempt at tawdry sophistication to entrap the country lad. Thieving from customers was typical of the trade, and in Westminster offenders were sent to Tottlefields Prison, which Saussure visited. The prisoners had to stand in two rows beating hemp and flax with heavy mallets, while a warden walked between the rows with a long cane to hit any shirkers. Their diet was bread and water, and there were no such things as prison clothes, so they wore what they were arrested in, which if the sentence were long meant an increasingly ragged appearance. Saussure saw a newly arrived prostitute in a magnificent silk brocaded with flowers, and the finest lace, who had been sentenced for stealing a customer's gold watch. Another, aged only about 15 or 16, had stolen money from clients. If a visitor offered any money to the prisoners the warder demanded half of it. Saussure's companion managed to get the girl released for 2/6 on the solemn vow that she would never steal or whore again, but two months later she was seen at the theatre as richly dressed as a duchess.

The Quakers were well known in London from their involvement in trade as merchants. To them fanciful clothing was impious, so the men wore big floppy hats with no loops or buttons, and very plain coats. Some even scorned shoe buckles and tied their shoes with cord. The women eschewed lace, ribbons, hoops, and frilled caps. Their cap was pleated on the forehead and made of silk, but bore no frills, while their hood (which prostitutes copied to mislead people) was also very plain. However, the quality of Quaker clothing was always very high, for they saw nothing impious about a thing being well made, or of good linen, silk and cloth. Religious toleration was now the rule in England, after the disputatious seventeenth century, and Saussure noticed that Jews did not have to wear distinctive clothing like the red hats Evelyn had seen on the Continent, although in Rome Jews had to wear yellow hats lest they be mistaken for cardinals. William III knighted a Jew for the first time in England in 1700: Sir Solomon de Medina, army contractor, financier and textile warehouse owner, for lending the government money.[18]

The most fanciful working clothes were found in the fashion world itself, on the dancing masters, perfumiers and perruquiers, and the place to see the latest modes was at the theatre. This had been the case in the previous century and continued down to this century, with the leading lady often attracting an audience as much for her clothes as for her performance in them. Thus when hair started to rise in the 1760s, the most extreme examples were to be seen on the stage, and on the engravings sold of popular actors and actresses. This trend was copied by maids in London, and then, in that 100-mile range around the capital, by some farm women, along with the bigger hats the styles involved. Beyond that range farmers' wives still wore the sugar loaf hat of 1660 in a slightly lower form, so that the hundred-year gap between metropolitan developments and the provinces still existed. Even so, printshops were beginning to spread to market towns, so those countryfolk within range of the town could see the plates of the latest look on market day, even if most of the style was beyond their pocket. Thus people in the towns and their regions were becoming a little more fashion conscious, although beyond that in the wilds matters remained static in dress.

Fanny Burney observed in *Evelina*, 1778, that the fashionable shops were quite theatrical places:

We have been *a shopping*, as Mrs Mirvan calls it, all this morning, to buy silks, caps, gauzes, and so forth.

The shops are really very entertaining, especially the mercers; there seem to be six or seven men belonging to each shop, and every one took care by bowing and smirking to be noticed; we were conducted from room to room with so much ceremony, that at first I was almost afraid to follow.

The ingratiating manners of bowing to customers and offering ladies seats as they contemplated the silks on show, were part of the seductive charm that Ned Ward had noted a hundred years before. At such emporia the sales assistants had to be smartly turned out, in clean coats, waistcoats, kneebreeches and silk stockings, and sporting the new high wigs, which for men rose in front. They were not so exaggerated as the female versions, which had a lot of padding, as *Evelina* recorded: 'I have just had my hair dressed. You can't think how oddly my head feels, full of powder, and black pins, and a great *cushion* on the top of it.' Even so the style was copied in the area around London by maids and by harvest women. Dressing the hair over a pad might need some help from a sister but the outline could be achieved, although for working women it had to be free of the plumes, jewels, ships, cascades, fruit and other fancies with which court ladies decorated their heads.

Fanny Burney also said that milliners (that is, dressmakers) were full of theatrical ways.

But what most diverted me, was, that we were more frequently served by men than by women; and such men! so finical, so affected! they seemed to understand every part of a woman's dress better than we do ourselves; and they recommended caps and ribbands with an air of so much importance, that I wished to ask them how long they had left off wearing them.

The dispatch with which they work in these great shops is amazing, for they have promised me a compleat suit of linen against the evening.[19]

Such rapidity in execution of an order was usual, the chore of the seamstresses upstairs who often had to work all night when a fine lady wanted something immediately. Their dress was a plain gown, an apron and a linen cap, as they sat sewing the enormous dresses and the mountains of trimmings which were the fashion. The paniers or hoops did begin to reduce during the 1780s, and the wide version was retained only at court, but the number of frills and furbelows did not decrease. French fashion was full of them, but the *robe à l'anglaise* had no frills and was decorated only with braid, and that appeared in Paris in 1784, when the English dislike of excess in dress began to make an impact across the Channel. Thus a London milliner would tell a client that frills were the height of French fashion, and the Paris milliner would suggest something simpler as being fashionable in England.

This was a common trick of the trade, to claim that something was the rage on this or that side of the Channel, which Horace Walpole said was often a blatant lie. The enormous hats of the 1780s were definitely French, and Sophie von La Roche was sorry to see their appearance in London, maintaining that the characteristics of national costume were gone, but a national difference over when hats were worn still existed. 'No breach of etiquette was quite so criminal in England as for a lady not to wear a hat outdoors. Even the lower-class women did,' so she felt compelled to acquire a hat and cap before venturing out in the London streets. Of course, she was expecting to find nymphs in the English national costume, but as it happened playing at shepherdesses had now been exported – to France where Queen Marie Antoinette was indulging in rural dress à la milkmaid and shepherdess.

Sophie had a front-row seat at the Haymarket when the new puffed-pigeon look made its appearance, in a clear example of a fashion being launched at the theatre, although its reception was rather rowdy, in 1786:

four ladies . . . entered the box during the third play, with such wonderfully fantastic caps and hats perched on their heads, that they were received by the entire audience with loud derision. Their neckerchiefs were puffed up so high that their noses were scarce visible, and their nosegays were like huge shrubs, large enough to conceal a person. In less than a quarter of an hour, when the scene had changed to a market-square, four women walked onto the stage dressed equally foolishly, and hailed the four ladies in the box.

The actresses had been quick to imitate the exaggerated style, and the fashionable girls' male escorts fled first, to be followed by the girls later when the ridicule was too much to bear. Even so, this puffed look came into vogue; puffing up a neckerchief was a simple thing to imitate, so it soon found its way around London, with plenty of maidservants willing to out-puff their mistresses.[20] Theatre companies took the new look to the provinces.

It was nearly fifty years since Saussure's visit, and the middle class mercantile women had changed to simpler fabrics than silk for summer:

[they] almost all wear black taminy petticoats, rather stiff and heavily stitched, and over these long English calico or linen frocks, though not so long and close fitting in the bodice as our tailors and taste cut and point them: here they are sensibly fashioned to the figure. Further, they mostly wear white aprons; though the servants and working women often appear in striped linen aprons. The caps really resemble those seen on English engravings, and simple black taffeta hats besides with black ribbons fitting right down on the head!

Obviously Sophie had consulted some magazines before coming from Germany. She observed that respectable women's feet were invisible, and that a new fashion for shoe laces was threatening the shoe buckle makers, which shows the mode imitating the Quaker shoe.

The century was well advanced before a concern over the fate of sweeps' boys began to be expressed. In 1760 'Ambulator' wrote to the magistrates of London and Westminster to protest at:

the number of chimney-sweeper boys that are to be met with in all parts of the town, without either shoes or stockings. It is to be concluded, that when their masters took them from their respective parishes, they, in some form, or other, bound themselves to provide them with some kind of clothing, to defend them against the inclemency of the weather.

He wanted sweeps who did not keep their apprentices decently dressed to be charged for a breach of contract, but no response came from the authorities. In 1785 Jonas Hanway tried to inspire action, maintaining that England was the only country which sent boys up chimneys. Elsewhere men did that job, or else two men pulled a bundle of brushwood on a rope through the chimney from top to bottom. Sophie von La Roche saw a sweep's boy aged only about six, but Hanway said they were usually apprenticed between eight and fifteen, and the poorest orphans and bastards were sold for seven years for twenty to thirty shillings – less than the price of a terrier dog. He argued that they were wretched:

we frequently see him, blasted with chilling cold, wet to the skin, without shoes, or with only the fragments of them; without stockings; his coat and breeches in tatters, and his shirt in smutty rags, sometimes with sores bleeding or with limbs twisted and contracted.

Hanway did not suggest that such jobs should be abolished, but he wanted all chimney sweeps to be registered to ensure that they looked after their boys, and he wanted the boys to be given a climbing dress of special kind. He was probably thinking of some sort of combination suit with a hood, possibly with trousers and rather like the old miner's hooded costume. Unfortunately, this philanthropic appeal also fell on deaf ears, so the ragged boys were still forced up chimneys, and sacks of soot were their only bed.[21]

In total contrast was the English reputation for cleanliness. Battista Angeloni wrote to a countess in Rome:

24. David Allan, 'The Edinburgh Salt Vendor', c.1788. All round the British coast, salterns produced salt from seawater in ponds and in boiler houses. This old vendor protects the contents of her basket with a cloth to keep it dry. Her hood, bedgown jacket and skirt are grey, probably the result of undyed cloth much worn. Once outside the town such workers would take off their shoes to save them.

What you have been told with respect to the English ladies, and women, in general is true, they have an external neatness in their dress, which is to be seen in no other nation; . . . This figure is dressed in the nightgown of England, which being often white, handkerchiefs and caps, as you will see, all of the same hue, gives an air of cleanliness beyond imagination.

He was most impressed that women of the upper rank were willing to dress down in simple clothes and aprons, unlike those in Paris who dressed as grandly as could be. It showed a modesty in avoiding the extreme mode which was the most important costume development in Britain in the eighteenth century. It explained why city ladies were prepared in the 1750s to dress like country nymphs and shepherdesses, as the Jesuit witnessed:

This dress, with their hats on in the public walks, communicates to a stranger, the most pleasing sensation, a kind of pastoral delight, a scene of old Arcadia, or like some of Watteau's pictures in the rural kind.

Yet this pleasant picture had its other side. If the French were overdressed, at least Frenchmen treated women as worthy companions for conversation, but Englishmen only treated women as temporary objects of joy.[22] This was a blinkered attitude: ladies were regarded as sweet and helpless, while no-one noticed the maids scrubbing the front step, or struggling upstairs with gallons of hot water, or scuttles of coal. It was one thing to dress like the working class, but quite another to help do their jobs. The sporting set, too, might like to dress like ostlers and coachmen, and talk to them, but as for their pay and long hours, that was another area not to be shared. Consequently many visitors were misled into thinking that Britain was more democratic than she really was. Dressing modestly was due to the Protestant Clothing Ethic, rather than to any empathy with the lower orders, and the contempt for the working classes felt by the upper levels in society were to lead to the rise of Radicalism and Chartism in the next century.

In his *Letters on the English and French Nations*, 1757, the abbé Jean Le Blanc was very critical of such dressing; for in Paris the lower orders tried to copy their lords, and in London it was the exact opposite:

masters dress like their valets, and duchesses copy after their chambermaids . . . that persons of distinction should take pride in dressing like their domestics, is a whim that borders upon irrationality. However there is no doubt, but it is from a principle of another sort of vanity, that many of the English affect to appear so modest in their dress.

Of course, he could not admit that the English were more godly than the Catholic French, or more humble, but it was the Protestant Church which preached simple clothes and simple churches, which affected labourers and aristocrat alike, and created a national mood.

Industry and the sea

The Age of Steam had begun in 1698, but there was no such thing as industrial dress yet and no legal regulations about it. The pioneers in this new industry were left to develop their own costume, such as leather aprons and clogged shoes to protect themselves from sparks. The heat of furnaces obliged men to work in shirts and waistcoats without their jackets on, but whether they preferred kneebreeches or trousers was a question of personal taste. The industrial revolution saw an important development for its future at Coalbrookdale in Shropshire. In 1708 the Bristol Quaker Abraham Darby leased an old blast furnace and reconstructed it. In January 1709 he first experimented with coke instead of traditional

charcoal to smelt iron ore. He tried other mixes of fuel, and built a second furnace in 1715, again using coke. This was important because charcoal meant burning wood and the forests were diminishing as a result, whereas coke was made from coal, of which there was an abundance in the region. By 1722 Darby had teamed up with the engineer Thomas Newcomen to make cast-iron cylinders for his steam engines. Newcomen's atmospheric beam engine separated the pumping unit from the boiler, and thus was a great improvement on Savery's engine. Newcomen's beam rocked 12 times a minute, and lifted 10 gallons of water up 51 yards at each stroke. The engines were installed at many mines, and the names of Darby cylinders and Newcomen engines spread together. The early use of coke did not produce an iron suitable for forging, but Abraham Darby II, the son, used a less-phosphorous iron ore which could be forged in 1748. Thereafter Shropshire started to produce more iron than the rest of the kingdom put together.[23] Not far away stood Birmingham, which Macky said in 1722 was the iron town for the whole of Europe, making swordhilts, screws, buttons and buckles. Liverpool had been given independent town status in 1698 by William III, and its new dock for 100 vessels was threatening to outdo Bristol as the major port in the west of England.

Defoe wrote that the miners in Derbyshire were called 'peakrills', and were 'a rude, boorish Kind of People; but bold, daring, and even desperate in their Search in to the Bowels of the Earth'. In wartime they were conscripted to undermine enemy fortifications. By now the special mining costume created in the sixteenth century seems to be dying out, as no-one commented on it, which is likely to mean that miners now looked too ordinary for comment, apart from their blackness with coal dust. In other words, they had changed over to kneebreeches for underground work and did not bother with hoods, so far as the men and boys were concerned. The women had probably gone over to kneebreeches too (as the theatre had), and like the men, they worked topless in the heat of the tunnels, or else wore their shifts under the kneebreeches. A kerchief round the hair would keep the dust out. On the surface, women and children with some men still sorted coal into sizes and sieved it, as in the ore industry. The women wore plain dresses hitched up to show the petticoat, with an apron on top, and a headscarf to protect the hair from dust when carrying baskets of coal on the head. The men wore kneebreeches and shirts, and sometimes old three-cornered hats. Aprons were still necessary for brickmaking, in sacking or canvas. Defoe found that 28 brickmakers in London used sea coal ash to mix with the clay to make their light 'laystallstuff' bricks, which needed less baking. This gave London boroughs a lucrative trade in garbage ash, and they charged garbage firms highly for the privilege of collecting it.

Defoe found little in the way of textiles left in Kent beyond Maidstone linen and Canterbury silk. Where there had been 300 looms, by 1724 it had dropped to 20, due to the flood of Indian silks, chintz and calico. Stroud in Gloucestershire had the best water for dyeing scarlet, and two to three million sheep fleeces were treated there a year. Leicester, Nottingham and Derby were stocking towns. Macky found Coventry a big, dirty weaving town, but was more struck by the effigy of Peeping Tom whose splendid blue coat trimmed with silver, black tie wig and laced hat were not correct period dress for Lady Godiva. Zacharias von Uffenbach visited London in 1710, and found a lot of children involved in the making of the famous English pins. He watched the weaving of plush, velvet, taffeta, damask, and flowered velvets for the royal state apartments, where children were also engaged to pull threads on the looms. London also wove girdles, gauze, ribbons, and silk handkerchiefs. The apron was still the most common working garment for weavers, usually in linen.[24]

Cloths and ready-made articles like caps, stockings and gloves were still carried around the country by pedlars. In 1705 the barrister Timothy Burrell of Sussex bought a pair of pink scarlet stockings for his daughter from a Scottish pedlar, which he considered a bargain. Shopkeepers in towns disliked travelling sales people, and in May 1685 had tried to introduce a bill into Parliament banning Scottish pedlars, hawkers and petty chapmen, in order to force customers to use shops. Roger North MP spoke against it, saying that taking goods out to the country customers increased sales, when country people could not visit the shops in town very often. No country housewife would ride all the way to town just to buy a ribbon, but she would buy it if it were brought to the farm. The House of Lords agreed, and threw the bill out.[25] Pedlars' weatherworn dress, often soaked by rain, continued to be rough homespun or second-hand garments, simple suits for men and simple dresses for the women, the latter using their aprons to carry articles in, as well as boxes and baskets. In the winter cold both sexes might wear the rough rug mantle or else an old overall/overcoat which had had previous owners and now featured a ragged hem and torn pockets. The head would be protected by any old hat in felt, or else a straw hat for women, still worn over the linen cap.

In the 1780s the overall coat did begin to be worn with trousers as the best outfit for travellers in rough country, for explorers, and by the cavalry on exercises in order to protect their fanciful uniforms. The outfit was worn as a protection against the weather and had nothing to do with industry. Trousers were also becoming more common among American settlers, for Lord Carlisle wrote on 21 June 1779 from Delaware in North America: 'The gnats in this part of the river are as large as sparrows; I have armed myself against them by wearing trousers, which is the constant dress of this country.'[26] Of course the Red Indians, Britain's allies against American rebels, already had their own version of trousers in one-legged trews which were attached to a belt at the waist and were not joined together in the middle. Europeans took over their type of one-piece trousers as the best answer to local conditions. A lot of British-made clothes continued to be sent across the Atlantic to dress settlers and slaves.

An illustration of the size of the wool industry as a basis of the economy can be seen in the clothier Samuel Hill of Halifax, who in three weeks in 1706 sold 1,000 cloths. He was big enough to employ

200 weavers, which meant 1,000 spinsters to supply the basic thread, for women continued to be the foundation of the system. The cloths were sent to fulling mills to be finished in urine, in the traditional way. Hill was large enough not to bother with cloth markets, but had his own contacts in England and abroad. Such markets had been held in the open, but in 1708 Halifax built a Cloth Hall, which was copied by Wakefield in 1710; Leeds erected its White Cloth Hall in 1711, with a Coloured Cloth Hall following only in 1757.[27] If England meant wool, Scotland meant linen, as Guy Miège observed in 1738:

Flax abounds in *Scotland*, so that besides what they consume themselves, they export great quantities of Linen, brown and whiten'd which is one of the greatest Manufactures of the Kingdom; and, if duly regulated and encouraged might save a great deal of Money in the Island, besides what it may bring into it. For the *Scots* have improv'd their Linen Manufacture much of late, and besides fine Linen, make very good Holland, Cambrick, Muslins, plain and strip'd, Threads, Dornick, Damask, Ticking for Beds &c. white and dy'd Threads, Laces, Tape &c.

He thought, however, that the Scottish women should be taught how to turn one pound of flax worth twelve pence into a fine linen lace worth £8, which is why he favoured more regulation of the industry.

The wool could not match England's, but Scotland produced:

Broad-cloth Coarse or Housewife's Cloth, Fingrims, Serges, Bayes, Crapes, Temmin, *Glasgow* Plaids, Worsted Camblets, and other Stuffs and Stockings for Home consumption and Export; besides their Tallow and Skins . . . They have come to a great Perfection in making Stuffs; and for Plaids, as has been mention'd already, they exceed all the World.

The raw wool from the Highlands and the Islands was brought to Aberdeen to the Wool Cross in the town centre to be sold, and the town made fine worsted stockings. This meant the sight of Highland dress mixing with Lowland. Of the Lowland men, Miège reported:

Their Clothes were made for Use, and not for luxury, their Stockings were never higher than the Knee, and they ware them indifferently of Linen or Woollen; their Breeches were most part of Hempen Cloth, and they had short Cloaks, as upper garments, of fine Yarn for the Summer, and coarser for the Winter.[28]

Presumably the jacket and shirt were worn under the short cloaks, in the same manner as south of the border.

John Macky wrote about Highland dress when he attended the Highland Fair at Crieff near Stirling in 1773, and noted that the chiefs were acquiring some civilized accessories:

The Highland Gentlemen were mighty civil, dress'd in their slashed short Wastcoats, and Trousing (which is, Breeches, and Stockings of one Piece of Striped Stuff), with a Plaid for a Cloak, and a blue bonnet. They have a Poynard, Knife and Fork in one Sheath, hanging at one side of their Belt, their Pistol at the other, and the Snuff-Mill before, with a great broad Sword by their side.

The followers were in belted plaids like women's petticoats, to the knee, and with bare thighs. Macky maintained that they stole everything, which suggests that he came from the Lowlands. The fair was the first time English cattle men had come to inspect the stock, and they bought 30,000 head at one guinea each. The Highlanders had never seen such money, and Macky said it showed the value of the Union. The Highlanders hired themselves to drive the cattle south for one shilling a day, but did not think about money for the trip back.[29]

Miège, however, noted a change in Highland attire with the introduction of more camouflage.

They delight most in Cloaths of several Colours, especially strip'd; the Colours they affect most, are Purple and Blue. Their Ancestors, as most of them still, made use of Plaids very much variegated; but now they make them rather of dark Colours resembling that of the Crops of the Heath, that they may not be discovered while they are on the Heath waiting for their Game.

The purple and blue were the colours of the heather, with which the new plaids were intended to blend. The Highlanders still slept in them in the open sometimes covered in snow.

Neither of the reporters deigned to notice women, but portraits show that the better-off women in the Highlands wore tartan dresses. They still wore plaids, despite complaints by the kirk that wearing plaids in church induced sleep. In Edinburgh the middle-class women looked English apart from the plaids, which were in many colours, unlike the black mantles so common on the Continent. The distinction between married women in linen caps and virgins wearing their hair down was still maintained in Scotland, although not in England. The poor Highland women had nothing better than the plaid as the basic body wrap, and possibly a linen shift; stockings were a luxury not for them, since they dug peat and fished on the beach.

Bonnie Prince Charlie upset all this in 1745. Miège's reference to variegation in plaids was also seen in the tartan suits, for at the battle of the Culloden some of the Prince's Highland troops were wearing as many as five different patterns. As Scots fought on both sides, the only way to tell who was who was by wearing cockades, white for the Young Pretender, and black for the Hanoverians. The red coats of the English Army were plain enough, and the Jacobites were beaten. To punish the Highlanders, the British government introduced the only clothing law in the century, the Act of Dress, in August 1747. This banned tartans, plaids, trews, little kilts, shoulder belts, and any greatcoats in tartan or partly-coloured plaid stuff, on pain of six months' imprisonment, or seven years' transportation for a second offence. The only exception was for soldiers in the Scottish regiments, for recruiting Highlanders was seen as a way of turning their bellicosity into service for the British government. While Highlanders were jailed for contravening the act, the gentry and the nobility continued to wear tartans and plaids because, as usual, they considered themselves above the law. In 1782 the Duke of Montrose persuaded Parliament to repeal the act, and the Duchess of Gordon, Jane Maxwell, took revenge by leading a fashion for tartan which was eventually to make the English wear tartan themselves. The Highlanders always insisted that their bare thighs were practical for acclimatization, along with sleeping outdoors when tending their cattle or hunting. The precise moment when a separate little kilt, the philibeg, was detached from the

plaid, is the subject of heated argument, but as the Act mentions them they were common enough to be recognizable as Highland dress. The vogue for tartan increased the amount of weaving work in Scotland. The napping that was done in England by waterwheels turning hammers, in remote parts of Scotland was done by tough-footed women who called it 'waulking the cloth', rubbing it to and fro with their heels against a board with runnels like a present-day draining board. They wore tartan dresses and capes with linen caps, if married, and their hair in a plait if unwed. The Lowland farmer-poet Robbie Burns helped to change the Hanoverian attitude to Scotland with his poems set to traditional tunes, helping to charm away the memories of the Forty-Five.

The sensation of the age was in Shropshire, when in November 1777 Abraham Darby III began the Iron Bridge, to an initial design by Thomas Pritchard who died in the October. The first iron bridge in the world, it attracted immense international attention, and attracted artists more than the advances in casting and and steam power that had made it possible. Cast-iron ribs were then used in the bridge at Preens Eddy downstream, and soon began to appear in industrial buildings. Critics said it would all fall down, but when disastrous floods on the Severn in 1794 washed away many conventional bridges, Ironbridge stood, and still does stand. Coalbrookdale produced iron wheels, iron rails, and iron pillars, and the Iron Age in industrial terms had begun.

There was still plenty of power in water, and in 1784 Samuel Gregg built a mill with a 32-foot diameter waterwheel of iron suspension, which produced one hundred horse power, at Quarry Bank, Styal, Cheshire, now a museum. That wheel worked until 1900. The indentures for some of Gregg's apprentices show that they received their clothes as well as food and training, in the traditional way. He produced cotton calico, and the Indian cotton which was too expensive for ordinary workers in 1700 began to drop in price by the 1780s, thanks to the gradual increase of production made possible by all the innovations in spinning machinery. The laborious yarn spinning done by millions of spinsters/housewives needed to be speeded up, and in 1764 James Hargreaves invented his 'Spinning Jenny', which spun eight threads, and by 1766 sixteen. A poor weaver, he was driven out of his native Blackburn by spinners and weavers, and opened his factory in Nottingham where he started to mass-produce cotton thread for the stocking trade. In 1771 Richard Arkwright opened his mill in Derbyshire with a roller-spinning machine which had to be powered by a waterwheel as it was too heavy for manual operation. The Bolton weaver Samuel Crompton produced a fusion of his predecessors' inventions in his spinning mule in 1779. Such developments met with fierce opposition and the burning down of mills, for the new techniques were always seen as a threat to existing jobs, rather than as an opportunity to increase production and make clothes cheaper. No longer were workers forced to wear rough wool and linen; cotton was coming down to their level. Moreover, a new cotton fabric had been invented: corduroy, a tough, durable textile. This coarse-ribbed cotton velvet was quickly adopted by labourers in town and country for their basic suits, and soon corduroy became the identifying livery of the working man.

The importance of water for transport received a boost in 1761 when the third Duke of Bridgewater asked his engineer to construct a canal from his mines at Worsley to Manchester. James Brindley solved the problems of locks by constructing an aqueduct to carry his canal over the river Irwell, without having to descend to it through a lock system. Since one horse can pull a canal barge full of coal weighing as much as 10 carts pulled by 10 horses on a road, the price of coal dropped from sevenpence to fourpence a hundredweight. Industry needs cheap fuel, and suddenly every industrial and commercial enterprise wanted to be connected to a canal system. The excavation all had to be done by labourers using picks and shovels, who put the earth into wheelbarrows for another set of men to run up wooden slats to the top of the bank where the earth was transferred into carts and wagons to be carried away. Consequently huge gangs, thousands of men, were involved, who lived in temporary accommodation like turf huts or wooden cabins, but they had to provide their own food and clothing, and only received a shilling a day. The contractors often paid them in tokens, which had to be exchanged for goods in the company shops. These were deliberately expensive, to keep the workers in short supply so that they could not afford to leave. Hobnailed boots, of course, were essential in so much mud, and rough corduroy suits were very useful here, along with a motley collection of Monmouth caps, felts and old three-cornered hats.

Canals were doubly useful, for not only did they make it cheaper to carry fuel to factories, but the barges could carry the finished goods to market as well. When Josiah Wedgwood built his pottery mills at Etruria near Stoke-on-Trent, he was very close to his fuel in the coal fields. His problem concerned the clay which had to come by sea from Devon up to the river Weaver and thence by land to the potteries. This was expensive, as was the despatch of the finished pots overland to the river to be sold, for the rough roads caused many breakages. Wedgwood asked James Brindley to connect the Trent with the Mersey, and this canal opened in 1777, so now everything he needed travelled smoothly by water – the coal, the clay and the pottery. Skilled labour was required to install locks: masons and bricklayers to build the surrounds, and carpenters to make the lock gates. These men were also needed to build the many bridges and aqueducts, and here aprons and smock frocks were still common. The types of barge varied according to whether they were used purely for inland waterways, or were coastal. In the Humber estuary the broad Humber sailing keels evolved, with a mast and sail, and the sailing barges on the Thames also became a distinctive type. Such craft used the coast, the rivers and some canals of the wider sort. Narrow boats evolved for the narrow canals, and as many of the eighteenth-century tunnels were very small, without any walkways, the barges had to be walked through by men lying on their backs and pushing against the roof with their hobnail boots. This was called 'legging', and some tunnels had teams of leggers whose boots must have needed frequent replacement. The term 'navigator' began to be used for the boat people and the excavators alike, and men from the Norfolk fens were most in demand for their experience in drainage. No special costume evolved; they simply wore the usual suits of the worker, as they had to supply their own. As towpaths were not common until the next century, there also teams of men called bowhauliers who would pull the barge upstream, scrambling over broken ground. Horses cost more than men did.

The barges were owned either by companies or by the bargemen themselves. Their dress was the normal working-class type for both sexes, with the new corduroy for men's suits becoming an institution into this century, and plain woollen cloth dresses for the women. Washing linen, however, was a problem in canal water, for the result was usually a muddy grey. Other jobs created by the canal boom were the lock keepers, the men responsible for the upkeep of weirs and flash locks, and carpenters, tinsmiths, and painters at the many canal boatyards, while the gradual introduction of horses led to more blacksmiths. As many trades already wore the apron it became just as common in the canal world, for almost every working woman wore one, as well as the carpenters, painters and blacksmiths. The engineers who designed this system of linking rivers and canals into an interlocking communication scheme, from the Thames to the Severn to the Mersey, differed in appearance from working men only in the better quality of their suits. These would be of a good broadcloth, and with an overall-overcoat for bad weather. The man who inspired the boom, the third Duke of Bridgewater himself, dressed with dark simplicity with only his buttons as an indication of rank: 'I remember his dark brown coat with gold buttons, the handsome rose of black ribbon which ornamented the tie of his hair, his placid but cheerful countenance, his manly and dignified form and carriage.' These would never be forgotten by those who worked for him.[30]

Whether men or women worked in any industry varied from town to town, as Arthur Young found on his tour of the north in 1771. Bedford lace was all women; Rotherham iron and pottery were men only; Sheffield plating and cutlery were men, women and children; Wakefield cloth was men only, as were the colliers; but Leeds cloth was men, women and children. Ayton alum production was men only; but Fremington lead mines employed men, women and children. Newcastle colliers were all males, and Carlisle cotton and checks were made by men; but Kendal stockings, cottons, linsey-wolsey and tanning were made by men, women and children. Warrington sailcloth, sacking, pins and shoes were made by all three, but Liverpool porcelain, stockings and glass were men only. Manchester fustian, check, hats and small wares employed men, women and children; the potteries men and women; Newcastle shoes and hats were made by adults and children, as were the porcelain and gloves of Worcester.[31] They wore the routine garments of the working class, never anything new, always home-made or passed on, and often only second-hand clothes were purchased. Exchanges between neighbours were also common, swapping the outgrown clothes of one child for another's. In industrial life there was little time for making garments so it was now mostly old clothes for all.

On the coast there was now more difference, for breeching had spread among fishwives. If the fishing fleet worked far away, they had to endure the same long separation from their husbands that sailors' wives underwent, as Fanny Burney found when she visited Teignmouth in 1773.

You see nothing here but women in the summer – their husbands all go out to the Newfoundland fishery for 8 or 9 months in the [year] so the women do all the laborious business such as *rowing* and *towing* and go out fishing yet I never saw cleaner Cottages nor healthier finer Children – the Women are in general Handsome none plain tho' tall and *strapping* owing to their robust work.

So she wrote in May, but by August she had seen their special costume:

Their dress is barbarous, they have stays half-laced, and something by way of handkerchiefs about their necks they wear a single coloured flannel, or stuff petticoat; no shoes or stockings, notwithstanding the hard pebbles and stones all along the beach; and their coat [petticoat] is pinned up in the shape of a pair of trousers, leaving

25. David Allan, 'The Edinburgh Fishwife', c.1788. Brightly striped petticoats were characteristic of the Newhaven area fishwives. This one has a bedgown jacket, and spotted headscarf over her white coif or 'mutch'. To carry a stone of fish on the back was usual. Here, too, shoes were put on only in town.

them wholly naked to the knee. Mr. Western declares he could not have imagined such a race of females existed in a civilized country.[32]

Sensitivity as to whether it was nice for women to do certain jobs which involved masculine-type clothing was a luxury that working women could not afford. Breeching their skirts was downright sensible for wading in the sea. The Catholic Church had long proclaimed that women should only work in the domestic situation, and Joan of Arc had been burnt for wearing men's clothes, among other crimes. This attitude, however, ignored the real position of working women. If their husband were at sea, the wife had to do everything at home, including his work. In the eighteenth century, opinion that women ought not to be strong workers was experiencing a revival, although this ignored the fact that many domestic jobs involved strength just as much as working in mines or fishing did. Fanny Burney's own mother had told her that it was 'unfeminine' to write novels, with hindsight a strange comment on an area where women outnumber men, and Fanny expressed a similar criticism in *Evelina* when describing the learned Mrs Selwyn: 'She is extremely clever; her understanding, indeed, may be called *masculine*; but, unfortunately, her manners deserve the same epithet; for, in studying to acquire the knowledge of the other sex, she has lost all the softness of her own.'[33]

Two trousered women of whom Fanny would not have approved were the pirates Mary Read from England, and Ann Bonny from Carolina, about whom Defoe wrote in 1724. Mary was raised in boy's clothes to fool her grandmother into continuing the weekly allowance of 2/6 she had paid towards the keep of her grandson, who had died. At thirteen she continued wearing the breeches and got a job as a footboy, but found it too dull, so she joined the Navy as a sailor-boy in trousers. It was the height of the war against French expansion, and most of the action was on land under the Duke of Marlborough, so Mary transferred to the infantry and fought with bravery. She next joined a cavalry regiment but fell in love with a Flemish officer and so was obliged to reveal that she was not the male soldier he thought she was. They married, and ran an eating house near Breda where Mary wore skirts for the first time, but her husband died, so she donned trousers again and went off to the West Indies to seek her fortune. There she was captured by pirates, joined them and rose to be captain of her own ship, given that she had naval experience behind her. When she was eventually captured she was engaged to a pirate and pregnant by him, which would have saved her from the gallows, but she died of prison fever. Ann Bonny was the daughter of a disgraced Irish doctor who abandoned his family and ran off

Ann Bonny *and* Mary Read *convicted of Piracy Nov.ʳ 28.ᵗʰ 1720 at a Court of Vice Admiralty held at* S.ᵗ Jago de la Vega *in y.ᵉ Island of Jamaica.*

to Carolina with a maidservant. While growing up in the colony Ann was courted by the pirate Rackan, so she donned sailor's trousers to follow him to sea, where she went on to join Mary Read's crew. Captured at the same time, she was saved because she was pregnant by Rackan, but he swung. Thus two decidedly strong, brave women wore the trousers, even if their jobs were outside the law. Their names are known, but there were probably others unnamed before them, who went to sea too in trousers.[34]

Sailors did not get a uniform until the nineteenth century, and there was still no such thing as the permanent naval or merchant seamen because all sailors were discharged at the end of a voyage – which is why the Admiralty did not want to give them a uniform. The size of the Navy varied enormously between war and peace, so that in 1710, about the time Mary Read joined it, the Navy had 313 ships and 43,950 men (and some women?), but when peace came again this was cut back to 67 ships and 6,637 crew in 1724. These enormous fluctuations went on all through the century, so

26. B. Cole, 'Ann Bonny and Mary Read convicted of Piracy Nov. 28th 1720 at a Court of Vice Admiralty held at St. Jago de la Vega in yᵉ Island of Jamaica'. American and British women in trousers, with short coats, baldrics to carry their cutlasses, and also armed with axes and pistols. However, they still wore the female coif to top the belligerent outfit. Female warriors go back thousands of years. The sea put women into trousers in the West.

that the advent of war would send the press-gangs out to impress 40,000 sailors from fishermen, colliers, labourers and the dregs of humanity. This is how lice were carried onboard and typhus spread. The naval surgeon Dr James Lind argued in 1757 that pressed men ought to be stripped of their filthy old clothes and given clean uniforms to prevent disease, but all he got was a uniform for his hospital patients to stop them deserting. Twenty years later other naval surgeons wanted a uniform of white waistcoats and trousers, a blue jacket and a round hat, with the ship's name on a belt. That appeal fell on deaf ears as well. Thus the dirty clothes and disease problem continued.

When Mary was on board the slop issue was grey kersey jackets with brass buttons and a red lining, red kersey breeches with leather pockets, red waistcoats of Welsh flannel, grey stockings, linen shirts and drawers, caps of leather or wool in red, and buckled shoes. The working rig was a canvas smock frock, wide breeches, and bare feet. The seamen did not have to buy the slops, so they would make do with what they had on when impressed. By 1737 the tarred hat was growing more common at sea, along with striped waistcoats, canvas trousers and a jacket with a neckerchief. If it was not a uniform as such, the sailor did want to look different to landlubbers, so the trousers and wide slop breeches were the traditional way to do it. This outfit was imitated among fishermen, too, as the jobs were interchangeable. Defoe observed in 1724 how the fisher smacks at Barking were conscripted in war to take pressed men out to the warships, to tender the fleet, and even on raids across the Channel to blow up Calais or St Malo.[35]

Macky described Portsmouth as the key to the kingdom, as it was the only town to have a regular fortification in the modern manner, designed for cannons by Sir Bernard de Gomme. It was peacetime when he visited the base in 1722, but he found 1,200 anchorsmiths, ropemakers, sailmakers, carpenters and victuallers in the dockyard. Defoe was equally impressed by the fortifications, and said the Navy made it a very prosperous town. Along with Chatham it was the arsenal of the nation, and a garrison town, so the gates were shut at nine o'clock every night. Poor César de Saussure came up against this problem when trying to leave England. Gales held him for days, and he found naval officers the most foul-mouthed and dissolute characters he had ever met. When the weather allowed him to be rowed out to the ship, the boat hit a buoy and sank, so Saussure had to swim to shore. As it was night, however, the town gates were shut so he had to descend to drying his clothes at a low tavern outside. He did find the sailors' diet satisfactory.

Diet concerned Dr James Lind who was the first director of the naval hospital at Haslar overlooking Spithead, the biggest brick building of its day. In view of the enormous numbers of men lost through scurvy, he tried to treat some sick crew members of HMS *Salisbury* in 1747, giving some the normal salted diet, and others oranges, garlic and lemons. The ones on fresh vegetables survived, the others died, and Lind published his findings, but it was forty years before the Admiralty agreed to issue lemon juice, so the enormous losses continued.[36]

Naval officers got a uniform in 1748. They were annoyed that Army officers already had uniforms, with the royal bodyguard, the Beefeaters, in royal scarlet livery, as were the new Guards regiments established after the Restoration, starting with the Coldstream Guards (which is why British troops were called 'redcoats'). The existence of red slop suits in the Navy in Queen Anne's reign is indicative perhaps of this jealousy. The Navy Club appealed to the Admiralty in 1746, and in 1748 the order was given that all officers above the rank of midshipmen should have a dress suit and a frock coat for undress. Midshipmen and students at the Portsmouth Naval Academy received one suit. In 1767 dress suits were abolished and the frock coat was elevated to use for all purposes. As in other liveries, differences in rank were shown by the collars, cuffs and buttons. The use of gold lace and embroidery on the cuff to show rank was introduced from 1783. Modification was made every few years, so the details varied continually, but blue, not royal scarlet, was the colour chosen, because the Marines had red uniforms. Of course officers considered themselves gentlemen, so they did not wear trousers but kneebreeches and stockings, not wishing to be confused with sailors and fishermen. Unofficially the hip-length jackets of sailors and all male workers were better for climbing up the rigging than frock coats so some officers borrowed this garment when they had to go aloft, but this was not granted recognition until 1825.[37]

The pay system continued to be unjust, with the tokens still issued, and men transferred from one ship to another losing all the pay due to them. At the end of the voyage when the sailors were paid off few of them could calculate what they were due, so there was no end to the dirty tricks of pursers.

Servants

The eighteenth century saw the appearance of scores of books on servants as the increase in trade and industry created a bigger middle class which needed to know how to manage its domestics. In his *Vade Mecum* for country gentlemen of 1717 Giles Jacob advised that a family, that is, estate, of 25 to 30 persons should have 8 to 10 liveried servants costing £50 to £55 a year. The bailiff, ploughmen, haymakers, husbandmen and harvesters would cost £80 a year in pay, and the mason, carpenter, smith, painter, saddlers and carrier £80. The clothing allowance for the gentleman himself should be £200 a year, nearly as much as liveries and wages put together. All employees were still called servants.[38]

In comparison, on New Year's Day 1722 the first Duke of Chandos had 93 persons in his palace Cannons near Stanmore, including his immediate family, his gentleman of the horse, his butler and valets, his black boy, the gentlemen ushers, the waiting pages, the Duchess's own pages and gentlewomen, under ushers, brewers, coachmen, footmen, postillions, stablemen, maids, cooks, and the postboy who rode a Welsh pony to the town house in St James's to collect the mail. The servants' diet was on Tuesday, Thursday and Sunday 21 oz. of beef, on Monday and Friday 21 oz. of mutton, and Wednesday 14 oz. of pork. The ducal livery was blue coats for the men, and blue stockings were added in 1727. In times of mourning it was blue edged with black. However, the baker received a green livery coat, vest and breeches. The gamekeepers wore shag frock coats, leather breeches, hats and boots. In 1723 the Duke spent £73 on livery, but the following year needed to economize and restricted full liveries to seven footmen, two coachmen, two grooms, one postillion, and two porters, the servants who were on

public show. The cost for plain liveries was £5 each, for laced ones £5.12s., and for the running footman who did not have a coat £1.17.2d. The Duke had to restrict expenses even further, for Cannons had cost a fortune to build, and in 1737 it was ruled that livery should be worn only between noon and six o'clock when guests were entertained, and plain frock coats otherwise. As another

economy the valets were ordered to curl and powder the Duke's wigs themselves and not send them out to hairdressers, which suggests just how free servants could be with the master's money. The Duke himself spread his purchases over many suppliers, so which tailors he used for livery and which for himself is not easy to say, but he patronized Bushy, Peter Carmo, James Thomas,

27. J.C. Ibbetson, 'The Sailor's Return Home', 1795. This fortunate sailor has got home without being press-ganged off his ship by the Navy. Trousers dominate sea life and the coast for men, along with fur hats or tarred hats. The wife has a mob cap and a fashionable red ribbon at the throat *à la guillotine*, and looks more modish than a country girl. Note the violin over the fireplace, the print on the wall and the pet parrot. Sailors had a wider view of the world than landlubbers.

Lewis Goulay, Humphreys, Alexander Jolly, Maxworth and James Mulville. Linen clothing for the household was made by the maids, but the linen draper was Hester Drew, and the hosiers were Sarah Beauvais, Jane Lucas, and Sarah Stanley. Dimity and diaper were supplied by Mrs Winchester. Hats and gloves came from Mrs Nixon and Sarah Maynold. Irish cloth was supplied by Johanna Tims, and brocade by Mrs Cocks. Nightgowns came from Eliza Probart, presumably for the Duke only. Women were very common in the underwear and fabric trades, but the Duke's wine merchant was Mrs Worth, and his butcher Mary Tomson.[39]

On his visit in 1784 the Duke de La Rochefoucauld stated that:

In general the English have many more servants than we have, but more than half of them are never seen – kitchenmaids, stable-men, maidservants in large numbers – all of them being required in view of the high standard of cleanliness. Every Saturday, for instance, it is customary to wash the whole house from attic to basement, outside and in.

To control the numbers of men in service the government had just introduced a tax on servants of one guinea a head; so while some nobles still employed 30 or 40 male servants for public show, the greater part of the work was done by the unseen, unliveried women.[40]

The richness of the liveries on show incensed many people. In 1720 Thomas Seaton complained that:

Much of unnecessary Cost is frequently bestow'd upon rich and showish Cloaths, or vain and gaudy Ornament, such as are both of them unsuitable, and above the Rank of a Servant in their Character to be cloath'd, or to be set off with; and they at once beggar themselves, and are the Objects of Ridicule to the Gentlemen or Ladies they serve, for the Affectation of Finery above their Place.

He also stated that servants should not gamble, drink, go to the theatre or play bowls at Marybone Gardens, which were common faults of London staff.

In 1725 Daniel Defoe attacked servants for their looking too fine. The maid from the country, he said, is engaged for £3 a year in town, the same wages as in Pepys's day, but hears of posts at £4 or £5 a year, so she moves on, and starts to dress too well:

Her Neat Leathern Shoes are now transform'd into lac'd Shoes with high Heels, her Yarn Stockings are turn'd into fine Worsted ones with Silk Clocks, and her high wooden Pattens are kickt away for Leathern Clogs. She must have a hoop too, as well as her Mistress, and her poor scanty Linsey Wolsey Petticoat is changed into a good Silk one, 4 or 5 yards wide at the least. Not to carry the Description further, in short, plain Country-Joan is now turn'd into a fine *London-Madam*, can drink Tea, take Snuff and carry her self as high as the best.

Tea was an expensive novelty. The Duke of Chandos paid 12/– a pound for green tea in 1724, and £1 a pound for Imperial tea in 1729, yet servants had a way of acquiring their masters' habits.

Defoe maintained that he had interviewed one maid who was so particular that she would not do any cleaning – that was the charwoman's job; she would not do any washing – that was the laundrymaid's duty or else could be sent to the laundry; she would not cook – that was the cook's department; she would not do any needlework – that was the chambermaid's duty; and she would not have anything to do with the nursery – that was the nurserymaid's. Evidently this jade just wanted to be a lady!

It was all too easy to mistake such creatures for their mistresses, as the Academician Pierre Grosley observed in 1772:

The servant-maids of citizens wives, the waiting women of ladies of the first quality, and of the middling gentry, attend their ladies in the streets and in the public walks, in such a dress, that, if the mistress be not known, it is no easy matter to distinguish her from her maid![42]

Carl Philip Moritz from Berlin was also surprised how maidservants strove to follow fashion, in 1782:

Fashion is so generally attended to among the English women, that the poorest maid servant is careful to be in the fashion. They seem to be particularly so in their hats or bonnets, which they all wear; and they are, in my opinion, far more becoming than the very unsightly hoods and caps which our German women, of the rank of citizens, wear. There is, through all the ranks here, not so great a distinction between high and low, as there is in Germany.[43]

Defoe argued that women servants ought to be liveried like the men to stop this confusion of the ranks.

Things of this Nature would be avoided, if our Servant-Maids were to wear Liveries, as our Footmen do, or if they were obliged to go in a Dress suitable to their Station. What should ail them, but a Jacket and a Petticoat of a good Yard-wide Stuff, or Callimanco might keep 'em decent and warm.[44]

He thought that the wearing of silk by servants was also bad for the native wool industry. In 1771 it was reported that Queen Charlotte wanted to see maids wearing badges or marks on their sleeves to distinguish them, but nothing was done. The independence of English servants amazed foreigners, but England was supposed to be the land of liberty. Abolishing livery was also no solution, as Count Frederick Kielmansege found in 1761–2, when dining with the Duke of Newcastle who allowed his footmen to look like men of quality:

At least ten to twelve servants out of livery waited upon us, of whom the majority wore long wigs, which would naturally make it difficult for a stranger to distinguish between guests and servants. Now, all these people, in spite of their fine clothing, expect their tips when you leave but to a gold-laced coat you cannot offer a solitary shilling; you must slip two shillings and sixpence into his hand.[45]

The count was equally surprised at Newmarket to see the British nobility itself dressed as plainly as horse dealers from Smithfield, but the British upper classes did not have to attend court so much as continental nobility, and spent a lot of time on their estates and at their stables in simple country clothes. To show their rank, they let their servants wear silk and gold lace, and the count was staggered by the amount of gold and silver plate displayed at Newcastle's dinner party. One could impress by one's accessories, especially the servants.

Padre Angeloni complained that English servants were the highest paid on earth, and the best fed, and as for maidservants insisting on tea twice a day, was there no limit to their presumption?

Grosley also felt the wages were too high, for a Welsh maid who could hardly speak English and only do simple cleaning, received six guineas a year, plus one guinea tea allowance. This beverage is one of the best examples of the way the servant class passed on aristocratic habits to their relations.

Jonas Hanway protested in 1756:

It is the curse of this nation, that the *labourer* and *mechanic* will *ape* the *lord* . . . To what *height* of folly must a nation be arrived at, when the *common people* are not satisfied with *wholesome* food at *home*, but must go to the remotest regions to please a *vicious* palate! There is a certain lane near *Richmond*, where beggars are often seen, in summer season, drinking their *tea*. You may see labourers who are *mending the roads* drinking their *tea*; it is even drank in *cinder carts*, and what is not less absurd, sold out in cups to *Haymakers*!

Keeping up with one's betters, however, had become a tradition in Britain. Hanway thought that splendour was on the increase and wrote in 1767:

It was a rare thing in my memory to see any gold or silver lace on the clothes of a domestic servant in livery; lace of wool, cotton or with a mixture of silk, contented us. Now we behold rich vestments, besilvered and begilded, like the servants of foreign princes.[47]

A response to all this criticism came from the poet-footman Robert Dodsley, who argued neatly:

'Tis true, internal Qualities conduce
To greater-Ends, and are of greater Use,
Than those which only serve for outward Show,
As powder'd Wiggs, clean Shirts, and such like do;
Yet these are necessary, and 'tis fit,
That those, whom Time and Business will permit,
Appear before their Masters always clean and neat,
But don't ye run into affected Ways,
And apish Gestures practis'd now-a-days;
Be decent, clean, and handsome, but not nice,
Respectful and well-bred, but not precise.
Preserve a Mean; but of the two Extreams
A Fop less odious than a Sloven seems.

Dodsley also countered Defoe's argument against servants wearing silk:

He enumerates several Inconveniences which he would persuade us arise from Servants wearing Silks, Cottons, and painted Linnens. And first, he wisely thinks 'tis detrimental to our Woollen Manufactures, not considering that there are very few Silks worn among Servants, but what are their Ladies Cast Cloaths, which if they were not to wear, would be sold to the old Cloaths-Shop, and worn amongst the common People's Wives and Daughters; and where then would be the Difference, with respect to the Woollen Manufacture?

Defoe also criticized housekeepers getting poundage of a penny or two in the shilling on goods supplied by tradesmen, but Dodsley, of course, was all in favour of poundage and tips, or vails, as they were called. The Scottish nobility attempted to stop vails, with mixed success.[48]

Lavish finery was of course restricted mainly to the servants of the very rich. Of the servants of the middle class Grosley wrote 'All the domestics of the citizens are dressed in plain, but good Cloaths,' and he was much taken by London coach drivers:

Coachmen, as a mark of distinction, wear an upper coat adorned with a long cape of two or three rows, each of which has a fringe. With this upper coat wrapped round them, their bodies bent, and their legs swinging backwards and forwards, they cut the same figure on the coach here as the modish coachmen who make the pavement of Paris sparkle.

He could discern no difference in livery dress between the coachmen of government ministers, aristocrats or merchants. The costume was the same, apart, probably, from colour. Grosley also admired the coachmen's self-discipline, for when 400 coaches converged on Ranelagh Gardens they formed themselves into files, without police or marshals, whereas in Paris such pressure of traffic would have ended in a vicious mêlée.[49]

They were not all angels, for at Shalstone Manor Elizabeth Purefoy complained that her coachman John had run off on hearing that a pregnant girl was charging him with paternity. Footmen could be difficult too, for she had to write to the mercer Woodford at Bicester on 3 June 1741:

I desire you will send mee in some time this week the following things (To Wit) 4 yards of cloath the same to the pattern wch is what I had of you for the last frocks. The footman who went away took his frock and wastcoat with him.

By 1743 she clearly had a new coachman who needed livery, as she wrote to her tailor Fell in Chipping Norton:

I desire you will make the coachman a frock the same coloured cloath to the pattern as near you can, & gold coloured serge paduaSa wastcoat. Pray let the serge paduaSa be better than the last was. It must not be a lemon colour, but a gold colour, & and the lining of the frock must be of the same colour; and let mee have it within a week or as soon as you can.[50]

Here the 'frocks' are frock coats, now regular among masters and male staff. They also feature in the accounts of the Reverend William Cole, whose man Tom Wood was also postillion, valet, woodman, footman, harvester and gamehunter in this parsonage. In 1766 we have 'Tom Allen the Taylor & his son making a Fustian Frock for Tom,' and earlier that year:

The Taylors here making Tom's livery, a white light coloured cloth turned up with Yellow & lined with the same & gilt buttons, & Yellow Plush Breeches, but his Postillion Coat is all yellow. This I have given above 30 years; for my father gave no livery at all . . . I might chuse as I pleased.

The parson's mother had been a member of Lord Montford's family, so he based his livery on his lordship's.[51]

Female staff received clothes of a purely functional nature, without the gilt buttons, lace or braid of livery coats, and were the peahens by comparison with the peacock footmen. Nan West, housekeeper to Timothy Burrell Esq., usually received her allowance in May. In 1700 it was 'two smocks for Nan West 5s. A chip hat 1s.6d. 2 blue aprons 2s.6d. Mending her fingers, 2s.6d. New shoes 2s.2d.' In 1701 she received '3 flaxen shifts for her, 10s.; stuffe for her gowne and petticote 12s.9d.; and for making the gowne, 2s.'. In that sort of situation she probably told her employer what needed to be renewed, and as he was a widower there was no likelihood of any silk dresses coming her way. The mended fingers were probably working fingers for use in cold weather, like gloves with the fingertips missing.[52]

Black pageboys were still dressed in turbans à la Turque with sometimes an aigrette, but the rest of the costume was usually conventional, with a frock coat, waistcoat and kneebreeches, stockings and buckled shoes. The only other exotic touch might be a sash or earrings. Native pages still often came from good families, in the mediaeval tradition, to be trained and educated and subsequently to be given some advancement, so these young gentlemen were often dressed as such, with good-quality wigs, linen and suits. Whether the pages still had to wear trunkhose or kneebreeches depended upon the taste of their employers for a historical or a modern look. Where the occasional black woman servant was engaged she was dressed as simply as other women servants in a plain dress and an apron, but she might have a touch of West Indian style in the bandana knotted on her head, instead of the linen cap of British women.

For running footmen Scottish youths were most in demand, doubtless because of their childhood in bare feet. When John Newte was on his way to Dumfries in 1785 he noticed lots of Scottish children running about with bare feet, and the women too, of course, but they now had stockings without feet called *huggers* – an early form of leg warmers. The smoke from the peat-burning gave them all a yellow hue, and he commented 'Their Dress, in general, particularly that of the old, is little graceful'.[53] Once employed as a running footman the young Scottish male could be dressed in considerable splendour, and the Duke of Chandos had one from the Highlands as the fleetest of foot. By the 1780s, however, the running footman was in decline, for the turnpike roads meant that coaches did not have to be massive vehicles to plough through mud, but lighter and therefore faster. The footman running as fast as he could would now be overtaken by carriages and phaetons dashing along at sixteen miles an hour. Furthermore, the Post Office had by now spread all over the country, so it could carry messages. It stopped using single postboys, who were often robbed, and introduced the first Royal Mail stagecoach on 1 August 1784, from Bristol to London in 17 hours, calling at Bath, Chippenham, Marlborough, Newbury, Reading, and Maidenhead, with four horses and fifteen changes. It carried an armed guard with a blunderbuss to see off any robbers, and so was safer than the solitary postboy or the running footman.

Just how fancifully dressed running footmen could be varied from employer to employer, but velvet and silk were common. According to the Revd George Ashby they always wore short silk petticoats weighted down with a deep gold fringe, but this was a sweeping generalization. The inn sign of the Running Footman portrays him in a short jacket decorated with frogging, a sash, kneebreeches with rosettes at the knee, and a black postillion's cap with the peak turned back and a feather, carrying his long cane with a silver top, inside which eggs and wine could be carried to fortify him *en route*. The Duke of Lauderdale's running footman also wore kneebreeches, as seen in the second chapter of this book, so the comment that 'Village Maids delight to see the Running Footman fly bare-ars'd o'er the dusty Road' does not apply to all of them.[54] All such male servants would astound country folk by the sheer colour of their liveries. The third Duke of Richmond's livery at Goodwood was yellow frock coats with scarlet collar and cuffs trimmed with silver. Lord Torrington sported dark blue frock coats with brass buttons and yellow breeches for his staff. The Earl of Carlisle favoured claret frock coats, and the Marquess of Bath mustard frock coats with black waistcoats and silver braid, silk stockings and silver buckles on their shoes for the footmen, and gold or silver lace on their three-cornered hats! What luxury they wore, what food they ate, and in some families they had a job for life, until they ended as the old man who banged the gong for mealtimes. Little wonder that servants in great houses were envied, with their brand-new clothes every year, while the average peasant never had anything new. From the outside it must have looked magical, but one could not see the women toiling away in the kitchens and the cellars as drab as could be; the cooks, scullery maids, laundry maids, brewsters and ciderwomen, all with their sleeves rolled up, all with aprons over their dresses, and their linen caps.

FOUR

The Industrial Revolution
1795–1845

Agriculture

For men the biggest change since the adoption of kneebreeches was the boost given to trousers by two movements. The first was cultural: the back-to-nature vogue and the cult of the Picturesque, with rural subjects the fashion, which led more men in the middle and upper classes to wear trousers because they were 'rural'. Because trousers were fashionable, countrymen now adopted them more widely, but on a gradual scale. The older generation, as might be expected, stuck to kneebreeches well past 1820, and it was the younger men who took to trousers. Even so, kneebreeches did not disappear completely, and today still can be found in the country on gamekeepers and hunters, as they are not long enough to get covered with mud. Trousers were a craze for the urban young, and were given much political significance by the French Revolution: the revolt of the *sans-culottes* (those without kneebreeches), the trousered peasants, against the aristocratic establishment. Thus any male who considered himself liberal and radical adopted trousers, preferably as tight as could be, although high society still insisted on kneebreeches for court and evening events. Of course, it was the region around the capital where trousers first became common wear, and were the mark of the young master who still expected his servants to wear kneebreeches.

In 1800 the concept of hiring fairs had still not reached Cumberland, where the requirements of the statute of 1350 were maintained almost to the letter, although some jollification had been added. John Housman observed:

Hirings for farmers' servants in the county are half yearly, viz. at Whitsuntide and Martinmas. Those who offer their services stand in a body in the market-place; and, in order to distinguish themselves, hold a bit of straw or a green branch in their mouths. The market being over, and fiddlers tuning their fiddles in the public houses, the girls begin to file off, and gently pace the streets, with a view of gaining admirers while the young men, with equally innocent designs, follow after, and, having eyed the *lasses*, pick up each a sweetheart, whom they conduct to a dancing room and treat with punch and cake. Thus they spend the afternoon, and part of their half year's wages, in drinking and dancing.[1]

The absence of tools to illustrate a job, and of aprons to indicate the type of domestic post, is striking, and the hiring had nothing to do with fairs, statute or otherwise.

Clearly such associations existed in the south of England, and by the 1840s were being condemned for their licence, when Francis Heath was praying that they would cease, in tones of Victorian disapprobation:

. . . the 'mops', 'hiring', or 'statute' fair . . . had not ceased to disgrace some of the smaller towns of the western districts. These fairs, annually held to enable servants, of both sexes, to be hired, were often the occasion of the greatest drunkenness and profligacy. Young girls dressed in their finest clothes, were exhibited like cattle to be hired by the would-be employers, who came to the fair to seek their services; and the scenes which frequently took place at the close of the day were too disgraceful for description. But, though the 'mop' fair had not then, as it has not yet, become an institution of the past, there were, happily, signs that its decline had commenced.[2]

He did not seem to care that this annual event in the West Country might well be the only time when

farm workers and servants came to town. In Cumberland newly hired employees were usually allowed a week to go home and mend their clothes before starting work at the farm, but Heath does not mention such a custom in the West Country. He stated that as late as 1842 clothing for the peasants was very inadequate, especially among the women. Too poor to afford more than one outfit, if they got soaked outdoors they had to go to bed while trying to dry their clothes, but the garments were likely to be still damp when they had to be donned next day. By then, however, the clothing club was beginning to creep in, usually run by the parson's wife, to which labourers' families could contribute a penny or threepence a week slowly to build up enough money to buy, second-hand, their Sunday or holiday outfit. It still meant, however, that at best the farm workers would only have two lots of clothes, and the best had to last a lifetime.

Heath interviewed a farm labourer aged 81 at

28. T. Uwins, 'Haymakers at Dinner', c.1820. Smocking can be seen on the farmer's smock frock, and it became a nineteenth-century tradition. More important was the invention of corduroy, seen in the suit of the young man on the ground with the hobnailed boots. Its strength and durability was a boon to workers. The old woman retains a black satin bonnet, but the young ladies have mob caps or poke bonnets. The girl by the tree wears the sleeveless bodice so common on the Continent and also found in Britain.

Marlborough in Wiltshire, who had started work in the previous century when he was eight. He said his life's wear had been smock frocks and corduroy kneebreeches, and he had always worked for twelve hours a day. A man of that age would not want a pair of new trousers even if they were given to him for nothing. An old woman of 65 had started farm work at 13:

she was arrayed in a sun-bonnet of bluish-green print – her dress, or gown, being of brown linsey at threepence-

29. Anon., 'Dorset Peasants', *c.*1840. More elaborate smocking back and front evolved, especially on Sunday smocks. The man with the pitchfork retains knee-breeches and gaiters, but his companion has gone over to trousers. The mother has a black satin bonnet over her coif, but the little girls have the tunnel-shaped sun bonnet which the Dutch had been wearing since the 1660s.

halfpenny the yard, set off by a blue apron made of material worth sixpence the yard. Coarse woollen stockings worn with their heavy boots are considered by farm women the most comfortable article of their kind.[3]

The apron was the most expensive article this woman was wearing, and so was probably her best apron, worn specially to be interviewed by the gentleman. The sun bonnet had a varied ancestry. David Allan's lace woman of 1784 had worn a black fabric bonnet with a wide brim to shield the eyes from the sun, and such bonnets were still being worn in 1820s. They predated the entry of bonnets into high fashion, which did not occur until about 1795. Fashionable bonnets were much narrower, the poke bonnet look; but one advertised in *Carnan's Ladies' Complete Pocket Book* of 1802 had a fabric hood gathered into a stiff brim

which was very round in shape, and this style transferred into the sun bonnets of the Victorian period. The farm woman or town trader needed to be able to see, as well as to shade the face from the sun, so this wide brim, of cane, became the basis of the later type of sun bonnet. The first kind had been black, reflecting the popularity of black taffeta hats in the 1780s, but after the regency the new version was more colourful, like the blue-green print Heath mentioned. They were worn very widely from Sussex and Hampshire up to Scotland, and on the borders were called 'uglies'. Certainly they were less elegant than the modish bonnets, and quite bulky in comparison, but they were a functional article of wear.

Of course the ancient straw hat did not disappear before it, and maintained a long run beside the sun bonnet. Their making was dominated by women, and the size of the industry can be seen from James Pigot's *Commercial Directory* for 1842. Chesterfield had 14 women straw-hat makers, and one man. Derby had 20 women, and no men, and Melbourne eight women. Bristol had 75 women, and about half as many men. Other towns with such hatters were Cheltenham, Gloucester, Worcester, Hereford, Monmouth, Newport, Oxford, Bath, the Potteries and Birmingham. It was obviously a big local industry, and straw hats must have been very common in summer.

The term 'mob cap' became more polite in the 1790s, having suggested sluttishness before then, and was now used to describe a lady's morning cap. This was simply the ordinary linen cap that women had been wearing for centuries, but in the expanded version of the 1780s to fit over the huge amounts of hair and padding. Worn with the traditional neckerchief, both in clean linen, it became known as the 'Martha Washington look' in the rebel American colonies, whose first presidential couple dressed with puritan simplicity, the general in a black professional suit, and his lady like any English housewife. Of course, working women, with only the one cap in most cases, could not afford morning and afternoon caps, so they wore the mob cap round the clock, and as it was very large this cap broke the established custom of never being seen outdoors without a hat over it.

This period suddenly saw a rush of books on the subject of the lower orders, inspired partly by the alarums of the French Revolution, and partly by artists in quest of Picturesque subjects. In 1796 Strutt's *Complete View of the Dress and Habits of the People of England* appeared, and in 1806 William Pyne published his *Microcosm* in which he attempted to record every type of job, tool, clothes, wagon, cart, and barge or crane, to assist artists both student and amateur with 'picturesque representations of the scenery of active life in Great Britain'. He followed this in 1808 with *The Costume of Great Britain, Etchings of Rustic Figures* (1815) and *The Costume of England, Scotland and Ireland* (1827). Thomas Rowlandson illustrated Combe's *Tour of Dr Syntax in search of the Picturesque* in 1813 and produced his *Character Sketches of the Lower Orders* in 1820, in which year T. Busby's *Costume of the Lower Orders of London* also came out. In 1839 J. Smith wrote *The Cries of London*, while Charles Dickens put his low-life characters in *Sketches by Boz*, illustrated by Cruickshank, in 1836, when his *Pickwick Papers* also began to appear, followed by life in the slums with the villain Bill Sikes in *Oliver Twist* in 1838. Lives which had been largely ignored now began to be studied in detail.

Pyne's *Microcosm* showed the Army still being followed by wagons piled high with tents, furniture, women and children. Soldiers' wives still nursed the wounded, washed the soldiers' clothes, cooked their meals, dressed their pigtails and sang and danced with them, as well as watching them being killed in action. These travelling nurses, housewives, and washerwomen wore the usual plain dress, mob cap, kerchief and apron in summer, although winter would see the addition of hoods, cloaks, soldiers' coats, or blanket mantles, as they trekked across the countryside in Spain and Flanders. Washing, as at home, was done at the river's edge and hung to dry on lines or spread on the ground. Pyne shows male haymakers stripped down to shirts, waistcoats and kneebreeches, but wearing smocks on top when taking their scythes to be sharpened by the grinders, who wore aprons. Leather dressers also needed aprons to protect their clothes. The year of his survey, 1806, was too soon for trousers to be seen inland, although he showed them on fishermen and sailors, and the spread of trousers became significant after the Napoleonic war ended in 1815. He showed firemen's helmets with a long neck-covering in leather, exactly the same as that which porters and coal heavers had developed. In *The History of the Royal Residences* of 1819, Pyne even showed the cooks in St James's Palace with white caps and aprons down to their ankles. All males, they wore shirts and kneebreeches otherwise. When he looked at Wales he found the women had created a specific look consisting of a hip-length smock worn over a skirt, with a belt or apron to pull it in at the waist. Over their linen caps they wore bowler hats, and the 1660s sugar loaf pointed hat had begun to disappear, except when it was part of almhouse livery.

When the Reverend Richard Warner made his walking tour of Wales in August 1797, he found that it was the country of blue clothes, unlike English russet and undyed cloth for the working poor.

Large parties of reapers also, amounting in the whole to two or three hundred, met us on their way into Herefordshire and Glocestershire, for the harvest month: remarkable in the uniformity of their dress, which consisted of a jacket and breeches of thick striped flannel, the manufacture of the country, and dyed almost invariably of a light blue colour.

The English had blue aprons, blue oversleeves, and even blue petticoats, but no blue suits, except at sea. The Welsh women were not dressed exclusively in blue, but it dominated:

The dress of the Welsh women is exactly similar throughout the principality, and consists of these particulars: a petticoat of flannel, the manufacture of the country, either blue or striped; a kind of bed-gown with loose sleeves of the same stuff, but generally of a brown colour; a broad handkerchief over the neck and shoulders; a neat mob-cap and a man's beaver hat. In dirty, or cold weather, the person is wrapped in a long blue cloak which descends below the knee. Except when particularly dressed, they go without shoes or stockings; and even if they have these luxuries, the latter in general has no foot to it.[4]

Shades of Scotland, and its barefooted women with their 'huggers', the footless stockings! Needless to say, the Welsh men wore shoes and stockings which were held up by red garters, but the Celts north and south evidently expected their women to be hardier than themselves. One local habit the parson noticed was that the men wore their kneebreeches open at the knee, perhaps to give a glimpse of those red garters. The blue could well date from Roman times, for they found the Ancient Britons daubed with blue woad, and the Welsh, the Cornish and the Bretons were the descendants of that ancient race. The Celtic word for blue is *glas*, from the Latin *glastum* meaning woad, and was one of the words adopted from the Roman conquerors, along with *pont, port* and *fenestra*. Bilberries or huckleberries were also used for blue dyes, and the preservation of this ancient colour as a national characteristic is quite probable. As other visitors to Scotland and Wales found, the local inhabitants prided themselves on their antiquity and would claim family trees going back three thousand years, to before even the Romans arrived, so it seems that a similar loyalty to woad was maintained as well in Wales.

Bedgowns were jackets, to the hip, and were a shorter version of the Indian gown and nightgowns of the seventeenth century which became outdoor wear. The bedgown was usually fastened with tapes down the front, for as it was home-made, buttonholing took too much time. It was not Welsh, however, and spread all across Britain. It is worth noting that the Welsh themselves laughed greatly at the sight of the Reverend Warner in his short spencer jacket, 'the coat without tails', as they called it, which Earl Spencer was said to have invented when his coat tails caught fire. The parson was being rather *avant garde* in sporting this, but he did come from fashionable Bath. The garment became more common on boys than adults, especially schoolboys in spencers and trousers, which at Eton became a uniform.

On his tour of north Wales the mineralogist Arthur Aikin observed that Welshmen rarely wore coats that had not been made and dyed in the principality. Flannel was Wales's biggest cloth industry; it was made mainly around Welshpool, and was dyed blue, drab (blue-grey) and brown. Flannel for export was taken across the border to Shrewsbury to be dyed and marketed, and then was sent to the Continent and to the West Indies.[5]

Bedgowns in the Lancashire area were described by the radical, Samuel Bamford. Born in 1788 he grew up in the country outside Manchester. His mother, Hannah, who died while he was still a boy, he remembered in detail: 'Her dark hair was combed over a roll before and behind, and confined by a mob-cap as white as bleached linen could be made, her neck was covered by a handkerchief over which she wore a bed-gown; and a clean checked apron, with black hose and shoes, completed her every-day attire.' His father was a cottage weaver of muslin, a specialized craft; his wife helped him by weaving, and winding bobbins, in addition to being a mother and housewife. Samuel was sent as a trainee weaver to his Aunt Elizabeth: 'She took snuff, wore a mob-cap, a bed-gown, a stiff pair of stays which stood out at the bosom, a warm woollen petticoat, white knitted hose, and shoes with patten clogs to keep her feet warm.' This, of course, was the north-west, where clogs were common, but it is interesting to see his aunt using them as pattens to protect her shoes. Sam himself went with 'bare legs and feet, bare neck and head', for he never wore stockings in summer, and his clothes were scanty except on Sunday when he had to wear a decent suit with a waistcoat, jacket and kneebreeches, his family being Methodists. He mentions local festivals, including White Apron Fair in late August at Middleton when the ladies paraded in their best prior to going to the alehouse and dancing later. On that day the men would want 'a bran new suit, wi' trindl't shurt', and the women 'a geawn made wi' tucks an' fleaunces; new shoon wi' ston up heels; new stockins wi' clocks; a tippt wi' frills o' reownd; monny a streng o' necklaces, an' a bonnit made by th' new mantymaker, the prettyist at ever wur seen, wi' a skay blue underside, an' pink ribbins.'

The local rush harvest was similar to the harvest festival seen by Hentzner in 1598. The last cartload

30. Thomas Heaphy, 'The Village Doctress', 1809. As doctors were expensive (and lethal!) the poor looked to the village wise woman. Some were charlatans, but others had a reputation for miles around. This labourer's corduroy jacket was now the norm. The nursing mother's wide-cut neckline was practical, filled with neckcloths. Aprons were worn by all country women, but the daughter has the new pinafore. Note the absence of cushions, carpets, and curtains, except on the box bed.

was topped with greenery, and the front was decorated with a sheet decked by the village girls with roses and precious items of silver like spoons, tongs and teapots, for glitter. From each hamlet carts converged on Middleton for a celebration, when best clothes, or new clothes, or at least clean clothes had to be worn. A country character of his

youth was the itinerant story teller, Old Alice of Bharla, who was always welcome, although the Bamfords were literate. She appeared 'her face half muffled, and her person concealed in an old brown cloak, and with sundry rags, bags and pockets swinging under her clothes'. She probably carried all her worldly goods upon her. Her dress recalls that of the simpler woman, who collected mush-rooms, watercress, nettles, dandelions, and hedge mustard to sell to the herbalists in town, walking 30 miles a day, and Alice may have done this, too.[6]

Across in Yorkshire the costume of the labouring poor was studied by George Walker in 1814, just when the fashion for trousers was beginning to spread inland. Naturally, he shows them on sailors and whalebone scrapers, in undyed canvas or blue, with undyed shirts or blue or red. The professional guide across the Yorkshire

Moors took to trousers because he was often out in the wind and wet, so developed a suit of jacket and trousers, over which he hung his game bag and a sling of shot. The Army was wearing trousers in plenty, which Walker showed on the 33rd Infantry Regiment of Halifax and on the North York Militia. A man out in the fields gathering the spiky heads of teasel for use in the clothing trade to nap cloth started to wear trousers, clearly for protection from the spikes, which would stick to the stockings if kneebreeches were worn. At alum cliff works the men hacking the alum out of the cliffside now wore trousers; so did men in the new factories, and schoolboys. Kneebreeches, however, continued to be worn by a lot of agricultural labourers, and by grooms and ostlers because they went well with riding boots. Smocks in Yorkshire Walker showed worn by shepherds, and by peat gatherers. Shepherds and shepherdesses both did a lot of knitting, from Scotland to England and Wales, to pass the time. In Yorkshire, Wensley Valley was alive with knitters, as the whole local population was engaged in it: men, women and children, and the shepherds too. The dress of working women in the county Walker showed to be the bedgown jacket in blue, worn with a brown skirt, brown stockings, and a yellow kerchief over the head topped by a round felt hat. The aprons were either dark blue or white. In Wales it was the bedgown which was brown, and the skirt blue or striped. Bedgowns were also worn by the new breed of women workers at seasides, now that dips in the briny ocean were said to be good for the health. Walker shows those at Bridlington, assisting young ladies from the bathing wagons, to be dipped wearing a dark shift. (Men swam in the nude, so they did not need discreet wagons.) When Count Kielmansegge had made his visit in 1761–2 he found that Southampton was supposed to be the healthiest place in the country with the best air, but now doctors were saying that immersion, and not simply sea air, was essential.

Another medical matter was the supply of leeches to doctors to do their bleeding of patients. Walker said that Scottish women specialized in this business, standing in ponds and streams with bare legs and feet to attract the creatures which they then put into little barrels. Accordingly their skirts only came to the top of the calf; otherwise they wore the bedgown either plain or else in tartan, with linen aprons and caps. Of course the village wise women avoided bleeding in preference to herbs, and they still dressed like other working women so far as the cap and apron were concerned, but often wore dresses rather than bedgowns, particularly in southern counties, to show a slightly superior professional quality.

In 1818 William Johnstone White started his *Working Class Costume*, covering Norfolk, Cambridgeshire and Middlesex. This was meant to be the first in a series of volumes illustrating the whole country, but proved to be the only one published. This near to London, costume was fairly close to fashion, even if the garments were second- or third-hand. The women had taken to sun bonnets, not hats over caps or kerchiefs as still lingered in Wales and Yorkshire. These bonnets were bulkier than the slim straw ones of high fashion, but they were bonnets, not hats, although White illustrated one woman going to market in a traditional flat straw hat over a linen cap, looking very 1740s. Bamford said that some bedgowns were skirted, meaning that they were long, and a number of wrapover long dresses in White are probably these skirted bedgowns. Younger girls, however, were striving to follow the slimline round gowns of the mode, with the high classical waist, even if, like the heather seller, their dress was more patched than elegant. The slender line of neo-classical taste was encountered by Fanny Burney in Paris in 1801 when she was reproved for wearing three petticoats, as fashionable ladies now wore only one, and some had even forsaken stays and shifts! As a middle-aged lady she resisted such semi-nudity, and so did working women of similar age, to whom wearing one petticoat smacked of rampant immorality, as did the absence of stays which of course was a characteristic of prostitutes. The revolutionary French might not object to wearing such indecent clothes, but on this side of the Channel the working class was very conservative and suspicious of novelty, which few of them

31. George Walker, 'Knitters in the Valley of Wensley', from *Costume of Yorkshire*, 1814. Everybody knitted in this area, from the shepherds to the old people. The woman has a bedgown and skirt, with an apron and neckcloth. She wears a hat on top of a headscarf like Welshwomen. Trousers have not yet spread this far, and the men retain kneebreeches.

could afford in any case. Consequently many working women of the older generation still wore several petticoats and stays, retaining a wider silhouette than their daughters. Some even still hitched up their skirts to show the petticoat in the way that was fashionable in the 1640s, and White shows one with a quilted petticoat that was last in the fashion in the eighteenth century.

Older men showed their conservatism by still wearing wigs, but White shows that none of them in his survey had maintained cocked hats; they had all taken up the new top hat that came in during the 1790s. Some were very battered and probably 20 or 30 years old, but top hats now ruled in Middlesex, Cambridgeshire and Norfolk, even if they looked odd on top of an old wig. Even George III wore them like that. So close to the metropolis

overall/overcoats were available second-hand, and many of the men in White's survey wore them with ragged hems, torn pockets and patches, so that here cloaks for men were going out. They were still worn by the women, however, and White shows only one lady in an overcoat. A double-breasted overcoat worn by a man with one leg was a military coat, brought no doubt from his regiment. Another military item reaching the populace was gaiters. Made in leather or canvas, they were common in the infantry, whereas the poor civilians had had to make do with sacking or straw as leg protectors, but by 1818 leather gaiters were spreading, and ex-army surplus was probably responsible.

Trousers White shows on the young men, particularly those in the construction industry. A navvy building the Archway at Highgate had a top hat, shirt, waistcoat, trousers and lace-up boots. A man driving the disposal carts was dressed the same, but had shoes. Norfolk reed cutters wore trousers, to roll up like sailors, and worked with or without shoes in the Fens. The 'King of the Fishermen' in the Fens was Isaac Garratt because he caught a 6 ft 7 in sturgeon in 1816, and so thrived on that reputation. He wore a smock over trousers with big leather boots that could be turned up at the flap, and a battered top hat. The mud huts such men lived in were often flooded and they wore their damp clothes for weeks on end before changing or drying them out, and like simpler women seemed to live to a great age regardless. One scruffy character in trousers with a striped waistcoat under his jacket was a sailor and must have got them from the slops stock because they were too long and becoming torn round the hem. White shows several smocks of varying lengths worn by labourers and drovers or cowboys, but they are all plain. Smocking had begun to appear, but only on the smocks of the wealthy farmer to begin with, and not until the 1810s did smocking feature on workers' smocks.

The most desirable cloak for women in England and Wales at working-class levels was a red one. In his diaries John, Viscount Torrington, commented on the cheerful sight of the red-cloaked women in Wales, which suggests that the blue cloaks mentioned by Warner now had a competitor. The observant Samuel Bamford described exactly how it looked and was worn in Lancashire: 'An ample crimson or scarlet cloak of the finest wool, double milled and of an intense dye that threw a glimmer wherever it moved, was put on, the hood being thrown over the head, cap, and handkerchief, and all drawn closely and comfortably round the face or left open as the wearer chose.'[7] Clearly it was not cheap, but something to save for and conserve, and distinguished that level of society from the ladies with silk shawls. Fustian and corduroy or flannel were the fabrics of the workers, broadcloth and silks those of the middle class.

The drive of people off the land into towns continued in England, and spread to Scotland with the notorious clearances. By legal changes the British government turned clan chieftains into landowners looking for profits, no longer guardians of their kith and kin, and tenants were forced out of farms, or had them burned down around their heads. Between 1800 and 1840, 350,000 Scots moved to the Strathclyde to look for work in Glasgow and Paisley, while others emigrated to

Canada and the USA or Australia. London passed one million in population, and abandoned villages were to be found from John O' Groats to Land's End. In his *The Glengary Evictions* of 1853, Donald Ross listed several case histories of the suffering caused by Mrs M'Donell forcibly shipping most of her crofters to Canada from Knoydart in Invernessshire. The elderly and infirm who insisted on remaining had their spinning wheels and other furniture flung out, their crops torn up, and their homes demolished. If they tried to build a hut from the ruins that was destroyed too. People were thrown out to make room for sheep, as there was more profit in wool and mutton.[8]

The Napoleonic Wars caused enormous demands for food, clothing and armaments but after peace in 1815, the business came to an abrupt stop, and caused a widespread depression, as often happens after a war. William Cobbett recorded the signs he saw of this in his *Rural Rides*. In November 1821 he wrote from Marlborough in Wiltshire on what he had seen around Farnham: '. . . women labourers (reapers) presented such an assemblage of rags as I have never before seen even amongst hoppers at Farnham, many of them are common beggars. I never before saw *country people*, and reapers too, observe, so miserable in appearance as these. There were some very pretty girls, but ragged as colts, and pale as ashes.' He blames the new size of farms as being partly responsible, for the big farmers bought out the traditional yeomen farmers and husbandmen and turned them into labourers through the power of paper money. At Gloucester he found things less depressed: '. . . the labourers themselves well as to dress and healthiness. The girls at work in the fields (always my standard) are not in rags, with bits of shoes tied on their feet and rags tied round their ancles, as they had in Wiltshire.'

When watching the mowing at St Albans he commented that the English did the mowing, the Irish the haymaking, but the Scots preferred to become gardeners. He was amused, when near the Royal Military College, Sandhurst, to pass its drying ground with an acre of land covered with washing lines of shirts and other underwear

32. George Walker, 'Scottish Leechwomen', 1814. The tartan bedgown of the girl on the left is the only native touch. Short skirts were essential for this job of collecting leeches for doctors. The white caps or coifs were worn throughout Britain.

blowing in the breeze. At markets he found that animals in 1821–2 were only fetching one third of the price they had brought in 1813 when the war was on. By 1830 wages and the dole had been cut back so much that farm labourers in the south were desperate and started burning ricks in protest. They also attacked the new threshing machines which they saw as a threat, but they killed nobody. The new Whig government acted just as harshly as Tory ones, sent in the militia, hanged nine labourers, transported 450, and imprisoned 400. While the radicals celebrated the first Reform Act of 1832, in 1834 six labourers at Tolpuddle in Dorset were transported to Australia for administering oaths of loyalty to a trade union (which was illegal). A national outcry ensued, and the men were brought back two years later. In 1838 the Charter of the People was born, for the masses were not satisfied with the Act of 1832, and demanded universal suffrage, the abolition of

property qualifications, and the payment of MPs so that the poor could stand for election. It took until 1911, however, for all such demands to reach the statute book.

Cobbett was a farmer's son and wore a smock in his youth. The sight of a sandy hill at Bourne in Hampshire reminded him of a game he used to play with his brother, when they took their arms out of their smocks and rolled down the hill as if in a sack, getting covered with sand. At Arundale in Sussex he saw another activity from the past, 'a woman bleaching her *homespun* and *home-woven linen*'. With the coming of cotton mills and industrial production, the ancient custom for housewives to make all their own fabrics was dying out. No doubt most women welcomed this development as the first labour-saving benefit to come their way, but Cobbett took a more sentimental view. It was in the American colonies that the tradition endured longest, for he had seen in New England and Maryland that farmers' wives did weave their own cloth and make linen. All the coats at Long Island races had been home-spun, but that continent was still only settled along the coasts at this date. The drive inland came later, and home-made clothes had to go with the settlers, who were thousands of miles away from mills. Indeed, American cotton had to be exported to English mills to be woven in sufficient quantity to begin to offer settlers some ready-made fabrics and cheaper clothes.[9]

Artisans and professionals

This period saw the battle between professional black and dandy colour at its climax – and black won. It was of course still the suitable tone for persons in responsible posts. Carl Philip Moritz had been impressed by the gowns and mortarboards at Eton:

Their dress struck me particularly: from the biggest to the least, they all wear black cloaks or gowns, over coloured clothes; through which there were apertures for their arms. They also wear, besides, a square hat, or cap, that seemed to be covered with velvet, such as our clergymen in many places wear.[10]

The clergy continued to be involved in education at

33. John Smith, 'Staffordshire Ware', from *The Cries of London*, 1839. The Staffordshire ware man commuted to London by canal. His smock is unusual in having a separate panel of smocking and beading decoration that was probably a family heirloom. He evidently likes his smocks very long, and this example also lacks the wide collar of country smocks. With it he sports a top hat and a black scarf, a hint of metropolitan style.

both university and scholastic level, and when Samuel Bamford was at Manchester Free Grammar School his teacher was the Reverend John Gaskell:

His dress was such as became his station – that of a curate of the Church – his coat, vest, and breeches were of fine black cloth; the latter article of dress being held below the knees by a brace of small silver buckles; his stockings were dark grey speckled; his shoes were also fastened with silver buckles; and his cravat and linen were neatly adjusted, and very white.

He does not mention a wig, but the Church of England continued to wear wigs well into the reign of Queen Victoria, which to foreigners looked like a weird masquerade. So did lawyers and judges, of course, the former short bag wigs and the latter Restoration perruques. Lawyers still wore black mourning gowns over sober suits, and judges were still in royal livery scarlet with white fur trim.

In medicine, too, black remained established wear for doctors, and for Bamford's apothecary, 'dressed in black, with thin grey hairs on his head, a white cravat and a dusting of snuff on his waistcoat'.[11]

The chief advocates of colour were those who were not interested in bourgeois standards and Protestant sobriety, such as George, Prince of Wales, and Alfred, Comte d'Orsay, to whom bright yellow waistcoats and blue coats were the thing. They also favoured a sporty look with skin-tight doeskin breeches like jockeys, and striped waistcoats like riding silks, along with many-caped overcoats copied from coachmen. The ensemble would be topped with the new top hat, and bottomed with riding boots. In London this was copied by the wealthy young, and by 1839 Dickens found that it had percolated down to builders' labourers as their Sunday best:

Pass through St Giles's in the evening of a week-day, there they are in their fustian dresses, spotted with brick-dust and whitewash, leaning against posts. Walk through Seven Dials on Sunday morning, there they are again, drab or light corduroy trousers, Blücher boots, blue coats, and great yellow waistcoats, leaning against posts. The idea of a man dressing himself in his best clothes to lean against a post all day.[12]

The look was spread around the kingdom by the

coaching fraternity. Coachmen wore big bouquets on drawing-room days at court, and innkeepers started to do so too, as a festive note with which to greet arrivals. Abbé Le Blanc would have been horrified. He thought it bad enough that the British aristocracy should dress down like servants, but now they were imitating coachmen and ostlers! The chief critic of such kaleidoscopic chaos was George 'Beau' Brummell, who single-handedly knocked middle-class ideals of cleanliness, neatness, and modesty in dress into the heads of the Prince of Wales and his cronies in the 'horsey' set. By insisting on sparkling linen, country washed and country bleached, and coats and kneebreeches or trousers of simple tone but perfect cut, he made restraint the dominant ethic in menswear down to today. He would not wear anything gaudy even for a gala occasion, and so the black evening suit came into being by 1810. His motto was that if a man's clothes were stared at, they were not good taste. Thus fashion began to calm down and tone down its products, with dark blue, brown and black for frock coats. By 1840 Comte d'Orsay admitted defeat and started wearing black coats and waistcoats with brown trousers and a black stock. Over the next twenty years labourers in London were to copy this, and it would then spread to the country, so that the upper class and the working class both started to dress like the middle class, which goes to show where the power now was.[13]

The streets were still full of entertainers, sellers, and beggars as of old, some of whom T.L. Busby examined in 1819. The mechanical fiddler was an American from Providence who had joined the Royal Navy. He lost his left hand at the Dardanelles and was granted a naval pension, but it was not big enough to support a wife and family, so he earned a bit extra by holding a violin in his hook, and the bow in his surviving hand, and going round the London fairs. He wore a blue jacket, blue trousers and a red cap to retain a maritime air. Another sailor, Owen Clancy from County Cork, had been shipwrecked off North America and lost both feet through frostbite. As he was not in the Navy he did not get a pension so had to beg on crutches, but was known for his cleanliness in his nankeen suit and

34. W.H. Pyne, 'The Slaughterman', from *The Costumes of Great Britain*, 1808. Leather and skin aprons dominate, as do leather gaiters with shoe flaps for slaughter work. The slaughterman's shirt and striped waistcoat would be appropriate to many jobs. The low-set seam in the sleeve was the ancient way to make shirts and tunics.

white linen, probably thanks to his wife.

Postmen now had uniforms: a red coat with blue facing and beige kneebreeches. They earned 14/– a week but had to provide two sureties of £40 before they could work in the Post Office. Mail coaches travelled overnight on the turnpike roads, arriving in London at dawn. Mail was sorted from 6 a.m. and delivered between 10 a.m. and 1 p.m. There were no postboxes, so people had to hand letters to the postmen and pay him a penny. Firemen still worked for the insurance companies, and the foreman of the Hope Insurance Company had a livery of crimson jacket, blue kneebreeches, and a crimson hat. The sight of a fire engine arriving at a fire and refusing to tackle it if it was not one of their registered houses gave way to more co-operation between companies, culminating in 1833 with the London Fire Engine Establishment, under superintendent James Braidwood from Edinburgh, who had 80 men and 19 fire stations. Staff were on duty for 24 hours at a time. Braidwood refused to allow new steam fire engines and preferred the old manual pumps, but their ineffectiveness was well illustrated in 1834 when the Palace of Westminster burned down and Establishment could only save Westminster Hall. It was financed by all the insurance companies.

Coal heavers and dustmen had improved on the porter's neckpiece by devising a cape-like extension to the leather helmet, which covered the neck and shoulders. Otherwise their dress was the conventional suit of jacket and kneebreeches. Dustmen announced their arrival with the cart by ringing a bell, more slowly than fire-engine bells. Handbells were also common among bakers, muffin makers, hot piemen, and other food sellers. All such items had to be carried on trays or in baskets, and the Thames was lined from Fulham to Staines with the huts of the basket weavers, who used the osiers growing there to make a huge variety of baskets, from bin-size to bucket. The journeyman prickle maker was the weaver who specialized in the deep prickle baskets used by wine merchants to store empties. Whole families worked together on basket weaving, and dressed the same as anybody else at that level.

35. W.H. Pyne, 'A Waterman to a Coach Stand', 1808. This licensed waterman has a large skin apron with two front pockets for tending the hackney horses. His rough coat could be of rug, the roughest of fabrics. His sheepskin hat and the sheepskin gaiters date back to Homer and the Bronze Age. Like most working men, he favoured a coloured neckcloth.

OPPOSITE ABOVE
36. W.H. Pyne, 'Coal Heavers', 1808. Leather hats with long neckflaps protect the neck and back from coal dust when carrying sacks. Otherwise the costume is similar to that of other workers, with the striped shirt, leather kneebreeches, gaiters and boots. They are sieving and loading the coal into sacks at the quayside.

37. W.H. Pyne, 'Dustmen', 1808. Their neckflaps are padded for carrying heavy dust baskets. In the previous century such pads were buckled on, but now they are made in one with the hat. Both dustmen wear ragged aprons, while gaiters keep ash out of their shoes. Patches and tears were common at this level of society.

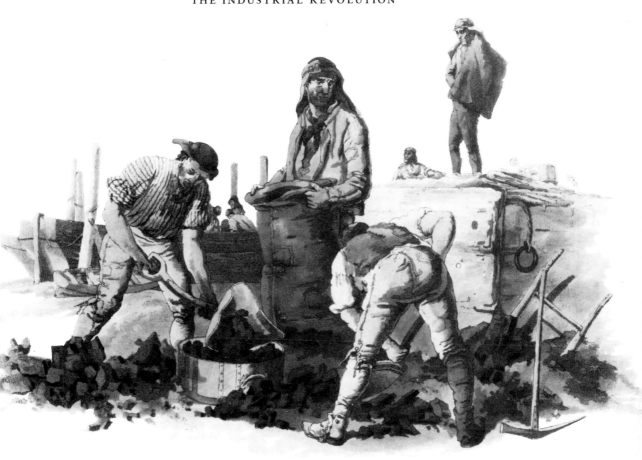

The 'hard metal spoon man' was William Conway of Crab Tree Row, Bethnal Green, who was interviewed by John Smith in 1839. He inherited his job from his father, and had 11 regular routes so that customers knew when he was coming. He walked 25 miles a day, six days a week, and needed a new pair of shoes every six weeks, which were made from old boot tops. His corduroy suit was often soaked, but dried as he walked.

Canal workers became known for smocking, for it was said in 1830, 'The Boatmen are usually in smock frocks, neatly worked, which are to them what finely worked collars are to ladies.' Once horses and towpaths began to replace bow-hauliers, the men started to wear smocks, dressing as drovers and ostlers did. Smocking the smock kept them occupied when waiting in a barge queue to unload or go through a tunnel.[14] This influenced some users of the canal system like the workers in the Staffordshire potteries, whose wares were conveyed to Paddington Basin by barge. Their men started to wear elaborately smocked smock frocks, although they were not well paid: 7/- a week for men doing a 12–14 hour day, 16 hours with overtime; women got 4/- and children 2/6 a week. The pots cost one penny at the factory, and fourpence at Paddington.

The streets were full of calls. 'Two bunches a penny, primroses', 'Milk below!', 'Sweet China oranges', 'Do you want my matches?', 'New mackerel, new mackerel', 'Knives, scissors and razors to grind', 'Fresh gathered peas', 'Round and sound, five pence a pound, duke cherries', 'Straw-berries, scarlet strawberries', 'Old chairs to mend', 'New love songs, only ha'penny a piece', 'Hot spice gingerbread, smoking hot', 'Turnips and carrots, ho!'. The milkmaids were usually Welsh or Irish girls who collected the milk with their yokes and pails from the cowkeepers on the edge of London, at 2/3 the barn gallon. By law they were only supposed to add one third of water. Their best town routes in the West End brought in nine shillings a week. Like many girls they were now wearing mob caps without hats, and still retained an eighteenth-century look compared to the slim line of high fashion. This forsaking of hats was more marked in Scotland, as K. Pennant observed on his tour, the account of which was reprinted several times. He thought the men very lazy, but along the Deeside remarked, 'The women are more industrious; spin their husbands' Cloaths, and get money by knitting stockings, the great trade of the country. The common women are in general most remarkably plain, and soon acquire an old look...by being much exposed to the weather without a hat.' There was a similar absence of hats in the Highlands, but of course women used plaids:

The women's dress is the *kirch* or a white piece of linnen, pinned over the forehead of those that are married, and round the hind part of the head, falling behind over their necks. The single women wear only a ribband round their head, which they call a snood. The *tonnag* or plaid, hangs over their shoulders, and is fastened before with a *brotche* (brooch); but in bad weather is drawn over their heads.

He noticed in church how women pulled the plaid right over the face, and thought it was to concentrate on the sermon, but pastors still complained that it was to sleep. In other respects the dress struck Pennant as now like English dress at that level. The Highlanders were still wearing plaids 'dyed with stripes of the most vivid hues', but as Miège found long before him, heather-toned plaids were worn too. The little kilt was now common wear, the *feil-beg*, but the ancient shoe, the *cuoran*, made of skin with the hair on the outside, was seldom worn now, ousted by English-type shoes. Of course, when Highlanders were driven into the towns they started to wear jackets and trousers, whereas back home trews had been the mark of the gentry and chiefs – the exact opposite to the position south of the border. Many became factory workers in the textile mills, the first of the mass-production industries.[15]

38. W.H. Pyne, 'Firemen', 1808. Blue was favoured by most London companies as their livery, with different coloured trims. The picture shows the leather helmets and boots, knee protectors, and the badge on the arm, like the watermen who were the first recruited firemen in London. The men on each side of the engine pumped by pushing the bar up and down.

Industry and the sea

Glasgow made nankeen and cotton. The Paisley silk mills had been started in the 1750s by an Englishman called Philips; by 1785 they were employing 15,000 people, and paying out £500 a week in wages at some mills. A new fashion at the turn of the century for silk shawls lasted right down to the 1860s, when Worth brought back fit, so Paisley silks had a boom period. William Cobbett visited Fulton & Son in 1832: 'It was all put in motion by a wheel, turned by three men; and there was a great number of young women and girls employed at the work; and all very neatly and nicely dressed.'[16] He was also impressed by the silk shawls and waistcoats at Bissett's which surpassed anything from India. A special apron was evolved in the mills, which Walker illustrated on factory boys in 1814. Made of white linen or cotton, it was put on over the head, and consisted of a sleeveless bodice back and front, with the normal apron starting at the waist in front. It was perhaps the first pinafore, and protected the clothes over the chest and trousers as the boys leant forward over the machines. It was also adopted by the mill girls and became traditional in factories.

While Robert Owen at New Lanark was a generous employer, many were not, and in 1802 Sir Robert Peel senior, a cotton manufacturer, introduced the first Factory Act to protect the health and morals of apprentices. In 1819, the year of the Peterloo massacre, the second Factory Act appeared, limiting the hours worked by children in cotton mills to 72 hours a week, while the lower age limit was set at nine years old. These hours were extended to other mill workers in the Twelve Hours Act of 1833, which established a few but the very first inspectors of factory conditions. In 1847 the Ten Hour Act was passed, again only for the textile industry. For general health, the Asian cholera outbreak in 1831 led to the first concept of sanitary institutions and health officers to tackle outbreaks.

At Totnes in Devon Charles Vancouver found the women spinning serge on machines like cotton in 1808. The area found its traditional markets for corduroy and serge in the Mediterranean blocked during the Napoleonic War, and had to switch to coarse beaver cloth which was made in the weavers' homes and sent to Exeter to be dyed, after which it was sold to the naval slop shops in Plymouth. Barnstaple was known for plain and spotted baizes, as well as coarse cloth for the kitchen and dairy. Such traditional centres for wool based on a county system were now faced with industrial centralization, and with competition from cotton, imported from the USA and Egypt and woven in Manchester; Manchester cotton began to oust linen and wool from many clothes and domestic furnishings. The big difference between the dress of the traditional home weaver and the mill worker was that the former wore an apron and the latter the new pinafore.[17]

By this time Britain had the world's best transport systems; the turnpike roads were the fastest, with stage coaches competing to knock an hour or two off the usual time from A to B. The mail coaches, with names like Quicksilver or Wonder, were indeed the wonder of the world, and in fact were faster than railways when they began. For huge loads, the canal system now covered 4,000 miles interlocking with rivers, carried over 20,000 barges, and thus employed about 60,000 people on the barges alone, not counting the boatbuilders, carpenters, iron makers, bridge and brick makers, and horse suppliers who serviced the system. It had

all been achieved by private companies, but the absence of government direction, a central plan and standardization meant that not all barges could travel on all canals, as the widths, the tunnels, and the locks all differed. In Napoleonic Europe such matters were to be more organized from the centre. Exactly the same lack of direction occurred as the railway system started, with the Great Western Railway notably not having the same width of rail as the Great Northern.

Several scientists tried to invent steam railway engines that would move under their own power. Richard Trevethick built and tried out a locomotive at Coalbrookdale in 1802, and in 1803 with another engine pulled 25 tons' weight at Pennydarren in South Wales. In 1809 he exhibited a locomotive at Euston Square in London, but it was still looked on as a fairground ride. Locomotives first became common at coal mines, and in 1814 Walker illustrated the engine built by Mr Blenkinsop at Charles Bradley's colliery near Leeds, which could pull 20 coal wagons on the rails formerly used by horses. Two such locomotives did the work of 14 horses. From 1814 George Stephenson built over 20 railway engines to carry coal, not passengers. The first public railway, the Stockton and Darlington in 1825, was built to carry coal from the Durham coalfield to the coast, and employed both static steam engines at the inclines and locomotives on the straight sections. The Manchester to Liverpool line was built in 1828 before the directors were decided whether to use static engines and cables, or locomotives. A trial of locomotives was ordered at Rainhill in 1829, and George Stephenson's *Rocket* won at the required speed of 10 miles an hour, still slower than a mail coach and four. The proposition of a passenger railway from Birmingham to London seriously alarmed the Post Office, the stage coach companies and the canal companies, and there was a fierce battle through Parliament before an act in favour was passed in 1833. The Birmingham–Euston railway opened in 1838, and the railway age had begun in earnest, although the 1840s was a time of economic depression.

This rather haphazard evolution matched that

39. George Walker, 'Factory Boys', 1814. The factory pinafore, which became universal in textile mills, had a bodice top and front apron in linen. Such boys had to crawl under the machines to clear up the fluff, as well as operating them. Their clothes were always second-hand, as there was little time at home for making.

of the canals, so there were no such things as company liveries in the early stage. Some canal companies had begun to give lock keepers a badge as they collected the dues, for example the Peak Forest Canal in 1806 provided 'an upper Waistcoat and a Badge thereupon to distinguish them from other persons', but this was not general. On the Stockton and Darlington line in 1825 the engine drivers wore top hats, jackets and trousers like the majority of urban working men. George Stephenson's crew on the *Rocket* had top hats and trousers, but with the short spencer jacket, probably because it had no tails to catch in the fire (although its inventor wore tails). The Liverpool and Manchester Railway was the first to decide on a livery, introducing the peaked cap for its engine crews, and copying the spencer jacket from

Stephenson, with trousers for the lower limbs. The navigators who had built the canals, the bridges and aqueducts were now in demand to build similar cuttings and embankments for railways, which were just as labour intensive. The proposed but unbuilt Grand Imperial Ship Canal from London to Portsmouth in 1825, it was estimated, would employ 20,000 labourers, cost £4,000,000 and take four years. Such figures now applied to rail.

Samuel Smiles, the economist, wrote of the first navvies, 'Some of the best came from the fen districts of Lincoln and Cambridge, where they had been trained to execute works of excavation and embankment.' Their life was an itinerant one:

During the railway-making period the navvy wandered about from one public work to another – apparently belonging to no country and having no home. He usually wore a white felt hat with the brim turned up, a velveteen or jean square tailed coat, a scarlet plush waistcoat with little black spots, and a bright-coloured kerchief around his herculean neck, when, as often happened, it was not left entirely bare. His corduroy breeches were retained in position by a leathern strap round the waist, and were tied and buttoned at the knee, displaying a solid calf and foot encased in high-laced boots.[18]

40. George Walker, 'A Yorkshire Miner', 1814. This white suit was probably undyed rather than clean, and suits were brushed and shaken, not washed. There is nothing unusual about the costume, as it is the now-traditional jacket and kneebreeches worn by most working men until trousers creep in again. The scene is Brandley's colliery near Leeds, with a Blenkinsopp railway locomotive. Such engines operated at mines decades before they carried passengers. The engine drivers here are dressed the same as the miner, although one has an early top hat.

This suggests his Sunday outfit more than his working one, when coats came off and mud-spattered waistcoats, shirts, breeches and then trousers were the norm. 'Jean' was another name for fustian-type fabric.

British navvies were shipped over to France, 5,000 of them, to build the first railway there in 1841. British engineers were now in demand to create systems from India to Argentina. The contractor Brassey shipped 3,000 navvies to Canada, and then 2,000 to Australia, to start their railways, while in 1854 he provided 500 navvies to

get the Army out of the mud of the Crimea by installing a railway. *Punch* showed a change in their costume, by then a woollen cap, often striped, a smock frock to the thighs, corduroy trousers and big boots. Smock frocks for mud were obviously better than plush waistcoats. American railways began by using wooden rails, so the English locomotives were too heavy, being designed for iron rails. Lightweight engines were therefore designed, like the Tom Thumb on the Baltimore and Ohio line in 1830. The first line in New York State, the Mohawk and Hudson, 1831, used stage coaches with iron wheels as the carriages. The engine driver wore a cap, a high-necked jacket and trousers. Difference in gauges was common here, too, and no standard was adopted until after the Civil War, when railways had proved their strategic importance. British navvies were highly paid, more than labourers or soldiers, and worked twice as hard as anybody else, astounding foreigners by their daredevil speed, which they attributed to a diet of beef and beer.

The miners dug the coal which enabled cast iron to be made into wheels, boilers, funnels, rails, station canopies, and bogies. Walker described the Yorkshire miner in 1814 as wearing a white suit bound with red, consisting of a jacket and kneebreeches, explaining this surprising choice of shade by the fact that miners had to wash every day, so their clothes were also washed frequently. This seems rather unrealistic. How many sets of clothes did he think miners had? Undyed fabric was of course cheaper than dyed, but a better reason for wearing white underground would be so that the miners could see each other, since they had only candles to work by. The safety lamps invented by Humphrey Davy and George Stephenson appeared in 1815. The Welsh miners had a costume of their own by now, for they wore a smock frock to the thigh, trousers, and a pillbox-type hat. In its basic elements this costume was very similar to the sailor's outfit worn by Weiditz in 1529, except that it lacked a belt. What was different was that this Welsh outfit was padded, in both garments. Parker's paintings of Northumbrian miners in the 1830s do not show these padded garments, for the men wear conventional if old and black coats, waistcoats, shirts and trousers, with either a kerchief tied round the head, or woollen caps. By the 1850s, however, padded clothes had reached the mines around Wigan, when photographs began to be taken of mining subjects. In that area clogged shoes outnumbered boots.

The Children's Employment Commission's report ruled that no children should work underground below the age of 10, from 1842. What shocked people even more was that women worked down there too, wearing only shifts, men's breeches or breeched skirts, and now, sexual high treason to the new Victorians, even trousers.

Several men told the Commission that it was brutalizing for women to work underground, and immoral for them to work alongside men. The Victorian ideal for women was a domestic angel devoid of strength and sexual feeling, a perpetual child in fact, so any woman who did not fit that ideal was presumably a threat. How poor women were expected to earn a living otherwise was given little thought. They ought to stay at home with the children, it was argued, ignoring the actual poverty which forced women and children to work. Inspectors went round the country to interview them. At Halifax it was found that Susan Pitchforth, aged 11, worked underground in only half a shift from her waist, black with coal dust, and saturated with water. Patience Kershaw, aged 17, dressed like a man, 'I hurry in the clothes I have now got on – trousers and ragged jacket; the bald place upon my head is made by thrusting the curves; the getters I work for are naked except their caps; they pull off all their clothes: all the men are naked.' Mary Barrett, aged 14, told the sub-commissioner, 'I work always without stockings, or shoes, or trousers; I wear nothing but my shift. I have to go up to the headings with the men; they are all naked there. I am got well used to that, and don't care now much about it. I was afraid at first and did not like it.' Sensational horrors, women and girls working with naked men! It had to be stopped; no females were to work underground, despite the fact that their employers said they did not fight like boys did. In future women could only work on the

surface sorting coal, or as bankwomen emptying the skips. In Staffordshire mines they also loaded the barges on the canal, which was outdoor work, so some cover was necessary:

These are substantially though coarsely clothed, and the head and neck more particularly protected from the cold. The work is laborious, but not beyond their strength. The clothing is obviously such that a girl cannot continue to wear it after going home. She therefore lays it aside and washes herself, and puts on more agreeable clothing for the rest of the day: the coarseness of the clothing, which prevents it from being worn after work, is an advantage.

Coarse, in the Victorian sense, could also mean trousers, and there are some photographs of girls loading barges wearing trousers. The miner Mary Glover, aged 38, of Ringley Bridge declared she preferred them:

I wear a shift and trousers at work. I always will have a good pair of trousers. I have had many a two-pence given me by the boatmen on the canal to show my breeches. I never saw women work naked, but I have seen men work without breeches in the neighbourhood of Bolton. I remember seeing a man who worked stark naked.

Showing her breeches indeed, and seeing men naked at work! – the Commission failed to understand that if a woman saw nudity every working day it became the norm. A woman who spent the day on all fours, crawling along pulling a line of coal trucks with a chain between her legs causing sores and weals would scarcely think about the subject. Who was interested in nudity when some tunnels were knee-deep in water, and water seeped through the roof, and when in the dry ones every movement caused clouds of coal dust to choke the company? It was a case of Victorian morality being based on lurid imagination rather than the grim reality. On the Continent, women in trousers still worked underground till the end of the century. But if the Commission felt that preventing females working underground would see an end to their wearing trousers, they were wrong, for the women continued to sport that 'masculine' garment on the surface.

Boys were allowed to go down the pit after the age of ten, and the dress of such youngsters in the Derbyshire mines was reported: 'Their clothing

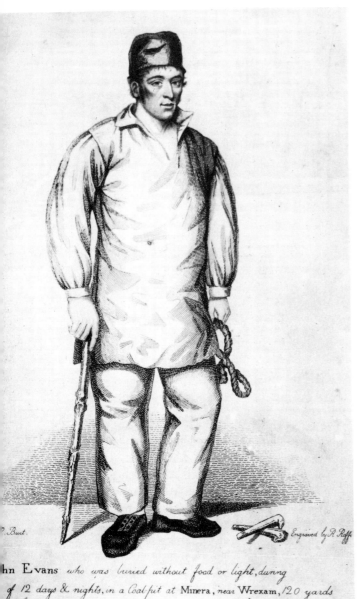

hn Evans *who was buried without food or light, during of 12 days & nights, in a Coal pit at* Minera, *near* Wrexam, *120 yards below the surface of the Earth,* September 27 *1819.*

41. A.R. Blunt, engr. R. Roffe, 'John Evans', 1819. The new Welsh padded miner's costume with its tunic top and trousers, not vastly different from sailors' outfits in 1529. Such padding protected the body against knocks, and made kneeling more comfortable. Over the next thirty years padded clothes spread to other mines. John Evans was commemorated for surviving 12 days and nights underground without food.

consists of a coarse flannel shirt or jacket, and trousers mostly of the same material. The jacket is thrown off in most pits, and only used where they are allowed to sit down to their dinner, or on coming out of the pit.' The geologist Joseph Prestwich, however, offered a more realistic description: 'The boys are dressed like the grown men in trousers, shoes and stockings, but with no other clothing, the heat not rendering more necessary.' They were used to haul sledges of coal by means of a rope round the waist up to the level where horses and carts waited. Shirts came off as well as jackets, and sometimes more.[19]

A new industry had sprung up in this period. In 1805 the American Benjamin Silliman found a chemist near Albany House, Piccadilly, who had installed a gas-making machine in the basement to illuminate his premises. This new form of lighting which was brighter than candles, and could illuminate a whole factory, made it possible for shifts to operate day and night. Gas lamps were installed outside Covent Garden in 1815, and on the stage at Drury Lane in 1817. Gas workers had entered the scene, but as usual there was no special costume devised for the industry at the start, so it was jackets and trousers for the first men.[20]

The ancient industry of old clothes was still thriving. When William Austin toured Rag Fair, Rosemary Lane, London, on 19 November 1802, he was accosted 15 times by Jews demanding, 'Do you want any old clothes?' One such dealer told him he could refurbish an old coat so well he could sell it back to its original owner. He claimed that he could tell a gentleman's coat because the back would be worn (from leaning against chairs?), and a writer or journalist's because the right cuff and the left elbow would be most worn, the one presumably from writing, the other from supporting the writer's head. As an example of merchandising initiative, he was told of a Jewish boy of ten who bought a gentleman's old clothes then stood outside his house bawling, 'Mr X's clothes for sale!', which obliged Mr X to send his servants out to buy them back again!

Dr Wendeborn found that the poor resisted clothes that were designed for them: 'All do their

1. John Wootton, 'View of the Severn Valley with Haymaking', *c.* 1715. Brownish clothes dominate for farm labourers ever since Edward III made them compulsory. Undyed cloth was also permitted but that soon became grey. After the Restoration women adopted red petticoats, as worn by the woman on the left, with the sleeveless blue bodice, white shift, and straw hat, which were to become a standard uniform in England.

2. J. C. Ibbetson, 'On the Road between Llandaff and
Pontypridd, with the Ruins of Castell Coch', water-
colour 1792. The wearing of blue was common
among workers in Wales, shown here in the blue coats
and cloaks, and stockings. The women keep to their
tradition of wearing men's hats, often over a
headscarf. A lime kiln stands beside the ruined castle,
which the Marquess of Bute had rebuilt in the 1870s.
The lime worker resting in the foreground wears the
basic uniform for a working man of a shirt and
kneebreeches, while the man by the horse has the
short coat of workers, for whom fashionable long
coats with tails were always impractical.

3. British School, 'A Pithead of a Coalmine with Steam Winding Gear', *c.* 1820. Coal transport by wheelbarrow, mule train and horse and cart, down to the coal barges on the new canal system, take the fuel to industry. Brown for workers continues, with white shirts. The woman carrying a basket of coal on her head has her skirt pinned up in the now-traditional way, but with a large pocket tied on in front to carry small coal. Underground the men dug the coal and the women carried it on their backs, but wore less clothing than on the surface.

4. John Frederick Herring, Senior, 'Springtime –
Ploughing', 1856. Smock frocks survived on
shepherds, and here on horse drovers, who lead the
teams. The ploughman and sower, however, have
gone modern in shoddy cloth suits, to the distress of
Thomas Hardy and Gertrude Jekyll, who bewailed
the loss of traditional styles before the influx of less
durable urban clothes. Hitherto country women had
made clothes in leather, corduroy and linen to last
from one generation down to the next. The scene is
probably the Essex coast, where Herring was based
before he retired to Tunbridge Wells.

5. James Hook, 'From Under the Sea', 1864. Botallack Tin Mine near St Just, Cornwall, where the men dug the ore and women on the surface sieved and washed it. Tin mines were the first to adopt helmets of compressed felt impregnated with resin. The men wear old suits, which the ore would colour the rust tone that Edward III had decreed for workers so long before. The girl's pinned-up top petticoat was standard from Scotland to Cornwall, and the hem was always shorter than the fashion.

6. James Hook, 'Crabbers', 1876. Hook spent the
summer of 1876 painting around Hope Cove,
Bigbury Bay, South Devon, where he depicted the
local crabbers. The man tackling the crabs wears a
well-oiled, short smock frock with canvas trousers,
while the one at the oars has the blue fisherman's
Guernsey of oily wool, canvas trousers and the long
leather boots which were oiled with goose grease.
Under the boots are knitted woollen leg warmers
similar to the loughrans worn by miners in the north-
east. Hats were waterproofed with tar.

7. Eyre Crow, 'The Dinner Hour, Wigan', 1874. Mill
owners banned fashionable crinolines and bustles
from their factories but allowed the modish hairnets,
as they kept the hair out of the machines. All these
girls wear the short-sleeved pinafore that developed
in the weaving industry, with narrow petticoats, and
clogs or bare feet. The shawls, which endured down
to the Second World War, were the last remainder of
the mantles so common in the seventeenth century.

8. William P. Frith, 'The Tenby Prawn Seller', 1880. All round Britain's coasts the digging for mussels and cockles and the netting of shrimps were female occupations, as was the carrying of the catch miles inland to market, while the men went fishing. The little hats in South Wales were to allow baskets to be carried on the head. Shoes and stockings were not worn at work, and were only put on when close to the town and market. Short skirts were of course practical for the beaches, with stout aprons. Shawls were common from Wales to Scotland. A similar costume survived into the 1930s, and people still work at digging for cockles and mussels, although in smaller numbers.

best to wear fine clothes, and those who cannot purchase them new buy the old at second-hand, that they may at least have the appearance of finery.' London was of course the place with the biggest supply of old finery, so the poor took advantage of the fact. The market was swamped in 1830 when *The Times* for 18 August advertised the public auction of the wardrobe of his recently deceased Majesty King George IV for the benefit of his pages (who had the right to it). Valued at £100,000, the wardrobe so flooded the second-hand trade that it only fetched £15,000, but the finery Wendeborn complained about was high-grade quality, even though the poor might have to wait until the royal suits had been through two or three other wearers before the price came down to their level. The size of the industry was shown by the opening in 1843 of Mr Isaac's Old Clothes Exchange in Cutler Street, with 7,000 square feet of second-hand dress. The Old Clothes Exchange run by Messrs Simmons and Levy handled exports of old clothes, with Ireland buying £80,000 worth a year.[21]

Recycling of linen into paper was long established, and this period saw an increase in the production of shoddy. This followed improvements in 1834 in the machinery which recycled rags of wool and cotton, but not silk, into yarn from which to weave shoddy, the cheap cloth for the poor. As with cotton, industry was making clothes cheaper. A fabric which was not cheap to begin with appeared after the clothier Joseph Everett was granted a patent on 23 June 1803 for his Salisbury Angola Moleskin, a soft cotton fustian which was shaved before dyeing and was as smooth as the coat of the mole. Once it was produced on an industrial scale the price came down, and moleskin joined corduroy as the fabric of working men's clothes.

The condition of seamstresses at milliners' and dressmakers' had come under the eye of the Commission on Children's Employment, and following the revelations of the terribly long hours of work in the industry for London's 15,000 sewing women, the Association for the Aid and Benefit of Dressmakers and Milliners was set up in 1843. To stop milliners forcing their girls to work day and night without a break during the season, the Association started to register seamstresses who could come in when demand was high. Their dress was the plain gown and apron, but the seamstresses and shirtmakers faced a new threat from the clothes being made in workhouses, where profits did not matter. In 1791 Wendeborn observed that there were 10,000 parishes in England, each with its little workhouse for 20 poor persons. The German thought this system established by Elizabeth I to help her subjects should be abolished. Similar views were expressed by George Nicholls in 1822, when he wrote: 'I wish to see *Poor Houses* looked to with dread by our labouring classes, and the reproach for being an inmate of it extended downwards from Father to Son.'[22] The idea that the poor had to be humiliated and punished for their poverty gained ground, and Nicholls became a Poor Law Commissioner in 1834. Small workhouses were closed down and their inhabitants herded into big central ones built like prisons with high walls. The nineteenth century believed in putting people into uniforms, so prisoners were no longer allowed to wear their own clothes, and the same applied to the inmates in the workhouse. Their own clothes were taken away, and they were put into striped uniforms like the convicts, and had their hair cropped short. Unmarried mothers had to wear plague yellow to advertise their depravity. Worst of all for the old married couples was the fact that the sexes were segregated, no matter how long they had been married, which caused much misery. As an example, the workhouse at Kingsbridge, South Devon, was built in 1837 to house 350 inmates and cost £6,000.[23] Actually to be given a set of rough clothes was better than wearing the rags of the poor, as was a regular meal, but administration varied greatly and there was a scandal in 1847 at Andover workhouse when the inmates were found to be starving. A few reforms were made and couples over 60 could now have a room, but few workhouses bothered to install them. The work provided was either the old beating of hemp and flax that prisoners did, or else making shirts, which undercut the professional shirtmaker struggling to make two a day for the princely wage of fourpence. There were also complaints in *Punch* that the prisons like Millbank Penitentiary made sailors' jackets and soldiers' greatcoats for 2¼d. and 5d. The Association for Dressmakers was followed in 1847 by the Society for the Relief of the Distressed Needlewomen, and this managed in 1850 to get the government to stop the making of cheap clothes in workhouses, although not in prisons. Henceforth the poor inmates made clothes only for the workhouse population.

Centralization also featured in policing. The solitary parish constable was joined with his fellows into a central police station when Sir Robert Peel, the Home Secretary, established the London Metropolitan Police Force in 1822, who were called after him 'bobbies' and 'peelers'. The first uniform was very civilian in style, with its top hat and tail coat, as if to assure the public that a new private army had not come into being. The period tackled the regulation of people long before it insisted on standardization of railway gauges or canal widths, no matter how essential that was.

The smock frock was too loose for a lot of jobs in factories involving proximity to moving machinery in which it might be caught, although it was still worn by the carters and bargees who conveyed the goods to the market. It still appeared in the construction industry and on road workers, who were busy digging up the surface for the new iron waterpipes to be laid. Cities were expanding rapidly, so the water supply had to be increased. Lisson Manor and Marybone Manor houses were demolished and their fields buried under bricks, but Bayswater was still a stream winding between farms with cows, ducks and sheep in 1798. It was, of course, a matter of individual choice whether a man chose to work in a smock frock or shirt sleeves and waistcoat, but as far as wives were concerned smock frocks protected the other garments from dirt and wear and tear. Rowlandson showed coopers wearing smocks and aprons on top as double protection, but at Whitbread's brewery aprons are more common in Garrard's paintings. This firm, in Chiswell Street, London, had in-stalled in 1785 a steam engine by Matthew Boulton and James Watt, of ten horse power; it was increased in power in 1795 and 1814. The brewery used it to grind malt and to pump water, and for Londoners it was one of the first steam spectacles; even George III and Queen Charlotte went to see it. It enabled the brewer to lay off 24 horses, and presumably their drivers and grooms too.[24]

Steam also appeared on the streets, as there was an attempt to introduce steam carriages, which it was argued were cheaper than trains since they did not require enormous railway constructions and could run on roads. Unfortunately, however, the gravel surface on turnpikes, which suited horses, got into the works. Goldsworthy Gurney designed several models, and even towed the Duke of Wellington to Bath in 1831, with the fireman and the engineer attired in top hats and tail coats like gentlemen. The engines were too fragile, however, so the steam carriage and steam omnibus did not catch on, although the more solid traction engine proved much more successful and became very common in farming, from the 1840s onwards.

Steam also appeared on the water, of course, with the invention of steam-powered launches, which led to new dirty jobs for stokers, and for ship's engineers. Very thick leather boots were worn by stokers amidst all the cinders and sparks of the boiler room, with a cotton sweatcloth round the neck to absorb the perspiration, and thick stockings for the same purpose. Flannel shirts were absorbent too, and duck trousers protected the legs in the heat. Out on deck the most important new fabric to appear was the oilskin, a cloth water-proofed with oil, instead of grease or tar. The Army used it first to protect its muskets during the Peninsular War, after which it started to be used for waterproof hats, and gradually for waterproof suits, and in 1834 Clark Russell Jack described the man at the wheel as dressed in yellow oilskin, which colour of course came from the oil. The oilskin rapidly became established as an essential outfit for rough weather at sea, and was adopted by sailors, fishermen, amateur sailors, and by the first lifeboat men, who appeared at Lowestoft in 1807 when the first effective rescue craft was launched. Many of Turner's coastal studies show that in less wild weather striped shirts were still popular for seamen and fishermen alike. Although when conscripted into the Navy men were still not given a uniform, when Samuel Bamford served as a sailor he said the term now was a 'blue jacket', not simply Jack Tar. This shows that blue jackets and white trousers were common enough to identify a sailor as being in the Fleet. C.R. Pemberton encountered the outfit in Liverpool in 1807 when he was recruited by 'two well-dressed sailors, that is to say, two clean white-trousered, neat blue abundant-button-jacketed, long pigtailed, mahogany-waistcoated, quid cheeked men', chewing tobacco. Certainly for public solemnities the Navy liked the men to look the same, as J. Brown of HMS *Victory* wrote in 1805, when he was selected to attend his admiral's funeral: 'There is three hundred of us Pickt out to go to Lord Nelson Funral. We are to wear blue Jackets white Trowsers and a black scarf round our arms, and hats, besides gold medal for the battle of Trafalgar Valued £7-1 round our necks.' Unofficially, a uniform was emerging, but the commanding officer could still put his crew into something different if he felt like it. The officers, of course, had uniforms, but still retained kneebreeches for class distinction, although cocked hats and epaulettes had now been added to the outfit. The non-commissioned officers wore top hats, well tarred, with the ship's name and shield on the front, but otherwise had the same jackets and trousers as the crew.

With equal unofficiality, women still had a way of appearing on ships. Strictly, naval nurses on hospital ships were male, because the women used back in Queen Anne's day had proved too drunken and dissolute to be dependable, but on the warships sailors' wives often emerged in times of battle to act as nurses and powder carriers, when the captains were very grateful for their help. Babies were born on board His Majesty's warships at the battle of the Glorious First of June, and the battle of the Nile. A French officer's wife was rescued from the sea, devoid of her clothes, by the English during the battle of Trafalgar, when she had to be

42. T.L. Busby, 'Shrimp Catcher of Hartlepool', from *Fishing Costume and Local Scenery of Hartlepool*, 1819. This girl has pinned up her dress to reveal a pair of kneebreeches for wading through the shallows. Girls doubtless adopted kneebreeches for the beach around 1700, but illustrators ignored them. This one has a short sailors' jacket, and Busby claimed that her long headscarf was particular to the Hartlepool area.

dressed in sailor's slops. In 1827 there were nine Petty Officers' wives onboard the *Genoa* at Navarino who acted as nurses, so they probably dressed in mob caps, gowns and aprons – unlike the others just mentioned, who were usually pretending to be sailor boys in trousers. When David Clark joined the Navy in 1795 he said there were women on all the ships to do the washing.[25] The designer Henry Angelo visited captured French prizes in 1794 when they were brought to Portsmouth and was horrified by the stench of the wounded. The ships' boys in hobnailed boots showed that they had been pressed straight from the plough.[26]

On the beach, girl shrimp catchers at Hartlepool were wearing kneebreeches under their short skirts, along with a sailor's jacket and a headscarf knotted under the chin, as drawn by T.L. Busby in 1819. They had not breeched their skirts, the practice which so shocked Fanny Burney, but had a separate pair of kneebreeches underneath, which would no doubt have shocked her even more. For wading in pools kneebreeches were more functional than trousers, so this Restoration innovation had reached the north-east coast by now, even if it took 150 years to get there. Obviously it may have arrived earlier than that, but as artists did not trouble to record the commonplace population very frequently before the Regency period, it is not possible to be more precise.

Needless to say, the wars against Napoleon caused enormous growth in the size of dockyards. The naval arsenal at Plymouth had been established in 1691, but when Charles Vancouver visited it in 1808 he found a staff of 2,741, consisting of shipwrights, caulkers, joiners, house carpenters, smiths, masons, bricklayers, sail makers, riggers,

43. Joshua Cristall, 'The Fish Market at Hastings Beach'. Fishermen sport their short jackets like sailors, and the wide slop breeches with sea boots; most have tarred hats, a few woollen caps. The fishmongers all wear smock frocks, which were little decorated in Sussex and Surrey, and the lengths could be long or short. The few women present might be fishmongers too, or else buying for large households.

riggers' labourers, scavelmen, labourers, quarter boys, oakum boys, pitch heaters, blockmakers, sawyers, braziers, plumbers, locksmiths, wheelwrights, coopers, cabin keepers, caulker keepers, and lastly carvers to make the figureheads and stern ornaments. Most of these jobs were apron dominated, although smocks for bricklayers and coopers were now a tradition. It might be thought that the dockyard dominated all employment in the town, but in fact at Portsmouth in 1841 the dockyard employed 34% of the workers while 45% were in dressmaking, hats and shoemaking. Some sewing machines had begun to appear, but the majority of clothes were still made by hand, so it was a labour-intensive industry. Sailors and soldiers received low pay so many of their wives had to take in sewing. London manufacturers set up warehouses in naval towns for which these wives did outwork. For the wives working at home, the dress was the domestic one of mob cap, apron and gown, usually with a kerchief.[27]

Smuggling was still rife along the coasts, and on 30 August 1818 a French rowing galley with 11 men landed goods on the beach at Eastney, thinking they were well out of the sight of Portsmouth town walls, but unaware that they were visible to the guard at Fort Cumberland. The duty officer waited until everything was on shore, then arrested the lot, and captured 1,132 yards of French silk, 19 Angola shawls, 11 dozen Angola gloves, 56 dozen kid gloves, 36 pairs of silk stockings, 42 snuff boxes, 225 yards of cambric, one fur petticoat, and 216 silk sashes. The usual punishment for smugglers (who of course dressed as, and often were, fishermen) was to send them into that floating prison, the Royal Navy.[28]

Servants

American visitors were astounded at the number of richly dressed footmen to be found in London, where their employers still liked to make a fine show. William Austin wrote home in 1802:

My attention was arrested, soon after my arrival, by a most humorous object, a chariot and *eight*; but to do

justice to the horses, four of the appendages to the chariot were not of their species: they were stout fellows such as Hannibal would have chosen for his companions through the Alps. Three of these gentlemen had their station behind, and so dignifiedly did they carry themselves, with so much lace were they puffed out, and so elegantly trimmed were their cocked hats, one might easily in the hurry of novelty have mistaken them for men of high rank.

Benjamin Silliman arrived on the King's birthday in 1805, so gala costume was to be seen on all sides. There was a parade of mail coaches with the driver and guard in royal scarlet liveries, as the Post Office was an appendage of the Crown. At night royal tradesmen filled their shop windows with lamps, while the aristocracy drove to court in their state coaches.

The livery of the footmen was also gaudy, and fantastical to the last degree. They wore lace not only on the border, but on all the seams of their garments, and their large cocked hats were surrounded with broad fringes of silver and gold.[29]

There was competition as to whether a coach carried two, three or four footmen, and the men were chosen for their height, good looks and good legs. They were the most public accessory displaying the importance of their master, so they were dressed up, whereas the invisible kitchen maids and cleaners were not. The eighteenth-century livery for footmen and coach drivers has survived down to the present day on royal coaches and on the Lord Mayor's coach in London, with cocked hats and laced seams still worn.

The German Dr Frederick Wendeborn was very critical of the role servants played in carrying fashion out to the regions, and blamed it on the improvement in trunk roads:

The roads were formerly bad, and travelling tedious and expensive; nor did the great and the rich so frequently and expediously, as they now do, go into the most distant parts of the kingdom, with their servants and attendants who carry the follies and vices of the capital, so successfully among the people who live remote from it.[30]

They certainly were a source of information on all the latest fads and fashions, and servants were still much envied by the labouring classes for their new clothes twice a year. At the wealthiest houses there was more than one kind of livery for footmen, the everyday, the semi-state, and the state livery, with increasing degrees of elaboration.

The career of the Scot John Macdonald shows just how many posts one servant could occupy if he wanted variety. He began as a postillion to Mr Gibbs in Edinburgh: 'I was fitted out with a green jacket, with a red cape, a red waistcoat, and a leather cap with the forepart lined with red morocco.' By 'forepart' he probably meant the peak of the cap. As he was only nine, he was strapped on to the horses to stop him from falling off. It was the style, he noted, for postillions on foot to put the whip around their necks.

Subsequently Macdonald became a cook to Colonel Masterson, with a speciality in soups. 'I usually put on a waistcoat with sleeves, with a white apron, and a cook's knife stuck before me.' This sleeved waistcoat in white linen was a lightweight jacket which seems to have been invented firstly for the heat of kitchens, although it spread more widely later to barbers and farm workers. It had the advantage of being easily washable compared to a thick cloth jacket, and was cheaper so that a cook might own two or three.

For a gentleman in Kent, Macdonald was butler, hairdresser and groom on the coach, then he changed to the town, to Mr John Crawford of St James's Street, who stated, 'I like my servants to go genteely', and gave him twelve pairs of silk stockings to wear with his livery. Macdonald next decided to improve his hairdressing qualifications, and spent four months working under La Motte, a leading London stylist, from whom he rose to the staff of the Hon. Keith Stewart. 'Our livery was the genteelest in London, richly topped with silver, and the coachmen and grooms turned out as clean as any servants in London.' Note the 'we'; servants identified the way they did things with the master. Finally, Macdonald transferred to the banker James Coutts, who complained that he had 20 servants but none who knew how to do his hair and wig, so Macdonald's additional expertise proved a boon. When he compiled his autobiography, this

postillion, cook, hairdresser, groom, butler, and valet called it his *Travels*, for his career had taken him to India, and Mr Coutts took him to Spain. There Macdonald married a Spanish girl and moved over into the hotel business, working at the Hotel de Naples in Toledo, which was a common thing for senior servants to do. Many an inn in England was run by former butlers, housekeepers, footmen, maids and cooks, with the stables run by former coachmen, grooms and ostlers. Sometimes kind employers set them up in such posts, like the Duke of Kingston and his circle.[31]

In 1799 the complaint about servants imitating their masters was still heard, but as Macdonald showed, employers liked their staff to look genteel. Since the Restoration a shoulder knot of ribbon had been the mark of the serving man, but by 1800 some bold employees were taking them off their livery coats so that they might appear more like gentlemen, and got away with it. Similarly, maids in town still sought to look like ladies, dressing in silk and muslin.

The appearance of the female domestics will, perhaps, astonish a foreign visitor more than anything in London. They are in general handsome and well clothed: their dress has the appearance of some taste . . . They are usually clad in gowns well adjusted to their shapes, and hats adorned with ribbands. There are some who even wear silk and sattin, when they are dressed.[32]

So Archenholz wrote on his visit, and this continued. Once photography came in, maids would insist on posing for portraits in their best bonnets and shawls, without an apron in sight.

It was not so easy for servants to give up wigs when their masters did, for this was a revolutionary thing to do, smacking of French extremes, and while the dandies in London were starting to sport their own hair, most men servants had to continue in wigs until the 1840s. Even when they were allowed to abandon wigs they still had to powder the hair to imitate a wig for gala occasions.

The agricultural developer Thomas Coke MP, of Norfolk, was quite happy to wear a smock when inspecting his celebrated sheep, and was indulgent to his staff, who were often the children of his tenants in the traditional way. When strapping

Polly Fishburn wanted to be a gamekeeper and horsebreaker that was all right by him. An expert shot, Polly was the terror of the poachers, and wore a man's hat with short hair, and a short skirt to allow for quick movement. In 1822 she was offered the post of nursery maid but preferred to transfer to Yorkshire with Coke's son-in-law and be his gamekeeper with a top hat, a greatcoat, a scarlet kerchief, her short skirt and boots, and her double-barrelled shotgun.[33]

Black servants were still rare, but the Duke of Sussex had two, of whom the smallest was his valet-de-chambre. At night Blackey, as he was called, got lost in the size of Holkam and ended up sleeping in a footman's bed. When the occupant awoke next morning he screamed aloud in fright that a devil had shared his bed, never having seen such a servant before. In that house silk and white muslin was the dress of the maids in the nursery, so no wonder the outdoor Polly declined it. The upper servants did not have to wear a livery now. Stewards, housekeepers, butlers, grooms of the chambers, valets and lady's maids could dress in a simply elegant way, in the manner later described as being a gentleman's gentleman or a lady's lady. The black evening suit appeared in 1810, and by the time Queen Victoria came to the throne had found its way to butlers, who were now indistinguishable from the guests, except that they wore evening dress all day. The exceptions in the upper servants were the cook and chef, who had to dress for the kitchen with aprons and white caps, whether male or female. Roasting cooks were usually male, general cooks female, as sometimes were the bakers. Confectioners usually came from France or Italy. Cleaning maids were expected to finish their jobs upstairs before the family and guests got up, and could be dismissed from their posts if seen. Their lot was really to be invisible, like the kitchenmaids. For unmarried maids the mob cap was still the major distinction from unmarried daughters of the house, who did not wear caps indoors and only donned bonnets when going out. It is still the tradition that the maid should have a head covering of some sort, no matter how vestigial, and regardless of her marital status.

For male servants, the most important dress concern during the Regency period was whether the master would allow them to wear top hats. The employer who liked his staff to look up-to-date did permit outdoor staff, the coachmen, postillions and footmen, to wear top hats, usually with a cockade at the side to denote servant status. Butlers were allowed to wear trousers by the 1840s, but the costume for footmen continued in most cases to be kneebreeches. Some employers, however, insisted on a historical livery because of the cult of the Picturesque. In 1828 Thomas Acland, Lord Holnicote, built the village of Selworthy in Somerset and told his pensioners that they had to look picturesque to live there, while Lord Ongley at Old Warden in Bedfordshire required his tenants to wear sugar loaf hats and red cloaks à la seventeenth century to give a historical atmosphere.

Every estate had its carpenters, blacksmiths, woodmen, gardeners and labourers, who still worked in their shirt sleeves and aprons. Some servants had more than one post, like Edward Barnes at Erdigg who was fisherman, forester and brewer. His master, Simon Yorke, had him painted in 1830, but wearing his top hat and tail coat with only an axe to denote his position as forester, and a sword to show his service in the Denbighshire Militia. The Yorkes were unique in having generations of servants painted, but the blacksmith, the gardener, and the butcher all put their hats and coats on to look their best. Only the carpenter, Thomas Rogers, was painted in 1830 at his lathe with his coat off, in his shirt sleeves and apron, doing his job.[34]

FIVE

The Heavy Industrial Age

Agriculture

Industry and nationalism both affected agricultural dress, and the spread of railways brought towns and country much closer together. The Smithfield Cattle and Sheep Society, founded in 1798, always met in London, so stock had to be driven huge distances to attend it, or be conveyed by canal. When the Highland Society was founded in 1822, it resolved to have its annual shows in other centres like Glasgow and Perth and not only in Edinburgh. This policy was copied by the Royal Agricultural Society of England when it started in 1837. The first of its shows was at Oxford, in 1839, then Cambridge in 1840, Liverpool in 1841, Bristol in 1842, Southampton in 1844, Shrewsbury in 1845, Newcastle-on-Tyne in 1846, Northampton in 1847, and York in 1848. Consequently farmers and labourers now had the opportunity to see not only the latest machines and the best breeds of animal, but the clothes worn by the engineers, salesmen and demonstrators: black professional suits. In 1860 the Bath and West Society, in order to raise public taste, introduced exhibitions at its shows of paintings, prints, cut glass, china, and photographs of the famous, which astounded the labourers who had never known so much finery existed.[1]

The battle between urban suits and traditional smock frocks could be literal, as Joseph Arch found. Born in 1826 in Barford, Warwickshire, he was the son of a shepherd, as he showed in his dress:

My clothing was of the coarsest. I had to go to school in a smock-frock and old hobnailed boots, and my work-a-day garb was the same. The sons of the wheelwrights, the master tailor, and the tradesmen were just becoming genteel, and used to dress in shoddy cloth. These peacocky youngsters would cheek the lads in smock-frocks whenever they got the chance, and many a stand-up fight we used to have – regular pitched battles of smock-frock against cloth-coat, they were, in which smock-frock held his own right well.

Dress was still a sensitive area because of the pecking order in village life. The squire came first, even in church, where he received communion first, and then the tradesmen, shopkeepers, the wheelwright, the blacksmith, and last of all the smock frocked farm labourers. This was one reason why Arch became a founding member of the Agricultural Labourers' Union in 1872, and an MP in 1885.[2]

Smock frocks began to be produced industrially, often in cotton drill or drabbet, a twilled cotton cloth, and using colour as well. Newark-on-Trent started to produce Newark blue. In the 1870s Richard Jefferies wrote of such blue smock frocks in Wiltshire:

Some of the older shepherds still wear the ancient blue smock frock, crossed with white 'facings' like coarse lace (smocking); but the rising generation use the greatcoat of modern make, at which their forefathers would have laughed as utterly useless in the rainstorms that blew across the open hills.

Jefferies did puzzle why shepherds used umbrellas in the village but not out at work, but this was probably because of those same winds.[3]

At the end of the century the garden designer Gertrude Jekyll agreed that smock frocks were very practical: 'The old carter's smock frock or

round frock, still lingering, but on its way to becoming extinct, is centuries old. No better thing has ever been devised for any outdoor wear that admits the use of an outer garment. It turns an astonishing amount of wet.'[4] The colours in West Surrey, she wrote, were ancient white, light grey, dark grey and olive green. This last could be the effect of oiling to waterproof the smock frocks, linseed oil being one of the liquids used for this process. Such green smock frocks were worn from Sussex to Hertfordshire, and Edwin Grey remembered them in his village of Old Harpenden in the 1860s and 70s:

When a boy, I remember, many of the men wore those 'round smocks', and quite a number of the boys too, and although I have never worn one myself, I was assured that they were very warm and convenient garments. These smocks were made of a very strong dark green material and were slipped on over the head. All the smock wearers who could afford it, had two of them, one for working in and the other for best, as it was termed, that is for Sundays and special occasions. Some of those who had only one would at these special times turn it inside out so that it appeared then quite fresh and clean. This rather long shirt-like garment also hid any imperfections in the underclothes, hence I applied the word convenient.

Some of the 'round smocks', especially those worn for best, were, many of them, elaborately worked from the shoulder downwards to just below the breast, having small blue glass beads inserted here and there amongst the smocking work near the shoulders.[5]

Several reversible smock frocks survive in Luton Museum's collection. Old Harpenden had both a clothing club and Sunday School Club for children's clothing, to help the villagers save for their Sunday-best smock frock or suit.

Smocking was most common from Newark

44. Joshua Cristall, 'Highland Drovers at Inverary', c.1840. Trousers spread among young men, although their elders stuck to kneebreeches or plaids and kilts. These all seem to be obeying the ancient law about boys not wearing shoes, into adulthood. A lot of country folk donned shoes only in town. The check-like tartans show none of the clan types that the commercially-minded were now inventing. Now cattle and sheep had to be driven only to the nearest railway head.

across to Worcester, Gloucester, Hereford, Warwick, and over into Wales, whereas the smock frocks in Sussex and Surrey were mainly undecorated, with only a little gathering at the neck. Those in the west had very wide collars. Such smocking was for the Sunday-best smock frock, which would be handed down for two or three generations. The patterns very rarely reflected the sort of job done, as these smocked smock frocks were for best wear.

The increasing reluctance of the young to wear ancestral garments annoyed the Quaker William Hartas of Danby in Cleveland. Girls turned their noses up at calico, and boys at leather breeches. The Reverend John Atkinson recorded the Quaker's wrath:

Why, when I was a lad there was a vast still sitting in their fathers' leather breeches, and more than I kenned had breeks their grandfathers had had for best, and there was a vast o' good wear in 'em yet. Mak' things last what they will is my advice to this meeting; and old-fashioned homespun and good leather breeks is baith very lasty.[6]

Gertrude Jekyll shared his opinion, complaining that the shops were full of cheap suits which soon became shabby, and were nowhere near as robust as smock frocks, corduroy or leather breeches to work in. Unfortunately the young could see how the middle class dressed at shows, and imitated them, even if only in shoddy cloth.

Smock frocks died out first in the industrial Midlands. Lady Josepha Stanley missed them when she married and went to live in Cheshire, having been brought up at Sheffield Park in Sussex where smock frocks abounded. When her husband died she returned southwards, and when she went to church in Buckinghamshire she was delighted:

6 April 1851. I had the pleasure of seeing the *smock frock* in numbers which I had not seen since I left Sheffield [Park] & everything here puts me in mind of those young days.[7]

Thomas Hardy was particularly distressed to see the change that took place in the 1850s to 1880s in Dorsetshire, as town wear ousted rural, and mass-produced clothes threatened home-made. The southern pattern of hiring fairs was still going, but how different they looked:

45. Anon., 'Market woman of Milnathort, Kinross', *c*.1860. Clutching the Holy Book against the demon camera, the old lady wears the common linen cap or 'mutch', with a triple-layered shawl pinned and tied about the waist with string. One striped petticoat is pulled up to show a dark one, a tradition since the seventeenth century. Her lace-up boots were preferred by many country women.

46. Nicol Erskine, 'Clout the Old, the New are Dear', 1886. Making clothes last was all-important for most workers. This Scottish shepherd must have a French wife, for her cap with the long side pieces is typical of the Auvergne. Her British cap is over on the chair. The books and table indicate unusual sophistication.

The hiring fair of recent years presents an appearance unlike that of former times. A glance up the high street of the town on a Candlemass-fair day twenty or thirty years ago revealed a crowd whose general colour was whity-brown flecked with white. Black was almost absent, the few farmers who wore that shade, being hardly discernible. Now the crowd is as dark as a London crowd. The change is owing to the rage for cloth clothes which possesses the labourers of today. Formerly they came in smock frocks and gaiters, the shepherds with their crooks, the carters with a zone of whipcord round their hats, thatchers with a straw tucked into the brim, and so on. Now, with the exception of the crook in the hands of an occasional old shepherd, there is no mark of speciality in the groups, who might be tailors or undertakers for what they exhibit externally. Out of a group of eight, for example, who talk together in the middle of the road, one only wears corduroy trousers. Two wear cloth pilot coats and black trousers, two patterned tweed suits with black canvas overalls, the remaining four suits being of faded broadcloth. To a great extent these are their Sunday suits but the genuine white smock frock of Russian duck and whity-brown one of drabbet, are rarely seen now afield, except on the shoulders of old men. Where smocks are worn by the young and middle-aged, they are of a blue material. The mechanic's 'slop' has also been adopted, but a mangy old coat is preferred, so that often a group of these honest fellows on the arable has the aspect of a body of tramps up to some mischief in the field, rather than its natural tillers at work.[8]

47. Anon., 'Hop Picking in Herefordshire', c.1890. In England traditional linen caps faced competition from the different kinds of sun bonnets. This kind with the frilled inserts were strengthened with cord or cane. Sacking aprons were ideal for field work. The man is in corduroy with a slop linen jacket. The girl behind him wears a loose dress that might be a kind of smock.

Francis Heath agreed that 1880 was about the date when even shepherds began to give up smock frocks, and adopted jackets and waistcoats in fustian and corduroy with corduroy trousers, just as labourers were doing. He stressed that peasant clothes were still never new, but handed down, or given by the farmer, or else bought at the second-hand shop, which is why Hardy found the suits and coats faded and mangy.

Light canvas slops, that is, ready-made jackets and coats, as distinct from sailors' breeches, began to be adopted by young farm workers in the 1870s for summer, although in winter they resumed thick fustian jackets, or the new short pilot overcoat in coarse cloth. Leather leggings or gaiters had become a tradition, and once trousers became common a leather strap was introduced to tie under the knee to pull the hem of the trousers up out of the mud. Edwin Grey was puzzled about how old labourers could have top hats for Sunday

best, but they said they were handed down when the farmer had finished with them. They wore wide-awake hats with a broad brim out in the field. In West Surrey Gertrude Jekyll said smock frocks were kept for Sunday, and by the end of the century ploughmen and labourers wore the white slop jacket for summer.

Grey was surprised how the men cut the feet off cotton stockings. Industry had made cotton stockings cheap and plentiful, but the old labourers preferred to wrap their feet in dock leaves and linen strips, as the stiff boots gave them sores. Hay was used to line the boot for warmth. In the wet, the boots were given a dressing of tallow candle grease to waterproof them. Women still wore pattens to keep their shoes out of the mud, and Pigot shows that Derby had four male patten and clog makers and four men patten-ring makers. Pattens lingered into the next century.

Barbers were rare in village life, so hair was

often cut at home or by the local groom with his horse clippers, but Old Harpenden had a woman who specialized in cutting hair and shaving men, Barber Grey. Sometimes there were women blacksmiths, usually carrying on their father's trade.

By 1870 a severe agricultural depression was beginning, as wheat from the opened-up American and Canadian prairies, transported by that British invention railways and steamships, flooded into the kingdom. Many farmers went bankrupt, including aristocrats, and a squeeze on wages was the result. The average farm labourer's wage was 9–12s. a week, and cottage rents were £4–£6 a year. Joseph Arch no longer wore a smock frock when he went to the first meeting of 2,000 labourers, summoned by word of mouth alone, to discuss founding a union. 'I was dressed in a pair of cord trousers, and a cord vest, and an old flannel jacket.' Later, in 1872, labourers wore their best clothes for a major meeting in Leamington, 'A poor best according to rich folks' notions no doubt, but smock frock and fustian jacket and shabby gown covered brave English hearts.'[9] The new Agricultural Labourers' Union voted for its first national strike for a living wage. The farmers expected to starve them out, for few labourers had any savings, but other unions sent money, the *Daily News* raised a fund for them, and recruiting agents turned up. Cotton mills wanted hands, and the North Eastern Railway wanted drivers and horse keepers at £1 or 23s. a week, so the labourers were offered a chance to leave the land. Furthermore, New Zealand wanted settlers, and so did Australia, where the shipping of convicts had ceased in 1852. New South Wales published a pamphlet in 1876 on its attractions; an eight-hour working day, and labourers' wages of £30–40 a year. Clothing could be had for the following prices: menswear: moleskin jackets 8s. to 12s., moleskin coats 12s. to 20s., moleskin waistcoats 3s. to 5s., moleskin trousers 4/6 to 9s., coloured shirts 1/6 to 4/6, socks 10d., strong boots 5/9 to 6s. Women's clothing: handkerchiefs 4½d. to 8d., straw hats 2/6 to 3/6, print dresses 7/6 to 12/6, flannel petticoats 3/6 to 8s., calico petticoats 4s. to

48. Thomson & Smith, 'Public Disinfectors', 1877, from *Street Life in London*. Professional black is worn by the health inspector; his staff have the new overall which had now been created for industry, since the factory acts had just begun to insist on protective clothing. The long jacket and trousers look back to naval and mining precedents.

8s., flannel per yard 2s., calico per yard 8d. to 9d., blankets 12/6 to 20s., and sheeting calico 1/6 to 2/6 the yard.[10]

No bedgown jackets were included in this list, and these had begun to disappear inland, although they lingered at the coast. Edwin Grey made no mention of them in his village in Hertfordshire. The women wore dresses in linsey wolsey, alpaca or flannel, but a second dress for best usually had some tucks and was a little more ornate, as it was

49. Chamberlayne of Marylebone Road, 'A Milkwoman from William Stoat's Alderney Dairy at 2 Upper Gloucester Place', 1872. Still loyal to the old linen cap, this indefatigable lady delivered milk in all weathers through Marylebone. The tartan shawl was her only protection from cold, apart from lots of flannel petticoats, plus the inevitable apron.

often second-hand, or else bought from the village dressmaker and then handed down as a precious bequest. Obviously the enormous crinolines of the 1850s and 60s had no place here, and few country women attempted that silhouette. White aprons abounded; every village woman seemed to wear one. Print dresses were for Sundays in summer, as were shoes, otherwise it was boots and pattens. Older women stuck to black 'coal scuttles', as Grey called their bonnets, which suggests the 1780s type

of sunbonnet. He did not mention print ones. Old Grannie Reid, who was the village nurse-cum-doctress, always put on a poke bonnet over her white cap, before going out, together with a three-cornered shawl, an apron and a dark dress. For dirty jobs it was now usual to make aprons out of sacks or sugar bags. General housework saw the apron in cotton print or check. The best apron was the white one, put on for the afternoon and going out. In the dairy a long apron with a bib was worn for milking.

Gleaning parties of women and children donned their oldest clothes, and what Grey called 'mushroom hats', the ancient straw hat with the brim turned down. Earbags were tied round the waist to carry ears of wheat, and when full the bag was carried on the head. The village was served by packmen, two of whom owned shops in St Albans, one of them a draper, and the other a maker of boots, an important item in working budgets.[11]

Bonnets did not conquer south Wales, because of the women's fondness for wearing men's hats. The Reverend Richard Warner referred to their beaver hats in 1798, and in 1807 Benjamin Malkin still found the custom in being. 'The dress in Glamorganshire is not so strongly marked as in most other counties, except that the women universally adopt the man's hat; but they wear it with very good grace and are remarkably neat in their attire.'[12] They wore such hats over their linen or muslin caps, or else over a headscarf, and once top hats started to come into fashion Welsh women adopted them as well, in the 1840s. In 1844 Anne Beale said that the Hollantide Fair in the vale of the Towey saw 'a black stream of hats; for a bonnet is as rare here as a Queen Anne's farthing'. Attempts to relate this top hat to the old seventeenth-century sugar loaf hats are nonsense because the shapes are completely different. The 'sugar loaf' always ended in a point, like liquid sugar drained into a cone. The top hat did not appear until the Regency period and was always tubular, and artists like Sandby and Ibbetson do not show Welsh women wearing such hats before then. When J.C. Rowland did his lithographs of Welsh people in 1848 the women were wearing a mixture, some still in old low straw hats, some in short top hats and others wearing tall ones. The wide brims on such hats developed later, and were a nineteenth-century introduction. In England some sugar loafs still survived, worn over white caps at the almshouses in Castle Rising, Norfolk, as the charity livery.

In her Welsh stories Anne Beale described the servant girl Rachel Lewis going to seek work. 'Her dark hair is bound across the forehead, under a clear muslin cap, and is always neat and glossy.' A 'striped flannel skirt, and loose bodice, the short sleeves, and clean white muslin neckerchief' completed the attire. She went to the hiring at the fair, as south Wales had copied southern England in this respect:

A crowd of females now gathered together in one place, dressed in their best woollen gowns, best aprons, best handkerchiefs, and best hats, as well as the men opposite, are anxiously looking about them and hoping that every farmer or farmer's wife who approaches, will view them with a favourable eye.

A less elegant lady in the short skirts of all working women was Corporal Davies's wife, who was known by her husband's rank or job, in the Welsh custom:

... coarse black worsted stockings, and thick shoes with wooden soles [clogs] made very conspicuous by short petticoats. The usual Welsh dress showing arms red and strong – a waist disdaining the foreign aid of whalebone-spread features – an eye without much meaning – a bronzed complexion – a somewhat flat nose – a cap, the strings of which are flying in the 'wanton wind' – a hat, the crown of which is much battered – and you have the whole figure of Nanny the corporal.[13]

By 'usual Welsh dress', showing the arms, she probably meant the bedgown jacket, which lingered on in Wales into the 1850s, but was not Welsh in origin. Thereafter check dresses become more common, like the 1855 red and black check flannel dress with buttons down the front, a blue check apron, a red cloak and a white cap conserved in the Welsh Folk Museum at St Fagan's Castle. The only reflection of fashion is a tiny lace collar, and some fullness in the skirt, which suggests that it came from a farmer's or tradesman's wife.

By now nationalism and antiquarianism were trying to discover traditional styles of dress, and what they could not find they invented. In Wales Elizabeth Hall, Lady Llanover, tried to find differences in colour and style between Gwent, Gower, Cardigan and Pembrokeshire in south Wales in 1834, but her drawings look very period with their puff sleeves. In fact she reflects the mixture of old straw hats and new top hats coming in when her essay was published in 1843. Shawls, aprons, kerchiefs, dresses, caps, check and cloaks are none of them Welsh in origin, but the most common colour she shows is blue, and that was the Welsh tradition. Anne Beale's Welshmen still had blue coats and blue handkerchiefs round the neck. The costume Lady Llanover created for her harpist Tomas was more Scottish than anything else, with its Scotch bonnet and plaid, worn with a check jacket with hanging sleeves, dark blue kneebreeches and red stockings, only the last two items having any Welsh character. It is now at St Fagan's. The big problem in Wales was the impact of Methodism which, like religions worldwide, stamped out any tradition older than itself, as the bard Edward Jones had complained in 1802: 'The sudden decline of the national Minstrelsy, and Customs of Wales is in a great degree to be attributed to the fanatic imposters or illiterate plebian preachers.'[14] The preachers imposed sober clothes and sober ways making merry Wales dull.

In Scotland, after Sir Walter Scott made it fashionable, Scottish dress began to be equated with Highland dress, but the Lowland Scots, the ancient enemies of the Highlanders, did not wear it except for plaids. The self-styled Sobieski Stuart brothers' *Vestiarium Scoticum* of 1842 tried to create tartans for every clan, including the Lowland families, but as the Gaelic scholar Campbell of Islay wrote in 1871: 'I do not believe that the distinctions which are now made as to Clan tartans ever prevailed at all, till Tartan became an important manufacture in Scotland in the reign of George the 4th.'[15] Smock frocks did not win general acceptance in Scotland, where the plaid was used to keep off the wind and rain, and this remained the dress of shepherds when they started

to wear jackets and trousers, always with a plaid over one shoulder. Edward VII favoured knicker-bockers and spats with stockings, and this was copied on many Scottish estates, with outdoor staff like shepherds and gamekeepers being given knickerbockers. Barefooted women were still common and many peasant women only put on shoes and stockings at the church door on Sunday before entering, having carried them there. Hats on women were still rare in Highland society. Mrs Ewen of Balloch pointed out that her mother and the minister's wife were the only women with hats in church; all the peasant women had only their white caps or mutchs in 1860, which of course could be covered by a tartan shawl or plaid in bad weather. One local custom consisted of a special dress for bankrupts, who had to wear a 'dyvours' costume, half brown and half yellow, with a hood, reminiscent of a fool's outfit; they could enter church only after everybody else.

50. Anon., 'The Express Country Milk Company of 26 Museum St. London'. Railways put many town dairies with their few cows out of business, and by bringing in vast quantities of milk overnight from the country ended the long tradition of milkmaids delivering milk. The Express Company delivered the milk over a large area by introducing horses and carts. The new milkman-drivers all have white overall coats and bowler hats, some with a badge.

Payment in kind was the ancient tradition on farms in Scotland, and the labourer had to pay for the rent of his 'cot' or house with the labour of his wife in harvesting, muck spreading, feeding, and cleaning out. In the south-east of the country these were called 'bondage women'. Out in the field they wore black straw hats over headscarves, short dresses and boots, although once sunbonnets came in they took to 'uglies', and then wore either. Ploughmen and labourers had to supply the woman in order to get the job.[16]

Urban habits, however, began to be copied in the countryside, to Thomas Hardy's annoyance:

The peculiarity of the English urban poor (which M. Taine ridicules and unfavourably contrasts with the taste of the Continental working-people) – their preferences for the cast-off clothes of a richer class to a special attire of their own – has, in fact, reached the Dorset farm folk. Like the men, the women are, pictorially, less interesting than they used to be. Instead of the wing bonnet like the tilt of a wagon, cotton gown, bright hued neckerchief, and strong flat boots and shoes, they (the younger ones at least) wear shabby millinery bonnets and hats with beads and feathers, 'material' dresses, and boot-heels almost as foolishly shaped as those of ladies of highest education.[17]

The young preferred shabby second-hand but vaguely fashionable clothes to any that meant traditional rural. Hardy had admitted how the traditional clothes lacked colour, being usually browns, mud-colour, leather-tone or faded snuff, with garments recut and remade, recycled from one generation to the next. Hippolyte Taine in 1872 also observed the urban appearance of English country folk: 'The villagers have more the appearance of workmen or small tradespeople; in truth, an English farm is as much a manufactory as any other, giving employment to day labourers and bailiffs.'[18] He found no example of the 'shrewd, defiant, yet astonished peculiarity' of French peasantry, proclaiming another species. Definitely not – the English felt that they were entitled to dress as well as, or actually like, their superiors.

Cleanliness was important when receipt of charity was involved, and one Dorset woman told Hardy, 'I always kip a white apron behind the door to slip on when gentlefolk knock, for if so be they see a white apron they think ye clane.'[19] Gertrude Jekyll felt that a boring, general standardization was taking place before her eyes, as industry began to impose a uniform range of clothes, but some local styles survived into the twentieth century.

Artisans and professionals

Black suits for professional men dominated urban society, with the black morning coat to the knee, the dark trousers and waistcoat, and the black silk

51. Anon., 'Boy with a Hurdy Gurdy'. Bare feet for children remained common into this century. Corduroy trousers and an old pilot coat complete the costume, with a piece of blanket to rest the hurdy gurdy on. His greasy hair has not been washed for some time. The capital was full of unwanted children trying to survive.

top hat as the uniform for a wide range of activities. All sorts of inspectors favoured the attire, from tax inspectors to school inspectors and sanitary inspectors. Anybody in an official position was required to wear it, and so did other officials like sports referees, station masters, bank managers, rent collectors, managers in shops and the new department stores, down to apothecaries and their assistants. The pharmacist Mr Higgins never allowed his assistants to go outdoors with-

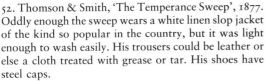

52. Thomson & Smith, 'The Temperance Sweep', 1877. Oddly enough the sweep wears a white linen slop jacket of the kind so popular in the country, but it was light enough to wash easily. His trousers could be leather or else a cloth treated with grease or tar. His shoes have steel caps.

53. Thomson & Smith, 'Cast Iron Billy', 1877. Horse bus companies did not use uniform liveries, except for railway company buses. The only identification for Cast Iron Billy is the badge and the whip, and he preferred a topper to a bowler. His route from Edgware Road to the Strand is still run by many buses today.

out their top hats on, based as he was in Crawford Street in the West End. Individual family shops now faced a threat from the new department stores, for the railway system with cheap day-return tickets enabled customers within one and a half hours' travelling time to shop in London, so that such stores could attract shoppers from Canterbury, Portsmouth, Bath, Birmingham, and Ipswich. Consequently the shops were much bigger, and mail order departments reached custom-

ers further afield. William Whiteley opened his draper's shop in Westbourne Grove in 1863, a new suburb and not based in the West End or City, the traditional centres for shopping. Calling himself the Universal Provider, he gradually expanded into groceries, dairy produce, meats, catering, ironware, laundry, hairdressing, and dry-cleaning, and kept a stable of 320 horses and 145 vans to deliver purchases over a range of 25 miles. The advantage of bulk buying also impressed some clerks in the Post Office in 1864, who set up the Civil Service Supply Association in 1866 and their shop in the Strand in 1868. The armed forces took notice and opened their own store, the Army & Navy Co-operative Society, in 1872, which was rather like a club for members of the services of officer rank only. Its mail order catalogue was much in demand throughout the Empire. The now-global scale of supply was illustrated by Arthur Liberty opening his East India House in Regent Street in 1875 to sell Japanese artefacts. The first Co-op appeared in Rochdale during the Hungry Forties, when the urban working class first organized its shopping power for its own advantage.

Such department stores traditionally required the staff to live in, either above the departments, or else in dormitories close by. The costume for such employees was most commonly black dresses for the girls and black suits for the male assistants. The hours were usually 8 a.m. to 8 p.m., and on Sundays they had to roam the streets as they could not stay in their rooms. Under the old apprentice system the shop assistant was provided with his clothes, but the employees were now hired on a day's notice of firing, rather than under an indenture, so they were not given their uniforms, even though they had to conform to the house livery black.

Underground, the expansion of London meant the construction of many new sewers, to which John Hollingshead paid a visit in 1862:

There seems to be only one costume for underground or underwater work, and the armour necessary for sewer-inspecting will do for lobster-catching on the coast, or for descending in a sea diving-bell. The thick worsted stockings coming up to the waist, the heavy long greased boots of the 'seven league' character, the loose blue shirt, and the fan-tailed hat, may be very hot and stifling to wear, but no sewer-inspector is considered properly fortified without them.[20]

By 'fan-tailed' he means the neckpiece at the back of the helmet which was now traditional for seamen, dustmen, and coalmen. The sewermen's hero was Mr Roe, surveyor of the Holborn and Finsbury Commissioners for Sewers, who intro-duced curved sewers, gratings, and manholes to prevent the build-up of poisonous gases in the old zig-zag type of sewer which had killed many a worker underground. In 1857 the Metropolitan Board of Works embarked on a comprehensive scheme for London.

The journeyman engineer Thomas Wright reported in 1867 on the new privilege of Saturday afternoons off work. At 1 p.m. the men would be waiting at the gates of the factory with their shop jackets or their slops rolled up under their arms. At the bell they dashed home for dinner, then spent the afternoon at the public bath houses to wash and change from dirty clothes into the clean ones for next week, donning a fresh pair of moleskin or corduroy trousers, and a clean shirt. They combined with this the top part of their Sunday suit, the black waistcoat and jacket, for Saturday night out at the pub or music hall. They had a penchant for big collars, scarves and cheap jewellery, worn with the new cloth cap and a muffler. Many working men shaved only on Sunday, so in the East End barbers were open on that day from 10 a.m. to 3 p.m.[21]

Second-hand clothing continued to be big business. Henry Mayhew visited the Exchange at Houndsditch, which cost $\frac{1}{4}$d. to enter.

Here meet all the Jew clothesmen, hucksters, dealers in second-hand shoes, left-off wardrobe keepers, hareskin dealers, umbrella dealers, and indeed the buyers and sellers of left-off clothes and worn-out commodities of every description. The purchasers are of all nations, and in all costumes. Some are Greek, others Swiss, and others German; some have come to buy up rough charity clothing and army coats for the Irish market; others have come to purchase the hareskins and old furs.

The mark of the dealers in arguing for bargains was that 'Everyone there is dressed in his *worst!*'

54. Thomson & Smith, 'Street Locksmith', 1877. Enter the woollen cardigan from the Crimean war hero; it was intended to go under coats and waistcoats, but this locksmith wears it on its own. Sacking aprons replace linen ones for dirty work. The man behind in the slop jacket sports a straw hat of a colonial pattern.

Slop shop owners hunted for old coats and trousers to turn into cheap ready-made suits, of the sort agricultural labourers were now buying. Outside, Jewish street sellers waited to buy garments off the dealers.[22]

Some builders' labourers still wore smock frocks in the 1850s and 60s, but of a very plain, undecorated kind, and so did dustboys sieving through the rubbish for anything recoverable. Mayhew gave his dustboy a fantailed sou'wester. Women in the dustyard wore black sunbonnets, or head scarves, bib aprons, short dresses and boots, with a shawl when cold. South Wharf, Paddington, to Bishop's Bridge Road was one such yard, where between 100 and 150 women and boys sieved rubbish for bits of leather and old bones or metal, which they put into boats. The residue was burnt. The lawyer Arthur Munby was fascinated by the tough working women, out of necessity so unlike the fashionable ideal. A dustgirl from Lambeth Yards he saw in 1862 had a man's corduroy jacket, a ragged cotton frock over a grey petticoat, mannish boots, and a battered bonnet, the whole thick with dust and ashes, and her apron, if once white, was now decidedly grey.

Mayhew visited some beggars in a cheap lodging house:

> ... never was so motley and so ragged an assemblage seen. Their hair was matted like flocks of wool, and their chins were greasy with their unshorn beards. Some were in dirty frock-smocks; others in old red plush waistcoats, with long sleeves. One was dressed in an old shooting-jacket, with large wooden buttons; a second in a blue flannel sailor's shirt; and a third, a mere boy, wore a long camlet coat reaching to his heels, and with the ends of the sleeves hanging over his hands.

One half-starved unfortunate had a check shirt so dirty that it looked brown, black and greasy clothes, and women's side-laced boots with the toes cut out so that he could get them on. Out of 50 beggars, 14 had no shirts, 5 no shoes, and 42 shoes that hardly held together. Deaths from starvation were a common fate, because it was not easy to get into a workhouse.[23]

The dressing of workhouse inmates like prisoners gradually gave way to grey clothes. Men now received coats, waistcoats, trousers, shirts, shoes, socks, hats and handkerchiefs. Women were given gowns, upper and under petticoats, shirts, handkerchiefs, shoes, stockings, caps and bonnets, and of course aprons, since working women were never seen without an apron, even if they were reduced to picking oakum in the workhouse. In his study of poverty in York at the end of the century, Benjamin Rowntree discovered that the average wage was 32/8¾d. a week. The minimum necessary amount of clothing for a year for the best-off worker came to 37/3, and consisted of boots, one new pair and repairs, 11/–; socks, four pairs at 9d., total 3/–; coat, second-hand, 4/–; vest, 1/6; trousers, one pair plus repairs, 7/6; shirts, three at 1/4 each, 4/–; overcoat, second-hand at 15/– should last three years, so 5/–; cap and scarf, 1/3. Thus even the better-paid still needed second-hand clothes for the larger items. For women workers the annual total was 31/10, comprising one pair of boots, 5/6 plus repairs at 3/6, total 9/–; no slippers as old boots preferred; ready-made dress, being a blouse, 2/– and skirt, 8/–, cost 10/–; aprons, four at 6d. each, 2/–; no other skirts; stockings, two pairs at 9d., 1/6; underclothes, one of each, 2/10; stays, one pair, 2/6; hats, cost 4/6, but should last three years, so annual total 1/6; jacket, 1/6; and shawl, 1/–. Clothes for children, depending on age, came to 13/– to £1 a year. Since birth control was unheard of at that level in society through lack of information, large families were common, and women dreaded sex lest it resulted in yet another child to feed and clothe. For two parents and eight children the clothing bill on the above budget would come to about £12 a year, out of a wage of about £72 which also had to pay for the rent, food for all, and coal for heat and cooking; and these figures were for the better-off workers.[24]

55. Thomson & Smith, 'Covent Garden Porters', 1877. A flattened type of bowler, squashed rather than specially constructed, is used for carrying baskets of flowers. The suits are the basic lounge suit in shoddy cloth, although the character with a velvet collar and a tie is probably a customer. Workers preferred a scarf or neckcloth to ties and starched shirts.

56. Paul Martin, 'Porters', c.1895. The leather pad has become enormous to carry piles of boxes or baskets, but seems in itself dangerously incapacitating, and trolleys began to take their place. The moleskin suits were another basic working uniform.

The many women sellers of fruit, vegetables, cottons, and matches to be found in the streets dressed very similarly in linen or cotton caps with a frill at the front, cloaks or plaid shawls, aprons, plain dresses to the ankle, and boots. As men were always paid more than women, several of the latter continued to pass themselves off as men. Helen Oliver began as a maidservant at a farmhouse in West Kilbride, Scotland, where she met a ploughman who turned out to be a woman in men's clothes, so in 1818 she 'borrowed' her brother's suit and went off to Glasgow to learn plastering. She worked as a male plasterer at Kilmarnock, Paisley, Lanark and Edinburgh, and was not exposed until she fell off some scaffolding

at New Buildings, Lord Moray's Park, Aberdeen. When a workmate undid her waistcoat to bring her round he found that she was a woman. Once she recovered she set out again, calling herself John Thomson, in search of more plastering or weaving. In 1866 Munby interviewed Helen Bruce, who since the age of 17 had worked in men's clothes as an errand boy, a shoplad, an oddboy at Newcastle docks, a stoker onboard ship to Leith, and a tallyman at an ironstone mine, had looked for a job in Hamburg but had to come home, and spent three years in London as clerk and copier. She said she did so for the money, and because men were not asked for references whereas women were, even for humble posts. She also preferred the convenience of male suits. The most successful such worker was Miranda Barry, who obtained an excellent degree in medicine at Edinburgh University as a man wearing male attire all the time, although she was tiny with red hair. She qualified as a surgeon (still a closed world for women) and became an army surgeon in South Africa, and in 1857 Inspector General of Hospitals in Upper and Lower Canada, with a salary only prima donnas could rival. On duty she wore the army officer's uniform of tail coat, epaulettes, trousers, and cocked hat, but used built-up boots to increase her height, and very high collars to conceal her soft neck. Off duty she wore the black frock coat and trousers of civilian doctors. A fine surgeon, she saved many lives, including one by a swift caesarian section, only the second performed in the West in modern times. She battled with authority over the treatment of prisoners and lepers, the use of unqualified people to dispense drugs, the treatment of blacks, and the lack of female nurses for female patients. During the Crimean War she met Florence Nightingale at Scutari and gave her a public dressing-down for wearing only her light linen cap outdoors in the fierce sunshine, so Miss Nightingale thought her a very hard man. What a contrast; Miranda Barry masquerading as a man all her life so that she could be a surgeon, and now Miss Nightingale reforming Army nursing as herself. The distinction lay in the area: male

professional posts, and 'feminine' nursing, which women could do as themselves.[25]

Even so, Florence Nightingale did not have an easy entry into nursing, as her family strongly objected. The wealthy were nursed at home; only the rest went to public hospitals with their rough nurses. There were very few schools for nurses. In 1840 the Quaker, Elizabeth Fry, founded her Institution of Nursing Sisters, but it was a rarity. The dress there was print frocks indoors, with large aprons, of brown holland for probationers, and outdoors the grey Quaker dress with a long black cloak and a black bonnet with a black veil and no trimmings. The nursing cap was copied from Elizabeth Fry's own white linen mob cap, reduced in bulk and confined by a ribbon. Miss

57. Anon., 'Miss Nightingale in the Hospital at Scutari', 1854, from Sarah Tooley's biography, 1904. The lady with the lamp and much determination favoured a black dress with a white cap, collar and apron. Elizabeth Fry and she were the first to insist on professional training for nurses, and their stress on cleanliness was enough to save lives.

Nightingale managed to get some time in a public hospital, picking up the basics as most nurses did, then in 1853 she was appointed superintendent of a sanatorium for sick governesses where she installed hot water, service lifts and bells for patients. A ruthless organizer, she got her big chance with the Crimean War, and set out with specially selected nurses. The French Army had nursing nuns, its English ally only orderlies. The hospital at Scutari proved to be a Turkish barracks with no ventilation and inadequate sewage disposal, so that patients died of typhoid and cholera caught there. Miss Nightingale installed new kitchens, new sanitation and ventilation, and introduced medical diets instead of Army cooking. The death rate halved. In her black dress, white cap, cuffs and apron she was adored by the soldiers as the Lady with the Lamp, but despite that image, no gentle angel could have tackled the Army and Whitehall unless possessed of considerable determination. Through the press the Nightingale Nursing Fund to train nurses began in 1855, and in 1860 the Nightingale School for Nurses at St Thomas's Hospital, London, opened. The Army Medical Staff Corps was established and so was the Army's Standing Committee on Sanitation in 1865, now that the Army was based all round the globe. An undated set of regulations in Miss Nightingale's scrapbook from St Bartholomew's Hospital states that probationer nurses would start at the age of 22 and 'will be required to provide for themselves, uniform dresses, caps, aprons, bonnet and cloak. They will have to pay for the washing of their own personal linen &c.'. Black was the usual colour for sisters' dresses, and grey for the rest, but hospitals loved different bonnets and caps. Agnes Jones took the trained nurse system into workhouse hospitals at Liverpool in 1865, and although she succumbed to typhoid in 1868, her work went on.

Cleanliness was the new idea, although Galen had said it was important in Roman times. In 1848 the Hungarian surgeon Ignaz Sammelweis at Vienna's maternity hospital introduced the practice of washing the staff's hands in chlorinated lime water, after a male colleague had died when he cut himself during an autopsy on a mother dead from puerperal fever. Twenty-five per cent of the maternity cases died from this infection. Sammelweis realized that it passed into the blood, regardless of sex, and that the nurses' and doctors' unwashed hands transferred it from patient to patient. The mortality rate at the hospital fell to 1%, but Sammelweis got the sack.[26]

Next there was Joseph Lister, a Quaker, who started to read medicine at University College, London, in 1844, when the students sported top hats, black coats, broad-black-striped peg-top trousers and muttonchop whiskers. He became a surgeon at University College Hospital in 1853, where the surgeons operated in their oldest frock coats stained with decades of dirt and blood. The wound dressers also appeared in dirty old coats. Lint dressings washed in unboiled water from the New River were applied to amputations, covered with oiled silk, and not changed for days. Gangrene was the usual outcome. In his oration on Lister in 1913 Sir Rickman Godlee declared, 'The nurses are nice and bright and clean, and so is the butterfly cap of the nun-like sister, but one cannot be sure that the same is true of her black flannel gown looped round by a rope girdle at the waist.' This might be just as dirty as the surgeon's.

Lister was very impressed by the work on microorganisms of Louis Pasteur and the two men became close friends, exchanging information. When Lister became professor of surgery at Edinburgh and Glasgow, he started to use carbolic acid to clean wounds after surgery, and to sterilize dressings, at Glasgow over the years 1865-9. The survival rate zoomed as a result. Lister introduced catgut for stitches which is absorbable by the body whereas the old silk and hemp were not. He began to insist on sterilized clothes for operating theatres, instead of frock coats and aprons straight off the ward or the street, and the white operating gowns and caps, the rubber gloves and overshoes of today, all followed from his ideas. He required the nurses' clothes to be made clean and germ-free by sterilization in heat. Although infection at hospital can still occur, Lister reduced the percentage tremendously, and in 1897 Queen Victoria created him a baron in gratitude.[27]

Top hats became common out in the street once they were passed down the market. Punch and Judy men sported top hats, and so did the groundsel man with his basket at his hip. Horse bus drivers also liked to wear top hats, once they began to appear on the streets from the 1820s, because coach drivers for the nobility wore top hats, but the latter had a coloured ribbon in a flat bow or bouquet, while bus drivers did not. Mayhew's street sweeper preferred a peaked cap, a short spencer jacket, trousers and boots, and his sweep also liked a peaked cap, worn with a smock frock to the hips. Dustmen retained their special fantailed helmets to protect the neck, together with short smock frocks, rolled-up trousers, and clogs, into the 1860s, but by the 1870s these were beginning to give way to suits and slop jackets.

When John Hollingshead looked at 'Ragged London' in 1861, he found that at London docks only 3–4,000 jobs were permanent engagements; the 25,000 dockers were hired only by the day, so their wages varied greatly. The men were mostly English, Irish, Scottish, German and some French, and dressed now in the uniform jacket, waistcoat and trousers. For women there was little domestic service in Whitechapel, skivvy jobs in coffee houses or gin shops at very low pay, and the most lucrative income was from prostitution. Angel Alley serviced the farmer's men who brought hay and straw into Whitechapel market twice a week. The classiest prostitutes were in the West End, of course, and Mayhew described the dress of those in the Haymarket, who included some German and French girls:

... black silk cloaks or light grey mantles – many with silk paletots and wide skirts, extended by an ample crinoline, looking almost like a pyramid with the apex terminating at the black or white satin bonnet, trimmed with waving ribbons and gay flowers. Some are to be seen with their cheeks ruddy with rouge.[28]

Here they could charge £1 a time. Even more expensive *horizontales* could be found at the Alhambra Music Hall and the Argyll Rooms, wearing as much as £150 in jewellery. In Whitechapel the charge was 2/6 to 5/−.

There was such an epidemic of venereal diseases in the mid-Victorian period that the Contagious Diseases Acts of 1864–9 tried to remove diseased prostitutes off the streets into lock wards to be treated and reformed by hard labour. There was no attempt forcibly to treat men, because of the fear that the soldiers and sailors might turn violent. Once sentenced, a prostitute was a convict and so could be shipped off to Australia in a cage, and on arrival handed to a settler. Transportation was abolished in 1852, when most of the Australian states objected to taking any more.

National uniforms for prisoners were introduced when Victoria came to the throne, and women received a jacket and gown, three shifts, three petticoats, three pairs of stockings, check aprons and two pairs of shoes. Male convicts had suits of jacket and trousers, with three shirts and three lots of socks to go with the two pairs of shoes. Drawers existed in the upper reaches of society, but as they are not mentioned, presumably they were not worn at this level. Prison officers received caps with a peak, buttoned tunics and trousers.

Industry and the sea

The Victorian belief in regulation spread also into industry, although it was at first left to employers to define what workers should wear. Fashion compelled mill owners to do so in the 1850s, once the crinoline made an appearance and mill girls began to copy this extremely wide style. Accordingly, on 9 October 1860 the mill owner Samuel Courtauld & Co. issued a notice:

DRESS

It is always a pleasure to us to see our workpeople, and especially our comely young women, dressed NEAT and TIDY; nor should we, as has been declared in a notice that has been put up at Bocking Mills, wish to interfere with the fashion of their dress, whatever it may be, so long as their dress does not interfere with their work, or with the work of those near them in our employ.

The present ugly fashion of HOOPS and CRINOLINE, as it is called, is, however, quite unfitted for the work of our Factories. Among the power Looms it is almost impossible, and highly dangerous; among the Winding and Drawing Engines it greatly impedes the free passage of Overseers, Wasters &C., and is inconvenient to all. At

the Mills it is equally inconvenient, and still more mischievous, by bringing the dress against the spindles, while also it sometimes becomes shockingly indecent when the young people are standing upon the Sliders.
FOR ALL THESE REASONS
we now request all our Hands, at all our Factories, to leave HOOPS AND CRINOLINE at home when they come to the Factories to work; and to come dressed in a manner suitable for their work, and with as much BECOMING NEATNESS as they can.[30]

Overseers were instructed to check all the girls for hoops, so from now on mill girls had to forego hoops and then bustles, when Worth launched them in 1869. They had to wear plain dresses with only a few petticoats, while shawls, often tartan, covered them in bad weather. Hairnets, however, were very fashionable in the 1860s, and this was an example of a good style; they kept the hair out of the way, so employers did not object to them and they became quite common. Aprons of the bib sort or else with cap sleeves and a front continued as the principal means of protecting the girls' own clothes.

George Smith, who in 1872 persuaded Parliament to ban girls under 16 and boys under 13 from working in brickyards, now turned his attention to the canals. About 100,000 people lived and worked on the canal system, despite the rise of the railways, and their itinerant life meant no school attendance for the children, and uneducated parents. Smith told the Royal Commission:

Their habits are filthy, disgusting beyond conception. I have frequently seen women in a half nude state washing over the sides of the boat as it was moving along, out of the water of the canal, upon the top of which has been floating all manner of filth. They wash their clothes – those that do wash – out of the canal water, and instead of their being white, or near to it, they look as if they had been drawn through a mud hole, wrung, and hung out upon the boat line to dry.[31]

What else could the poor bargewomen do? The barges carried no water tanks, so the only water for washing was the canal beneath, and, in any case, what was Smith doing watching women at their ablutions?

The *Birmingham Daily Mail* for 5 and 12 March 1875 examined canal workers. 'The brawny fellow in the bright plush waistcoat, huge lace-up boots and fur cap, who drives the horse and shambles sulkily along, and the faded woman in rusty, rugged attire, half masculine, half feminine, who steers.' The half-and-half reference is probably to the occupation of steersman, rather than to clothes, for in the 1870s the most common dress for women on the canals was the tubular form of sunbonnet, a plain dress, an apron and laced-up boots, the same as country women. The men began to abandon smocks in the 1870s in favour of either the short smock frock to the hip or else knitted jerseys, which made an appearance in photographs then.

In Wales the Good Works Commission in 1869 found the women workers at ironworks, where they were still concerned with sorting out the ore, dressed in 'coarse, sleeved pinafores, handkerchiefs tightly bound, battered hats bristling with frayed feathers, blue stockings, and, in some instances masculine overalls',[32] which was now the term for canvas trousers. If teamed with a short canvas smock, those became the industrial pair of overalls in the modern sense, now for protection in a factory, as distinct from protection from the weather.

The illustrated magazines of the period show the workers evolving different types of protective wear, as the law did not. Initially it was still the apron, as in William Bell Scott's *Iron and Coal*, where the Tyneside iron workers hammer the glowing metal with leather aprons as their only protection; peaked caps, blue flannel shirts to absorb the sweat and canvas trousers complete the costume. At Mare & Co., iron shipbuilders at Blackwall, London, in 1854, the men dealing with the molten metal were wearing leather overtrousers to the thigh, and a hard cap with a very deep peak coming right down over the nose, to shield the eyes from the glare. Trousers were the industrial norm for men now, in contrast to the firm's wagoners, who were still wearing kneebreeches and smock frocks, in rural style. When Hornsby showed their mobile steam engine and threshing machine in 1851 the engineers were in trousers and jackets; their customers in kneebreeches. At the Great Central Gasworks in 1876 the men in the retort house were wearing face masks against the heat, but otherwise they were dressed in the usual shirts and trousers. In light work factories it was different, of course, with no protective garments necessary. At J. Smith & Sons' clock shop in Clerkenwell in 1851, all the young men making clocks wore the traditional apron, with a waistcoat, shirt and trousers as the uniform outfit, but variety and individuality showed in their hats – some top hats, a few peaked caps, a square paper hat and a Scottish bonnet.

At Hinks and Wells' pen-grinding shop in 1857 the all-girl-staffed room had about a hundred of them sitting at overhead-powered grinding wheels sharpening pen nibs. Their very full skirts showed that crinolines were not banned here, and these girls were fashionable in the style of their hair, swept back into buns, with shawls, white collars and aprons. No protection against flying pieces of metal was provided, although the finely ground metal dust could get into the eye. A girl could protect her eyes only by wearing glasses, if allowed, as there were no goggles yet.

The economic depression of the 1840s saw many navvies out of work. Henry Mayhew interviewed one of 28 at a refuge for the houseless at Playhouse Yard, Cripplegate:

. . . a fine, stoutly built fellow, with a fresh-coloured open countenance, and flaxen hair – indeed, altogether a splendid specimen of the Saxon labourer. He was habited in a short blue smock frock, yellow in parts with clay, and he wore the high lace-up boots, so characteristic of the tribe, but the boots were burst, and almost soleless with long wear.

He had started on the railways at the age of nine as a greaser, then drove wagons when the London to Birmingham line was being built, but lost his job when the decline set in. There was fierce competition from farm labourers and weavers wanting his job, plus a huge influx of Irish labourers willing to work for almost nothing. He felt defeated.

At the railway companies, the directors were in professional black frock coats and top hats, but the station staff received liveries as company servants. An anonymous description complained in 1892

that station inspectors were slack: 'They are in uniform certainly, but it is often a very plain one, and the wearers do not add to its official character by habitually wearing the ordinary hard felt hat', instead of the topper. Porters were chosen for their height and fitness and thus were often farm labourers in origin.

The new hand can generally be told by the look of discomfort he cannot help showing in appearing in corduroy and brass buttons for the first time. It is surprising how neat some porters can appear with one uniform a year, which includes two pairs of trousers, and equally surprising how slovenly some are before their clothes are three months old.'[33]

One porter whose livery uniform was late told his superintendent he would go over to the charcoal system, blacking his skin with charcoal where it showed through the holes. This was in the West Riding of Yorkshire. The railway engines and carriages also had company liveries: mustard-green for the London–Brighton, Derby red for the Midland, crimson lake for the Isle of Wight Railway Company, green for the Great Western.

An early supplier of railway liveries was the tailor Walter Berdoe, of 69 Cornhill, London. He wrote to the directors of the Stockton and Darlington Railway Company in September 1841 about his waterproof cloth coats: 'Several Railway Brother Companies have adopted it, including the New River Company, the North Midland, the Birmingham and Blackwall Railway Companies &C, the latter orders I have in course of execution.' He offered to let them try out one of his greatcoats, price £3, available in long or shorter versions. Their response is not on file.

The Blyth and Tyne Railway Company considered its clothing policy on 13 October 1855. Topcoats were to be given to drivers and firemen every four years. Cleaners in the locomotive sheds were allowed seven to eight yards of check flannel, and the boiler smiths who cleaned out the fireboxes were to receive eight yards. The allowance to wagon greasers was to be abolished, as the company felt their pay was high enough. Enough flannel for a pair of trousers was to be allowed to the locomotive cleaners and boiler smiths, in view of the dirty nature of the work. The livery for the London and North Western Railway was green, and was supplied by C. Hebbert, army clothiers of 8 Pall Mall, whose price list was as follows: for the Superintendent of Police a green superfine frock coat with rich silver collar, silk shirt linings, and silver buttons, 75/–, and a pair of superfine green trousers 23/–. Inspectors of the company's police received superfine green dress coats with silver collars and buttons, 56/9¼, and superfine green trousers 23/–. Ordinary policemen received a green police dress coat with worsted collar and metal buttons, green police trousers, 13/11, and police greatcoats with embroidered badges, 28/9. The foreman porters at Euston and Birmingham stations received superfine green frock coats with silk shirt linings and silver buttons, 49/0¾, superfine black waistcoats, 14/10¼, and superfine green trousers, 21/9½. Ticket collectors were given a superfine green frock coat in plain Prussian-colour *serge de laine*, with shirt linings and silver buttons, 49/0¾, and superfine green trousers, 21/9½. Gangmen and foremen porters at country stations received superfine green jackets with the LNWR badge and buttons both in silver, 39/2¼, superfine green waistcoats with shalloon backs and sleeves and silver buttons, 14/10¼, with trousers of stout milled cloth, 21/9½. Brakemen and guards received jackets in stout milled cloth with worsted-embroidered badges and metal buttons, 30/9, waistcoats of stout milled cloth with fustian sleeves and back and metal buttons, 15/6, and trousers of milled cloth, 21/9. Brakemen also received shaped greatcoats of stout milled cloth with check kersey lining, 78/10. Ordinary porters received green corduroy jackets with worsted-embroidered badges and metal buttons, 13/2, green cord waistcoats with fustian sleeves and back and metal buttons, 10/7, and green cord trousers, 6/10. Chief guards were classier in superfine green frock coats, with the badge and buttons of silver, 58/6, and green trousers, 21/9½, plus a shaped greatcoat at 78/10. The under guard also wore a green frock coat and trousers in superfine, but with a worsted badge and silver buttons, 46/2.

Railway liveries were usually given out twice a year, as at stately homes, and on 1 March 1878 the South Eastern Railway Company issued its 'Uniform Clothing' regulations. In May its policemen would receive cloth coat, jacket, vest, trousers, or a tunic and trousers, hat or cap and belt. In November they would receive another pair of trousers. General railway staff were to have corduroy-sleeved vests, trousers and caps in May, and jackets and trousers in November. Overcoats were given out every two years, a more generous rate than the Blyth and Tyne Company, to station masters, inspectors, policemen, guards, brakemen, cartmen and boys, and head porters. All old liveries were to be returned to the station master, with the company buttons left on. The finery was very much for public display; engine drivers and track workers were not given tailored superfine cloth. They usually wore the jacket-and-trousers suit with waistcoats, but in bad weather would add pilot coats, oilskins, leather jackets, and in hot weather the slop jacket of cotton.[34]

The observant traveller through Tredegar or Blaenavon in South Wales would see the mine tip girls in their calf-length short dresses of sacking-like cloth, red worsted stockings, and lace-up boots with hobnails and tips and toecaps of steel. They often tied a scarf about the head and wore a hat on top, but unlike their rural sisters did not copy men's headgear. They liked some feminine touch such as artificial flowers, feathers, badges or beads on their hats, as a faint echo of fashionable glory above their coal-black faces. Women were still common in the iron industry in breaking the ironstone, hammering away for twelve hours a day and six or seven shillings a week in 1865. Sackcloth-type smocks were common here too, but cotton overalls – trousers – were sometimes worn underneath. Trousers had also begun to be worn by the women brickworkers who shovelled the fuel, with the same rough smocks as their sisters above, but a greater variety of headgear, from wide-awakes to mushroom straw hats or bonnets, but with the same touch of a ribbon or berries as decoration. Trousers also spread to Lympstone in Devon, where the women gathering

58. Louisa Millard of Wigan, 'A Miner and his sister', 1869. Both wear the padded trousers from Wales with clogs, but otherwise they are differently dressed. The pitbrow woman with her shovel and sieve has a shirt, a waistcoat and a padded skirt, with a linen cap topped by a scarf. Her brother has a moleskin jacket and waistcoat, shirt and peaked cap, along with his pick and safety lamp.

While the eighteenth century had not concerned itself with the wearing of kneebreeches by women underground at the mines, the Victorians made several attempts to stop women surface workers from wearing trousers. By the 1860s the Welsh type of padded mining costume had reached the industrial Midlands, and women surface workers took to padded trousers for the reasons that they were warm outdoors, and their narrowness was safer than wide skirts which could get caught on moving machinery or coal wagons. For the top part of the body they wore either a bedgown jacket, the shift and a waistcoat, or, most often, the new short smock frock to the hip. A padded hood protected the head, and clogs the feet. The miners tended to favour a cloth jacket and waistcoat over the shirt, the padded trousers, clogs, and peaked caps on the surface, much of which was of course stripped off once below. The big distinction in the wearing of trousers by both sexes in mining was that the girls wore a padded apron like a mini-skirt over the strategic zone, plus their hoods. In 1865 the women found a new enemy in the National Union of Miners, when some of its members, notably those in Northumberland and Durham, wanted to turn the whole of the coal industry into a closed shop for men only. They petitioned Parliament, claiming that employing females was the source of 'degradation and gross immorality', but could supply no evidence of immoral behaviour to the committee of enquiry. The lawyer Munby wrote on behalf of the pit women who worked to support families, keep elderly parents, and because husbands had been killed or injured in the mines. The committee accepted this argument and did not ban women from their surface jobs. Victorian propriety, however, would not leave the matter alone. In April 1874 the *Pictorial World* tried to raise a scandal by stating that pit girls in male attire were a repugnant spectacle:

All were attired in male habiliments, but some had thrown aside their coats and jackets, and merely wore coarse shirts and trousers, the brace being passed, sailor fashion, over the shirts. Several of the women were using the pick, others were busy with their spades, and a few were engaged in sifting coal.

mussels and cockles wore canvas overalls when Munby visited them in 1861, along with linen caps, bonnets, shawls, and blouses, so that from the waist upward they looked like demure maidens in a very conventional Victorian way, but were masculinely shocking below. To the Victorians, trousers were masculine by association and cultural segregation, regardless of all the trousers worn by women from Turkey and the Balkans eastwards.

The fuss seems to have made the girls gradually lengthen their mini-skirts, for by 1887 the girls in Lancashire mines had skirts and aprons to just below the knee, with the trousers showing only below that. This was the date of the latest attempt to get women out of the industry, this time by Labour MPs, again using the argument that women in trousers were immoral. The serious press, however, responded by asking what right Parliament had to throw some 4,500 women out of work? The Rational Dress Society had entered the scene. After its foundation in 1881, its president, Lady Haberton, argued that all women should wear trousers. The Revd Harry Mitchell of Pemberton near Wigan, mining country, said trousers for women was the dress of the future and praised pit girls as pioneers. This was a rare prophecy that time has proved right. In May 1887 Munby led a delegation of pit girls to see the Home Secretary in London, six out of the party of twenty-two wearing their trousers and clogs. They were told that the government would not interfere in their work, except to stop them having to move railway wagons. The trip had been proposed by the Revd Harry Mitchell, and the argument was defeated – until the next century.[35]

59. Gilly, 'Belgian Pit Girls', 1862. While British women were banned from working underground after 1842, on the Continent they continued to do so, wearing this early kind of overall with a jacket and trousers. Their little bonnets are less effective than the British women's hoods. The photograph was taken at the surface, as cameras could not operate underground in 1862.

60. Thomson & Smith, 'Workers on the Silent Highway', 1877. One bargee shows the short smock frock in linen or canvas that many men adopted for dirty work in towns, here worn with corduroy trousers. His crewman has one of the variety of knitted sweaters that had begun to appear. Peaked caps were widely worn by miners and railway men too. The cloth cap did not become common until after the turn of the century.

A special dress for a special man underground was that of the 'penitent', who had the risky job of igniting the fire damp found in many mines. Covered in wet sacking to prevent him catching fire, he had to crawl along holding a long taper ahead of him. Mines were now so deep that the old practice of carpenters lining shafts with wood gave way to brick lining by shaft sinkers. As this could be wet work, they adopted the seaman's fantailed sou'wester and sometimes a cloak, both in oilskin, to protect the working suit beneath. Most miners,

however, regarded safety clothes as unmanly and resisted them. Death by the age of 50 from silicosis among miners was common, while lead glazers in the Potteries got lead poisoning, metal tool grinders got iron filings in their lungs, and mill girls got asthma from the fluff off the textiles, along with swollen legs, ulcers, enlarged veins, fallen arches and turned-in ankles from standing all day. Smaller metal work went to women who turned out brass and steel nails, pins, screws, chains, steel pens and hooks-and-eyes, often in small sheds. Their clothing was not sensational, consisting of the plain dress and sacking apron with a shawl, but in 1882 and 1883 both the National United Nut and Bolt Makers' Association and the chain unions tried to restrict and prevent women from doing 'unsexing' work.

At Welsh slate quarries like Dinorwic in Caernarfonshire the men and boys lived in wooden huts out at the quarries during the week, and returned home to the family on Saturday for the weekend. Most of them wore canvas trousers (overalls), with cloth jackets and waistcoats. Shirts without a collar and tie were most common, but when the quarry clerk Griffith Jones turned up with his camera in the 1890s a few donned ties, albeit without collars. Generation distinction showed principally in the hats, for the older men mostly wore bowlers and trilbies while the younger generation were going over to cloth caps as their uniform headgear. On Saturdays they piled on to the slate wagons, to be taken home by the train that conveyed the slate to Port Dinorwic where it was loaded on to slate schooners and coasters.[36]

Along the coasts, oddly enough, there was no attempt to stop cockle girls, shrimp girls, or fishwives from wearing either very short skirts, kneebreeches or breeched skirts, probably because the custom was well established since the seventeenth century, and so was less sensational than the pit girls' adoption of trousers to replace kneebreeches. Breeching was well established along the Yorkshire coast, although it was a matter of individual taste whether a girl breeched or kept her skirt untied. The method was to pull the back

61. Walter Fisher of Filey, 'Flamborough Views, Bait Girls Breeched', c.1860. The bait girls Molly Nettleton and Sally Mainpiece breeched their skirts in the ancient manner, rather than adopting kneebreeches. One has an apron for the sake of modesty, but not the other. Victorian males would travel miles to see the sight but these girls could give them the whistle. Jackets and blouses form the top part of the costume, headscarfs are used, and thick woollen stockings with stout shoes protect the feet. The girls' agility up and down cliffs was astonishing.

of the skirt forward and pin it up, then to tie string around the knees to form breeches. In the 1850s and 60s the wearing of several petticoats in imitation of the crinoline led to a very full effect when breeching, but the 1870s slimmer line reduced that effect. The rest of the attire was cotton frocks over red kirtles, black or grey woollen stockings, and stout shoes or fisher boots, with shawls if it were cool and pilot jackets when it rained. Headscarves were most usual on the bait girls, who wore cushions under them for carrying baskets on their heads. They often carried a stone of fish on the back, but from Staithes to Flamborough the biggest demand was for bait, mussels or limpets, which the women gathered in all weathers to supply the herring fishing fleet, and had then to put on all the hundreds of hooks on the fishing line. At Scarborough the girls liked to wear hats on top of headscarves when not carrying anything on the head, for instance when mending nets, preparing bait or knitting. Sometimes sun bonnets were favoured, as at Filey. Tucks at the bottom of the skirt had been fashionable during the Regency era, and not surprisingly the style lingered on much longer away from the capital. At Filey Arthur Munby collected a photograph of Janie Crawford, 15, wearing a short skirt with eight tucks visible on the petticoat in 1871. At the port of Cullercoats near Newcastle-upon-Tyne the girls or fisherlasses did not tuck their skirts, when Munby got a photograph of them in 1875, but in 1881 when the American artist Homer Winslow visited the village they were doing so, and it became a tradition down to the First World War. They preferred the old bedgown jackets to a frock, still tied together with tapes to avoid having to make buttonholes.

Between 1843 and 1847 the Edinburgh photographic pioneers David Octavius Hill and Robert Adamson took many studies of fisherfolk at Newhaven, only a mile from Princes Street. It showed the women still wearing the striped petticoats which David Allan had depicted in 1784, but much wider in bulk to keep up with the trend for increasing width in skirts. The main difference was in the way the upper petticoat was pulled up to reveal the lower. In 1784 the front of the under petticoat was revealed; by the 1840s, probably because of Victorian sensitivity over decency, this was reversed and the apron and petticoat were lower over the woman's unmentionable zone in front and higher at the back. Pilot jackets were favoured for warmth and because they cushioned and protected the other clothes from the dripping baskets of fish on the girls' backs. The fishermen mostly wore the short sailor's jacket in dark blue, and white duck trousers with a tarred hat, top or bowler-style, for they liked to imitate the Navy, especially after the heroic wars against Napoleon and the French. Sea boots as long as riding ones were well painted with tar or grease for waterproofing. As the calotypes had to be taken in sunlight they do not record the dress for bad weather, but oilskins were around. The Newhaven fishing community was increasingly squeezed by the expansion of Edinburgh docks, which was to undermine the local style.[37]

Writing in 1865, James Bertram said that the Newhaven fishwives favoured brightly coloured petticoats in red or yellow stripes, and continued:

The Scottish fishwomen, or 'fishwives' of Newhaven and Fisherrow, as they are usually designated, wear a dress of a peculiar and appropriate fashion, consisting of a long blue duffle jacket, with wide sleeves, a blue petticoat usually tucked up so as to form a pocket, and in order to show off their ample under petticoats of bright coloured woollen stripes reaching to the calf of the leg. It may be remarked that the upper petticoats are of a striped sort of stuff technically called, we believe, drugget, and are always different colours. As the women carry their loads of fish on their backs in creels, supported by a broad leather belt resting forwards on the forehead, a thick napkin is their usual headdress, although often a muslin cap, or mutch, with a very broad frill, edged with lace, and turned back on the head, is seen peeping from under the napkin. A variety of kerchiefs or small shawls similar to that on the head encircle the neck and bosom, which, with thick worsted stockings, and a pair of stout shoes, complete the costume.

Sir Walter Scott had taken George IV to see the Newhaven fishwives, and the King complimented them on their handsome looks. Queen Victoria also paid them a visit, so their costume was relatively famous, and thus self-consciously worn. By 1883, when Bertram wrote a booklet for the Great International Fisheries Exhibition in London, the costume had slimmed down from the wide skirts of the 1840s and 60s, following the fashion for a leaner line. It was still a plain dress over striped petticoats, but these were fewer in number. The lace-edged 'mutch' caps were still present but cloaks and hoods had replaced the stout duffle jacket.[38]

Fisherrow was five miles from Edinburgh, so these fishwives had a longer trip to deliver the freshly caught fish, there being no fishshops before refrigeration. It was recorded that three of them carried a creel of 200 pounds' weight of fish in relay between them, and did the distance to town in under three quarters of an hour. Similarly in relay, another three carried 200 pounds from Dunbar to Edinburgh in five hours. Munby was amazed by the loads working women had to shift. Hannah West, a ballast digger of Upnor, Kent, had to quarry clay for vessels to use as ballast, hacking it from the quarry and wheeling it down to the quay, being paid one penny per ton shifted. She could earn one shilling a day because she moved twelve tons; each ton meant eight wheelbarrow loads. At the fishing villages the fishermen's paraphernalia hung outside the cottages: nets, lines, and oilskin unmentionables (trousers), together with the dozens of blue stockings worn by the womenfolk. In 1865 Bertram said the fishermen wore 'white canvas trousers and their Guernsey shirts' (the term for knitted sweaters before they were given a name of their own).

Of the fishermen at Eyemouth, Peter Anson wrote:

... every fisherman and boy at Eyemouth wore a pair of loose-fitting blue serge breeches, tied at the knee with tapes, over which were drawn a thick pair of long woollen stockings reaching well above the knee. On shore the heavy leather sea boots were replaced by slippers. A hand knitted guernsey [sweater] and blue bonnet, shaped not unlike a tam' o shanter, with a blue tassel on top, completed the ordinary 'rig' of the Eyemouth fishermen about 1850 or 60.[39]

Scottish bonnets appeared more on the boys on shore in the Hill and Adamson study, and as the century advanced glazed straw cutter hats and sealskin caps replaced top hats, bowlers and bonnets. At Wick the fishermen were described as 'stalwart fishermen clad characteristically in north waster, fearnought jackets, and high fishing boots'. Of the women the only comment was to the 'peculiar brevity of their lower garments'.

The introduction of steam drifters and trawlers in the 1880s allowed fishermen to follow the herring on all its migrational routes. The gutting, salting and packing was women's work, and the Scottish fisherlassies followed the fishing fleet down the coast from the Shetlands and Wick in June, to Fraserburgh in August, and down to Yarmouth and Lowestoft for the autumn. It was hard outdoor work, but they thrived on it, and knew more of the real world than most Mayfair ladies. They, too, hitched up the top skirt, or petticoat as they called it, to show the under petticoats, but of course aprons of oilskin or sacking were necessary when gutting herring. A tartan shawl was the usual head covering. By the turn of the century the shipbuilders were wearing slop suits in cotton or canvas over their waistcoats and trousers as a form of protective overall, along with cloth caps and lace-up boots.

Fishwives still controlled the marketing and handled the money, which led to some Victorian complaints that they unsexed their husbands, as if there were any choice when the men were out at sea catching the fish. For bad weather the costume at sea was the same in shape as it had been in 1529, being trousers and tunic. One such, exhibited at the International Fisheries Exhibition at Edinburgh in 1882, was made of tanned sheepskin and is now in the Royal Museum of Scotland. This ancient form of waterproof outfit was still being worn in the Faroes in the 1920s. For warmth under it went a knitted jumper in fawn and pink wool, while knitted socks, and a knitted hood and gloves protected the extremities. It has been claimed that by now fishermen had some 84 different patterns for sweaters, but the most common type by the 1890s was the navy blue gansy, the Shetland sweater. 'Fearnought' jackets dated back to Captain Cook's voyages in 1772–84, being stout woollen cloth garments worn at sea. The nineteenth century introduced several styles of knitted woollens. The 'cardigan' of 1855 was named after the Earl of Crimean fame and consisted of an over waistcoat with or without sleeves. The 'guernsey' was a seaman's knitted vest or shirt in 1851, usually in blue or striped versions. The 'jersey' was worn under the shirt to begin with, and was a long-sleeved tunic for athletes, women and sailors from 1836. The 'jumper' in 1853 meant a light jacket or shirt made of canvas, serge or linen, and was used for dirty jobs at sea. 'Sweaters' were originally for horses as a kind of horse blanket, but by 1882 athletes were adopting a knitted woollen version to train in and sweat. The term 'pullover' meant a hat cover; it was the 1920s which used it to mean a knitted over shirt garment. So many middle-class scholars were looking for local styles that it made local communities feel self-conscious about looking too peculiar, or else strive to respond to the quest by inventing elaborate systems that their ancestors had not thought of – hence the catalogue of sweater types. Knitted leg warmers to the thigh were another characteristic of fishermen's attire to go underneath the heavy leather boots.

For all fishermen and merchant sailors, the first concept of a permanent Royal Navy in 1852, instead of one that expanded or shrank according to the wars in hand, relieved them of the danger of impressment. In 1857 this new permanent Royal Navy gave a uniform to its sailors, and as the merchant navy liked to copy the Fleet they followed suit. The basic outfit of smock frock and trousers was the same as in the sixteenth century, but now the frock, or blouse, as it became known, had to be tucked into the trousers. It was navy blue serge for northern climes, and white drill for southern ones, with a blue collar showing three white stripes. In 1858 the Royal Navy Reserve included in its manpower coastguards, seamen pensioners, and the merchant marine, so they could still be called up in an emergency but at least not in the haphazard manner of former years. Officers, being gentlemen, had gone over to frock coats from 1828, and they had actually adopted

sailors' trousers the year before, which, along with cocked hats, formed their full dress right down to World War II. Sailors were allowed canvas or straw hats, but much preferred the latter, with ribbons hanging down the back.[40]

Servants

The middle-class household with an income of £1,000 a year should have a cook, an upper and under housemaid, and a man servant, wrote the editor, journalist, mother and wife, Isabella Beeton, in her *Household Management*, which ran through many editions. She decreed that £750 a year would permit a cook, housemaid and footboy; £500 a year only a cook and housemaid; while £300 a year meant only a maid-of-all-work, as did £200–£120 a year. Liveried staff were the footmen, under butler, coachman, grooms, pages and footboys. Upper staff still did not wear livery; nor did gardeners. Of footmen, Mrs Beeton wrote:

The footman in livery only finds for himself in stockings, shoes and washing. Where silk stockings, or other extra articles of linen are worn, they are provided by the family, as well as his livery, a working dress consisting of a pair of overalls (trousers), and a waistcoat, a fustian jacket or a white or jean one for times when he is liable to be called to answer the door or wait at breakfasts; and on quitting his service, he is expected to leave behind him any livery had within six months.[41]

The working dress was for when the footman was cleaning the boots, knives, silver, lamps or doing general polishing; the livery for waiting at dinner, in households without a butler or bootboy. Mrs Beeton was not so specific in her instructions about maids except that they should be neat and clean. It was a print dress in the morning, and black in the afternoon, with a clean apron for serving tea. Grey for nannies was the most usual.

John James entered service in 1895 as a footman to the Countess of Camperdown, but nearly made a disastrous mistake in thinking that a visitor 'clean shaven and not very smartly dressed' was an applicant for the post of butler. It proved to be the immensely rich Duke of Westminster, still display-

62. Anon., 'Maid of all work in the City', 1856. The airs and graces of English servants amazed foreign visitors. This young maid, with her frilled cap under her bonnet, has stuck in a flower, but otherwise in her striped dress and apron makes no pretensions to fashionable glamour – although many of her sisters did. Though simply clothed, she is better dressed than many a woman farm worker, and is closer to the fashionable silhouette than they could ever be.

ing that upper-class British fondness for dressing like their servants which had so disgusted Abbé Le Blanc in 1747. In 1897 James moved on as first footman to the Marquess of Landsdowne, who was grand enough to have the full three liveries. These consisted of the everyday livery of a black evening dress with black kneebreeches and white stockings; the semi-state livery, with eighteenth-century type coat with frogging and loops, kneebreeches and waistcoats in the Landsdowne colours, with white stockings; and finally the full state livery for riding on state coaches, with cocked

hats and grey stockings combined with the semi-state coats. One chore concerned hair powder. James wrote in 1949:

Footmen of the younger generation should be thankful that this daily powdering of the hair has gone out of fashion, for it was indeed a very unpleasant business. After the hair had been moistened, soap was put on and rubbed into a stiff lather, and the combing was done so that the teeth marks would show evenly all over. Powder was then applied with a puff and the wet mess allowed to dry on the head until it became quite firm. In the evening the hair had always to be washed and oiled to prevent it from becoming almost fox colour, and I remember I was hardly ever free from colds when this hair powdering was the regulation.

The dampness, of course, stopped the powder from showering the soup when the footman was waiting at dinner, but such a soapy mixture on the scalp all day must have caused some outbreaks of dermatitis. In 1912 James escaped footman's hair powder when he became steward to Princess Louise Duchess of Argyll, and now dressed in a suit and unpowdered hair.[42]

134

63. Anon., 'Indoor and Outdoor Staff on a farm in Ross', *c.*1900. Large farms, as well as the nobility, employed servants. Here the housemaids are all identifiable from their tall white caps, dark dresses and bib aprons, while one has a broom and another a bucket to underline their roles. The outdoor women have mostly sacking aprons and shawls, although the one with the flat white headdress must be an Italian immigrant. The men are all outdoor staff in slop suits and peaked caps, and only one in a hat.

The Duke of Queensberry was reputed to be the last peer to employ running footmen in fanciful liveries. In 1851 two running footmen preceded the sheriff and judges at the North of England Assizes, and in 1856 the Austrian ambassador still had 12 running footmen on his staff in Saint Petersburg, but this was the decade when they began to fade out. The Post Office in London could deliver a letter posted in the City to Kensington on the same day, so it was not a matter of need for any peer to continue to run a personal messenger service.

Furthermore, Alexander Graham Bell, the Scottish-born inventor, founded his Bell Telephone Company in Boston in 1877. L. Sholes invented a writing machine first marketed by the Remington & Sons company in New York in 1874, so that typewriters, telephones and women secretaries all speeded up communications, and they did not require any ornate liveries.

Hippolyte Taine was impressed by the size of British menservants:

They wear white cravats with large faultless bows, scarlet or canary-coloured kneebreeches, are magnificent in shape and amplitude, their calves especially are enormous. In the fashionable neighbourhoods, beneath the vestibule about five o'clock in the evening, the butler seated, newspapers in hand, sips a glass of port; around him ushers, corded lackeys, footmen with their sticks, gaze with an indolent and lordly air upon the middle classes passing by. The coachmen are prodigiously broad-shouldered and developed; how many yards of cloth must be required to clothe such figures?[43]

He was clearly describing semi-state coloured liveries. As to bulk, servants in wealthy houses still received more meat in a week than peasants could afford in a year. Lackeys had to 'match', so they were chosen for equality of height and legs. Street urchins used to stick pins into their calves to see if the superb shape were real or padded. Such servants were for show. The scullery maid in plain cap and dress with a sacking apron sweated unseen in the basement, amidst dirt, grease, raw meat, filthy dishes, and cholera lurking in the water. The women toiled while the liveried males paraded.

Maidservants were not supposed to look too fashionable, and *Punch* printed cartoons showing maids being told off for wearing crinolines, and then being expected to wear their mistresses' discarded crinoline cages as soon as the shape changed, causing them to knock over many a knick-knack. Munby's collection of photographs shows a Lambeth maid in 1861 donning her best bonnet with flowers, and a most stylish mantle decorated with ruching, her hair gleaming with macassar oil. Most had plain frocks, but some tartan, check or striped dresses. One maid even wears make-up, which suggests she might have been a part-time prostitute. Munby married the general servant Hannah Cullwick, who worked for a tradesman, Henderson, of 20 Gloucester Crescent, Paddington. He had encouraged her to keep a diary of her busy life, cleaning all the grates and the coal scuttles, fetching the coal, cleaning the whole house, scrubbing the kitchen, and cleaning the area and the street. She had to wait on the housemaid and boy. She had two days off between 1870 and 71. Her black straw bonnet she had owned for years. She had two shawls, one grey, one tartan, of her own. Her mistress should have provided the cotton dress, white cap and bonnet, and the aprons. Her richest time was Christmas, for tradesmen still paid the servants their allowance or poundage on the goods supplied, and Hannah was also the cook. Her marriage to the lawyer Munby in 1873 only lasted six years, since he treated her as a servant in London, and only dressed her as his lady wife on holidays, then expected her to change back into her grey cotton

dress and apron in town at the station. This double life she found impossible. Munby felt that there was a beauty in women working hard, for tiny wages, but their reply would no doubt have been unprintable.[44] Since women usually outnumber men they could not all be domestic angels, but had to toil as servants and anything else. The big difference between the appearance of women servants and men servants was that the women followed the fashionable silhouette, while the footmen were frozen in the style of the eighteenth century. Only butlers were up-to-date in their evening dress with trousers.

White clothes in the kitchen grew out of the natural tone of linen, and the long-sleeved waistcoats (that is, light jackets) from the need for lightweight garments in high temperatures. The chef's cap developed from the flat caps worn by cooks before the Regency. Once top hats came into vogue, and the very high bowler hats of the 1870s, this was reflected in the increasing height of chefs' hats. When Lady Lucy Bridgeman photographed her servants at Weston Park in 1851, the chef's hat was only some five inches tall, but by the end of the century it was a good foot tall. White garments, of course, also reflected Lister's stress on clean linen in hospitals, and when Escoffier became chef at the new Savoy Hotel in 1889 he insisted on clean whites in the kitchens. His commission from tradesmen was 5%. His pupil chef Eugène Herbodeau said Escoffier insisted that cooks should not only wear white coats and check trousers indoors, but that they should be just as smart off duty, with hats, collars and ties. Escoffier introduced specialization among his chefs which made the Savoy and the Carlton Hotels during his time a mecca for Edward VII and society, with standards many private houses could not equal. His boss César Ritz was equally keen on cleanliness, and insisted on white ties and aprons for his waiters, and black tie for his *maître d'hôtel*. The luxury hotel was now the model which stately houses had to equal, and a top chef could name his own price.[45]

SIX

Into the Twentieth Century
1900–1945

Agriculture

Some smock frocks survived, for when Barclay Wills interviewed old shepherds in Sussex in the 1930s, Michael Blane, born in 1843, still wore his because he did not care about looking old-fashioned at his age. His wife made them, but his last one he had made with buttons down the front so he could open it, as he had got tired of trying to pull them on over his head. In bad weather he wore an old fleecy white overcoat. Some shepherds had doghair hats, very solid, but hot in summer, so they carried little red caps in their pockets to change over. Jack Cox said he used to wear smock frocks in his youth, but when carrying hurdles he used to change into a slop jacket in sacking stuff, and he also had one of the little red hats, as hurdles would knock other hats off. Mr Copped himself wore a corduroy suit and gaiters and a hard felt bowler hat, but his father had always worn smock frocks, blue ones – not slate blue but what he called 'butcher's blue' – on top of his corduroys. He would have loved to have one of his overcoats, so thick and rough and fleecy white. When he was young it had been possible sometimes to get old army cavalry cloaks, which kept one nice and dry. Mr Wooler, born in 1856, said his usual dress was a smock frock and a white corduroy suit. George Humphrey, born in 1864, stressed how much of the clothes making was still done by the mother:

Father and us four boys made five to dress, and we all wore corduroy – buff colour – and corduroy gaiters too. We all wore smock frocks over that – blue ones. My mother made all the clothes (and looked a long time at a shilling before spending it), but the stuff was good then!

We couldn't afford leather gaiters; she made us cord gaiters to match the suits and lined them with canvas, and they kept out as much wet as the leather gaiters I buy now do! Every year, after harvest, mother went to the shops and bought a big roll of corduroy, and canvas, buttons, thread and things, and we all got a suit in turn. She made our smocks too, all tuckered up proper, with big turn-down collars, and pockets that'd take a rabbit easily without showing it, if you walked upright. Overcoat? Well, yes, we did have one of a sort, but anything had to do. We had good suits and smocks, and there wasn't much money left for overcoats.

The excellent weatherproof white fleecy overcoats had been made in Lewes, all by hand, by a woman who used two needles to produce watertight seams. She charged 32/6 for them, but since her death the coats were no good. For those with some money in the pocket, smock frocks could be bought at Lewes fair on 21 September, when lots of shepherds would arrive in their smock frocks and go to Browne and Crosskeys in the High Street for gaiters, overcoats, and smock frocks. Slate grey linen was the most common colour in Sussex. All the shepherds complained that modern corduroy was of poor quality and lacked strength, while the remade shoddy suits and coats now so common did not last.[1]

Writing in 1910 of shepherds in Wiltshire, W.H. Hudson said Isaac Bawcombe always worked in a slate blue smock frock, blue worsted stockings and a broad white felt hat. A woman who wore smock frocks was the wife of the shepherd Caleb, who sported a mannish hat, a smock and leggings, with a shawl, for working out in the fields. There were probably other women who did the same, as the dark oiled smocks were waterproofed. Old Isaac was able to retire into a charity for six old men in the parish of Bishop which had its own livery: a felt hat, boots, brown leather leggings and a long grey overcoat with a red collar and brass buttons. By the time H.V. Morton visited Midhurst in Sussex in 1939 the vicar said smock frocks had died out with their wearers, although they had been a common sight when he was a boy. Pattens for women had also vanished in his time. Calling at the local antique dealer, Morton bought some embroidered Georgian waistcoats for a mere five shillings, but found nothing of agricultural antiquity.[2]

Over in the Fens, Arthur Randell wrote that his mother made all the family shirts for the males, but not the suits, so they were clearly better off. She made rugs with sugar sacks as the base, with wool woven through, and sacking rugs were also used as horses' blankets. Sacking from ten-stone sugar sacks was used by the women for potato-harvesting aprons. On their heads went sun bonnets which were called hoods by the Magdalen villagers. Made from white, coloured or flowered linen, they had a thin cane sewn into the front to hold the brim up, and a double or single frill at the back to protect the neck from the sun and the wind. He was looking back to 1901–18, but said that some sun bonnets were still being made in the Fens in 1969.[3]

There were clearly several types, of which the oldest was the white linen tunnel-shaped bonnet with a neck frill worn in the Netherlands in the 1660s, which spread into this country as far as Guernsey. The black straw bonnets of the 1780s lasted into the 1870s, but black straw hats began to take their place. Uglies descend from the 1770s calash which had several bamboo hoops inside so that it could be collapsed back like a carriage hood. Uglies were mostly black cotton or silk, and were still being worn during the First World War. The hoods of Arthur Randell's Fenlands were very common in the nineteenth century, but in shape do not appear to date back beyond that. Gertrude Jekyll stressed that sun bonnets and straw hats were for working in; Sunday best in 1904 in Surrey meant a black satin bonnet worn over the white linen or cotton cap with its frill at the front. She said that the hood type of sun bonnet could have 13

64. *Country Life*, 'Norfolk Smock Frock', 1902. Made in 1870, this smock frock has been passed down to the twentieth century. There is smocking down the front, at the cuffs and on the pockets, and this is the coat version favoured by some wearers. Elderly shepherds continued to wear smocks into the 1930s. The neckcloth was common for many kinds of workers in country and town.

rows of cord and three rows of frilled corded inserts sewn into it, across the centre from ear to ear. This shows that cord strengtheners were used in Surrey and cane in the Fens.

The First World War was the great divide. Smock frocks in the Fens were very common until then, with the shepherds doing most of the smocking themselves in their huts during lambing time, but after the war they began to fade out. The village bootmaker continued to be important for working boots, which were still given weekly

65. Anon., 'Market Women at Donegal'. Mantles survived longest at the Celtic fringe, as plaids in Scotland and these blanket-like mantles in Ireland. The bare feet, aprons, and skirts shorter than the fashion were common outside the cities, and date back centuries. The men have the shoes and boots.

coatings of mutton fat or neatsfoot oil. At Magdalen he wore a stout bibbed gabardine apron, shirt, corduroy trousers and wide-brimmed slouch hat, with the exotic touch of gold earrings because he would have liked to be a gipsy. The old still did not like socks in their boots, like the local drover, Jerry Ling, who wrapped his feet in rags before donning his boots. He used to drive the cattle and sheep to the railway at King's Lynn, for which journey the blacksmith made the bullocks pads to protect their hooves. Turkeys and geese would be driven through a bed of pitch and sand to give their feet a protective surface before being marched to market. The blacksmith was identifiable by his thick leather apron, and liked twill trousers, a linen shirt and small cap. The pedlar from King's Lynn would walk round the villages fourteen miles a day, carrying on his head a wicker hamper of four to five stones' weight, full of tape, buttons, shirts, socks, and cotton reels. The tinker walked a similar distance a day in his slouch hat, thick boots, and white bib apron under his coat, carrying a rush bag like a carpenter's, with his soldering irons, tin sheets, wire to mend kettles, and pots and pans. He made Mrs Randell's loaf tins, cake tins and roasting tins. According to Richard Jefferies, the mighty boots took cobblers six months to make, with all the hand-stitching, nails and plates. Occasionally itinerant sales people might have a bicycle or a donkey, but not very often. The

motorization of such services came in after the war.

The lightweight slop jacket in canvas or cotton was well established by now, and was often blue or natural, but in the Yorkshire Dales yellow ones were commonly favoured. A clean one had to be donned for sheep clipping, as it was an occasion in the farming calendar. In the north they were called 'kitles' instead of slops and can still be seen on older farmers from spring to autumn. Farming overalls in the modern sense appeared in the 1930s, gradually ousting aprons for everything.

Hiring fairs were on the decline in the south, but twice yearly hirings continued in the north until the Agricultural Wages Act of 1924 put an end to them. Tailors like the Wilkinsons of Brough used to attend the hirings at Barnard Castle, to sell ready-made breeches and leggings, and take orders for corduroy suits for work, and cloth suits for Sunday best. After the Act stopped this standing for hire, the tailors took to bikes and cycled round the dales to find their customers.

Braces were the mark of sailors in the nineteenth century but after 1900 were found everywhere, and were termed 'gallowseys' in the north-east. In the summer many pairs of braces were on show out in the fields but labourers never removed their shirts no matter how hot it was, since that was not proper, and suntans were not fashionable until the Twenties.

It was also bad form not to wear a hat, so caps and straws were common into the 1940s. Leg ties or knee strings were termed 'yokes' in Yorkshire and 'yorks' in Teesdale. Rubber Wellington boots appeared in the late 1920s and made such items as leggings and ties unnecessary, but it was a slow changeover. Clogs were more common in the north on farms instead of boots, and were still worn into the 1940s.[4]

At the onset of the First World War women had to take over farming on a larger scale, to replace the men called to the front, especially for activities like ploughing, and operating horse-drawn machinery such as corn-drills, reapers, and binders. Tractors like the Ivel, smaller and more manoeuvrable than heavy steam traction engines, appeared in 1902, but few were bought by farmers before the 1920s. It took the war to make people more motor-conscious, including the Army itself, which began with thousands of horses but by the end had gone over to lorries. This meant in 1918 a lot of surplus military vehicles becoming available for farmers. The women who had to drive such vehicles mostly donned dungarees. In the seventeenth century this term had meant a coarse Indian inferior blue calico used for sails, but after a storm had torn the sails the sailors would use them to make trousers, so that by 1849 it was common to talk of 'dungarees' as sailors' trousers. Gradually they were imitated on land as overall trousers, which of course were also made in sailors' canvas. Exactly who added the bib top is unknown, but it could well have been a woman acting for herself, or for a son or husband who wanted some chest protection. Thus on the farms a woman now doing a man's jobs wore his trousers too, in Scotland with their uglies to display some feminine aspect, and with other kinds of bonnets further south.

For women to run estates and farms while the men were at war was an ancient tradition going back to beyond the Crusades. (See Appendix II.) In 1915 women's county committees were set up to encourage more women to work on the land. Village women said that they would take on more

66. Anon., 'Bondage Women at West Pilton, Midlothian'. In order to get a job himself, a labourer had to supply a woman to help with harvesting. All these girls wear 'uglies', descended from the eighteenth-century calèche. Sacking aprons for sorting potatoes were usual, but some seem to have sacking bodices too, put on over the dress or blouse. Traditional short skirts are accompanied by sturdy boots. The men have slop jackets, in the main, and cloth caps are beginning to replace the maritime type of cap.

67. Anon., 'A Farm in Lothian', c.1914. The women take over, and are mostly wearing the new dungaree trousers with a bib top combination. Four are wearing 'ugly' bonnets and two the English type. The women wearing skirts have tight jodhpurs underneath. During both world wars women had to replace men in many jobs previously closed to them.

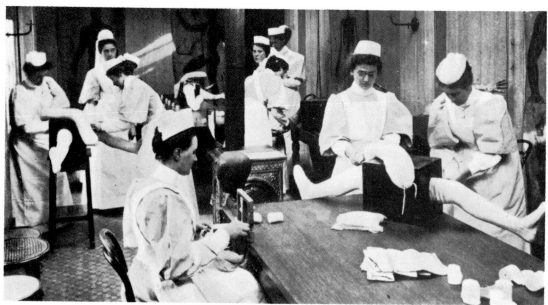

68. Anon., 'Walthamstow Telephone Exchange', 1910. The new century introduced a variety of jobs that gave women more choice: as secretaries replacing male clerks, as typists, as telephone operatives, and in more posts in department stores. The majority of such girls wore white blouses and dark skirts, although some preferred dresses. Ties and bow ties were also sported by the independent woman of the new century.

69. 'A Bandaging Class at Tredegar House', 1906, from Sarah Tooley's *History of Nursing in the British Empire*. Tredegar House was the Preliminary Nurse Training School for the London Hospital. Teenage girls were not accepted. This uniform was obviously designed about 1895, judging by its large leg-of-mutton sleeves. Making uniforms fashionable always means that they have to be redesigned sooner or later. The starched collars were a discomfort copied from men in the professional classes.

70. Anon., 'London General Omnibus Company Ltd', *c*.1910. The bus companies still do not provide uniforms. This conductor evidently likes a straw hat and a buttonhole. The driver still sticks to a top hat, like Cast Iron Billy in the previous century. Both have their licence badges. In 1933 the General, the LCC trams and the Underground were formed into the London Passenger Transport Board.

farm work if they got some help over clothing, so in 1916 the Board of Agriculture and the Co-operative Wholesale Society agreed to supply clothing to them at wholesale prices. By the end of the year, however, the Co-op said staff shortages made it difficult to continue, so the women's branch of the Board of Agriculture took over the sale. This help with clothes caused the number of women working on farms to treble. On 1 January 1917 the mobile Women's Land Army was set up to go anywhere and do any work. As this was an army the girls were given uniforms, with two overalls, a hat, one pair of kneebreeches, one pair of boots, one pair of leggings, one jersey, one pair of clogs, and a mackintosh. Later in 1917 they also received another overall, another hat, one more pair of breeches, and another pair of boots and leggings. The total value of the uniform was £7, and wages began at 18/–, for a beginner, rose to 20/–, and then to 22/– in 1918. The overalls were light cotton coats, worn over the jersey, kneebreeches and leggings, and hats had to be worn on duty. The girls carried out hay making, thatching, ploughing, sheep shearing, wood cutting, driving wagons and tractors, harvesting and machine repairs. School-boys, teachers and priests were also called out to help dig the potato crop or to pull flax, but as they were not in the Land Army they had to wear their own clothes. Kneebreeches for Land Army girls were clearly all right with the government, but it did not put them into trousers, although farm worker girls not in the army wore what they liked, which was often dungarees.[5]

Women's war work won them the vote in two stages, but they were thrown out of their jobs once the men started coming home to the 'land fit for heroes'. Many old jobs were now shrinking, for motors and lorries did not need blacksmiths, horses and grooms, but new types of workers. The multiples were opening branches in the country, and pre-packed food from the 1870s soon included margarine, meat products, pickles, biscuits, jams, chocolate, cocoa and ketchups, sold in the Inter-national Tea Co., the Home & Colonial Stores, Lipton's, and the Maypole Dairy, which all could undercut the local shopkeeper by their mass

71. Keeping & Co., 'Mr Morrish, chimney sweep of Bude, Cornwall', 1900. The one-piece overall arrives, in tough cotton, to fit over a shirt or vest and trousers. The cloth cap is beginning to spread through the working class, and some women wore them too. Connecting rods for the sweep's brush have at last replaced little boys.

OPPOSITE ABOVE
72. Anon., 'Aircraft builders at Ransomes of Ipswich', 1916. Women were wearing overalls in factories by the First World War, usually a coat to the knee and trousers, with elasticated or unelasticated caps. Some of these girls wear wings, probably as recognition for completing targets, rather than for flying. One has adopted a male tie, and a handkerchief in the top pocket, to show that she is a professional.

buying and selling. The same mass supply happened in clothing, with Hepworth's ready-made suits for men in new cloth replacing the remade shoddy outfits that country workers had had to buy before. George Oliver's boot and shoe warehouses offered more working pairs of boots than farm labourers had seen in a lifetime. Livestock fairs were less necessary, as multiples like the Co-op owned their own farms or else bought direct from the farmer, so that the drovers driving herds to town were replaced by trucks and trains.

Mass culture began in the cities, with the music halls letting everyone hear the same songs, then came the film industry, showing the same films in several different countries at the same time. This made country people even more aware of fashion,

for the films were often very glamorous stories where everyone wore evening dress. This struck J.B. Priestley very forcibly in 1933–4 on his tour of England. At Boston in Lincolnshire the local girls would have looked local in 1913, but by the 1930s they were copying Hollywood's Greta Garbo and Constance Bennett and were 'almost indistinguishable from girls in a dozen different capitals'. Hollywood and the USA he blamed for the Americanization of Britain into a cheap sort of Blackpool.

This is the England of arterial and by-pass roads, of filling stations, and factories that look like exhibition buildings, of giant cinemas and dance halls and cafés, bungalows with tiny garages, cocktail bars, Woolworths, motor coaches, wireless, hiking, factory girls

looking like actresses, greyhound racing, and dirt tracks, swimming pools, and everything given away for cigarette coupons.

The sight of an enormous excavator at Lincoln worried him, for it did the work of 800 navvies. What was the point of inventing a machine that put 800 men out of work? How could they buy clothes and food? How could an economy function properly with so many people without jobs? That problem is still with us.[6] Similarly, the introduction of milking parlours took the dairy out of the hands of women. The Universal Cow Milker by Lawrence & Kennedy improved on earlier efforts considerably in 1900, and by 1914 the milking of 50 to 60 cows simultaneously was possible. Machine-driven harvesting machines meant that the whole village no longer had to turn out to help. Instead of 40 men and women toiling in a field the number shrank to a couple, so what could village youths do for work but join the drift to the towns? In the eighteenth century most of the population was in the countryside; by the 1851 census half had moved into towns, and by 1900 three-quarters were in towns, and only one-quarter was left out in the

73. Anon., 'Women delivering coke', c.1916. All kinds of deliveries had to be taken over by women. These girls working for the South Metropolitan Gas Co. in Greenwich have been supplied with a uniform consisting of a long jacket, a peaked cap, a short skirt, gaiters and boots. Some companies provided overalls with trousers, which were probably better for the job.

country. This drift meant empty schools, shops with no customers, fewer doctors willing to live in such an empty area, and the gradual decline of rural society that still goes on. With the decline went traditional costumes, the various types of sun bonnets and shawls, the traditional fabrics like corduroy, the linen smocks and gaiters, and the leather breeches. Queen Victoria continued to wear the white cap of a married lady until her death, but not so society ladies of the younger generation, who only put on hats for outdoors, and started to appear bare-headed inside the house. By the 1920s this was being imitated in the country, with some wives and grandmothers denying their married state indoors. It was part of the cult of youth, and in 1927 the couturier Jean-Charles

Worth declared that 'today all women are young'. They tried to be, with forays into town to Woolworths and Marks and Spencer to find something fashionable, while make-up ceased to be exclusive to prostitutes, for film stars wore it and country girls copied them. The biggest change had arrived.

In September 1939 Nazi Germany and its ally the Soviet Union started the Second World War with their joint invasion of Poland. In November the USSR invaded neutral Finland; in April 1940 the Nazis invaded neutral Norway, and in May the neutral Benelux countries. Neutrality protected nobody as the Fascists and the Communists divided Europe between them. This time, with the example of the First World War to guide the government, the Women's Land Army was refounded immediately, and given uniforms consisting of a hat, jumpers, shirts, ties, kneebreeches, woollen stockings, boots, wellington boots, and this time trousered denim dungarees. Petrol rationing meant a come-back for horses for ploughing and harvesting, although the girls driving had to steer round huge blocks of concrete, sewer pipes

74. Anon., 'Leland Tiger outside Cadby House', c.1926. Lyons teashops opened in 1894 to cater for lady customers, who were not allowed into restaurants on their own. The waitresses were always given a black dress with a white collar, cuffs and apron, black stockings, and the white cap inherited from maid servants. Here it has the low waist of fashion, and modish liveries began to dominate many jobs. The men delivering bread and cakes wear the overall as a coat, with dark red trim at the collar and cuffs, and a peaked cap.

and similar obstructions put there by the Local Defence Volunteers to stop German aeroplanes from landing. Road signs disappeared, road blocks and pillboxes were erected, black-out was imposed, and food rationing arrived. To increase food production, marshes were drained, playing fields were ploughed up, golf courses planted, allotments set up everywhere, and some London squares even kept pigs and chickens. Between 1939 and 1941 four million extra acres were brought under cultivation. The Women's Land Army was helped at harvest time by city volunteers. Since the Germans dropped lots of incendiary bombs on the

crops, hay ricks were made smaller and less close together, and the Youth Service Brigade would help to put out fires in their school uniforms with a hanky tied over the mouth. Boys did the beating out and girls carried the water. To get a souvenir from a downed German bomber was their ideal.

In remoter parts of Wales and Cumbria standing for hire lingered into the 1950s, despite the law on a minimum agricultural wage. There labourers were only paid at the end of the year worked, so that was the time to settle up with tailors and bootmakers, and to get drunk. There was still one man in twenty on the land in 1950, but this figure had fallen to one in a hundred by 1980. The old labourers who had to train all the newcomers from the towns stuck to their traditions: heavy corduroy trousers, boots, leather leggings called 'buskins' in Suffolk, and corduroy waistcoats with a cloth back. The old sleeved waistcoats in corduroy were so thick a jacket was not necessary. In that part of the world knee strings were termed 'eightsies', and tied-up trousers were 'at half past eight'. A wagoner said he still got his clothes once a year in May: a summer suit of the slop kind in light cotton called a blewett (as it was blue), or else a greyett, which had the trousers lined or half-lined. Clogs were essential during the war because of the shortages, and while most had rounded toes, the ones in Lancashire were duck-toed, like a wedge, in front.[7]

OPPOSITE ABOVE

75. Anon., 'Making Christmas Pudding', c.1926. The Royal Arsenal Co-operative Society Preservatory coping with the Christmas demand. Under the health regulations all workers have to wear overalls and head covering, but these overalls have the fashionable low waist, so in the next decade they will have to alter.

76. Anon., 'Filling Jars with Marmalade', 1934. The Royal Arsenal Co-operative Society Preservatory's new uniforms, with the higher waist of the 1930s, and smaller caps. These girls all wear sacking aprons made from sugar bags to protect their gleaming whites. Short-sleeved uniforms are a problem for those who feel the cold, and one girl has kept her jumper on. Hemlines now go up and down according to the vogue.

Artisans and professionals

Professional black continued strongly up to the First World War and immediately afterwards, as so many people were in mourning. Half-mourning in dark grey could be worn after two years of deepest black, and during the 1920s grey suits became more common. The battle was on between frock coats and top hats versus lounge suits, bowler hats and trilbies. Lounge suits and turn-down shirt collars both appeared in the 1850s as casual undress for country holidays when Edward VII would wear them out of town. Gradually, of course, they crept into town, notably among the artists who found the short jacket more convenient to work in than the frock coat, and consequently it spread among the literati and sophisticated. At the same time lounge suits became very popular among the working class. They wanted to wear suits, even if in shoddy, and the short jacket and trousers were the modern version of the hip-length jacket and kneebreeches that they had been wearing since the seventeenth century. The lounge suit had none of the inconvenience of long frock coats, so the workers adopted it in great numbers to such an extent that black lounge suits were accepted as Socialist suits, worn by some into the 1950s. In 1937 George Orwell spoke of 'office workers and black-coated employees of all kinds', showing how common black still was in offices, banks, and institutions. He was criticizing Socialists for demanding a dictatorship of the proletariat – the manual workers – and not including all the underpaid, lowly 'middle class' clerks, commercial travellers, and lower civil servants. Attempts by middle-class ladies to devise a dress for Socialist women failed, however, for their loose aesthetic gowns were too expensive for a way of life where fashion was still second-hand. No manufacturer undertook mass-produced fashionless gowns, for advanced ladies argued that fashion should be abolished, but the workers themselves still tried to copy it, and one of the chief reasons for the regular supply of second-hand clothes was that the original owners wanted something more up-to-date. Without the existence of fashion there would have been fewer clothes available for the poor.

When Gordon Selfridge opened his London store in March 1909 it was intended to be a palace for shoppers, and the male staff had to wear black suits and the women black dresses with high necks, and long sleeves in serge with black woollen stockings. After the war in the Twenties the girls were allowed lighter dresses, to the knee after 1925 but still in black; by the late 1930s, however, they were allowed white blouses, black cardigans and black skirts. The men still had black suits. This was typical of all temples of merchandise at the time. Outdoor staff were employed in delivering to customers daily with horse-drawn vans which were not phased out until the end of the 1930s. The drivers were dressed as coachmen in riding breeches and boots, with a buttoned double-breasted tunic and peaked cap which was also given to motor van drivers later. The commission-aire between the wars, Arthur Stratten, ex-army, designed his own uniform with a peaked cap, a frock coat with medal ribbons, trousers, and of course leather gloves for opening doors. The lift girls on the celebrated bronze-fronted lifts were attired very like chauffeurs and coachmen with

77. 'Express Dairyman', c.1935. Milkmaids are now extinct. This man retains some equine character by wearing jodhpurs under his long apron, although he pushes a handcart and does not have a horse and cart. It is cold enough for him to need his own jacket over his company overall coat. Many firms now used uniforms, with only the coloured collar, cuffs and cap as differential features.

BOTTOM LEFT
78. Victor Stewart, 'Digging up the Tram Rails at North End, Portsmouth', 1940. The Second World War has begun, so people are urged to save metal. Rubber boots now occur for any outdoor work. Most of these labourers wear light slop suits, one has a trilby and all the rest cloth caps, now almost universal for workers in the British Isles. If warm some would strip down to the shirt and waistcoat, but no further. The neckcloth still carries on.

79. Victor Stewart, 'A Direct Hit on Stanley St., Southsea, 24 August 1940'. All over the country cities suffered in Hitler's blitz. Tin hats, and overalls with wellington boots, appeared everywhere. The RSD (Rescue, Shoring & Demolition) are needed here.

kneebreeches and gaiters and a long tunic, although their peaked caps were larger.[8]

The outbreak of war in 1914 threw 40,000 women out of work in the luxury end of the market, so Queen Mary founded her Women's Emergency Corps to do anything needed. The first women off to France were the forces' nurses, but soon more had to be called for, with quick training courses, and the age limit raised to 45 to cope with the huge casualties. They wore capes, coats, skirts to the ankle on their dresses, and lace-up boots. A variety of headwear settled down to a long white veil down to the back as the principal form. White coats and rubber gloves and rubber boots were now the basic medical costume for operations, with masks and white caps all sterilized. The appeal went out, wrote H. Usborne in 1917, for women to be bus conductors, canteen operators, clerks, carpenters, club leaders, commercial travellers, crèche matrons, dental mechanics, doctors, factory inspectors, gardeners, district messengers, grooms, health visitors, health almoners, inspectors for the NSPCC and the LGB, investigators, lamplighters, mail van drivers, masseuses, midwives, motor drivers, munition workers, nurses, organizers, patrols, police, pharmacists, postwomen, relief officers, sanitary inspectors, school nurses for the LCC, taxi drivers, teachers, telephonists, tram conductors, voluntary aid detachment superintendents, and to join the Women's Auxiliary Corps. Some of these posts involved uniforms consisting of a mannish jacket with four pockets and a belt, a skirt to the calf, boots, a shirt and a tie, with a variety of soft or hard caps, some peaked, depending on the post. In the main, officialdom preferred women not to wear trousers, so lady inspectors on the railways were mannish as far as hat and jacket were concerned but wore skirts below that. Not so the women porters handling the milk churns; they, not being in uniform, wore their own man's soft peaked cap, dress and apron to the ankles, sometimes with a shawl. Lady tram conductors did adopt very wide trousers with their mannish jackets, although on the buses the lady conductors usually wore skirts.[9]

Women were anxious to help with policing, but

80. Victor Stewart, 'Three ARP Wardens with a motorized fire pump on a wheelbarrow', c.1942. Tin hats and one-piece overalls were issued to men and women alike, this time. Once again women had to take on all sorts of work, and 'make do and mend' was the call, so improvization had to produce this sort of help for fighting fires.

81. Victor Stewart, 'Land Army Recruiting', 1942. Bring back the girls! but this time the Women's Land Army gets dungarees, as well as shirts, ties, hats, jumpers, corduroy kneebreeches, socks, shoes and wellington boots. This form of national service lasted until 1949, after the war. The advert also shows riding breeches as part of the uniform.

82. Victor Stewart, 'Volunteer Ambulance Drivers', Fareham, Hants, 1940. Since there was some initial confusion over the issue of uniforms, some of these girls wear their own mackintoshes, but the cap was the identifying mark. The one on the far right has trousers on; these became increasingly common to save stockings. The vehicle belonged to the Hampshire County Council.

when officialdom proved unco-operative, Miss Damer Dawson founded her own corps in Grantham in 1914. In November 1915 the town council appointed the private corps into their official police force to help with general work and the guarding of munition factories. The lady inspectors had the male peaked cap with silver braid, but the women constables wore a sort of low-set bowler; skirts to the calf, boots, shirts, ties, and mannish jackets were common to both.

Voluntary ambulance drivers had hats like an Australian trooper with one side turned up, but otherwise it was the mannish jacket to the hips, a shirt, a tie, a skirt to the calves, and boots. If one should wonder at the wearing of shirts and ties by women, it was because officials wore them, and it was felt that to carry out that function women had to look like half men, above the waist. Lots of women worked as solicitors' clerks during the war, issuing writs and subpoenas, and filing documents, so not surprisingly some wanted to study the law and become barristers, but they were refused. It took a campaign to get the Sex Disqualification (Removal) Act passed in 1919 before the first female student got into the Middle Temple to read

law.[10] Here, too, ties and shirt-like blouses predominated among women in offices and courts.

There were economic depressions immediately after the 1914–18 war, and again in 1929 through into the 1930s, so it was little wonder that the homecoming heroes felt disillusioned. It caused J.B. Priestley to declare in 1934: 'The dole is part of no plan; it is a mere declaration of intellectual bankruptcy . . . Labour Exchanges stink of defeated humanity.'[11] George Orwell tried out in person what it was like by becoming a tramp in 1933. He sold his suit at Lambeth for something older:

The clothes were a coat, once dark brown, a pair of black dungaree trousers, a scarf and a cloth cap; I had kept my own shirt, socks and boots and I had a comb and razor in my pocket. It gives one a very strange feeling to be wearing such clothes. I had worn bad enough things before, but not at all like these, they were not merely dirty and shapeless, they had – how is one to express it? – a gracelessness, a patina of antique filth, quite different from mere shabbiness. They were the sort of clothes you see on a bootlace seller, or a tramp.

My new clothes had put me instantly into a new world. Everybody's demeanour seemed to have changed abruptly. I helped a hawker pick up a barrow that he had upset. 'Thanks, mate,' he said with a grin. No one had called me mate before in my life – it was the clothes that had done it. For the first time I noticed too how the attitude of women varies with a man's clothes. When a badly dressed man passes them they shudder away from him with a quite frank movement of disgust, as though he were a dead cat. Clothes are powerful things.[12]

Indeed they are, dividing the established from the hopeless. Orwell tried a night at the workhouses or 'spikes', as tramps called them, where they were stripped and searched for money. Anyone with more than eightpence was not allowed in. They were supposed to take a bath, but many tramps said hot water was weakening. For sleep grey cotton nightshirts were provided, but there were no beds and they had to sleep on the floor. In the morning their own clothes were returned and they had a medical. Most looked undernourished. On leaving they were given a meal ticket worth sixpence. The Victorian policy of punishing the poor and inadequate continued to be enforced.

Orwell had also tried working as a washer-up in hotels in Paris, in the filthy sculleries beyond the chandeliered dining rooms. Pencil-line moustaches were very fashionable in the Thirties, but Orwell was ordered to shave his off. Customers wore moustaches; waiters and washers-up did not. Even though the waiters wore evening dress with tail coats, white ties and shirts, they could not resemble the clients completely. The cooks, who did not appear in the dining room, did wear moustaches just to show their superiority over waiters. A large mirror outside the scullery was for the waiters to groom themselves before appearing in public. If Old Etonian Orwell expected to find an absence of class distinction or status marks among the workers he was mistaken. The kitchens of such establishments as the Trocadero in London were enormous, but Escoffier's whites were fully established, following Lister's impact on cleanliness. Chef's hats a foot or more high, white coats and white aprons, although trousers could be of grey canvas or cotton, were universal.[13]

H.V. Morton visited the slums in 1933 for the Labour Party.[14] One old man wore old clothes of both sexes. 'He had no coat. He wore a woman's knitted jumper, brown and tattered. There was a big tear in his right trouser leg, through which a sharp white hairless kneebone protruded.' An old soldier told him that the trenches were better than his cellar home, where his pallid wife in a sacking apron battled to keep clothes and home clean against Liverpool dirt. A string of washing across the room was typical. How amazing, he wrote, that in an age of electricity, of chromium, of trans-Atlantic flight, and worldwide radio, the poor were still living like Saxon peasants. Orwell wrote: 'Trade since the war has had to adjust itself to meet the demands of underpaid, underfed people, with the result that a luxury is nowadays almost always cheaper than a necessity. One pair of plain, solid shoes costs as much as two ultra-smart pairs.' This still applies, for the fashionable shoe is not designed to last, and the durable stout shoe is expensive. He estimated that 20,000,000 people were underfed, but most homes had radios, women had artificial silk stockings, and people had chocolate, cinemas, fish and chips and did the football pools.

In Lancashire Orwell saw the women on the coal dumps: 'dumpy shawled women with their sacking aprons, and their heavy black clogs, kneeling in the cindery mud and the bitter wind, searching eagerly for tiny chips of coal'. Near Wigan Orwell noticed a slum dweller in her 'sacking apron, her clumsy clogs, her arms reddened by the cold . . . She had a round, pale face, the usual exhausted face of the slum girl who is twenty-five and looks forty, thanks to miscarriages and drudgery'. Large families were common throughout society with women still having children into their fifties, until Marie Stopes opened her first birth control clinic in 1921 to teach the secrets of the few to the many.

The two million unemployed in the Thirties received less and less. The single man got full benefit so long as his insurance stamps lasted, at 17/– a week, then he went on to the Unemployment Assistance Board which gave him 15/– for 26 weeks, and lastly on to the Public Assistance Committee which gave only 12/6 a week, and spied on any activity, however innocent (such as looking after the neighbours' children), that might in theory bring in some more money. Here, too, second-hand clothes predominated, never anything new, and the likes of overcoats and mackintoshes were unaffordable luxuries. The poor were lucky to have a scarf. As for thousands of years, when the only outfit was washed the wearer had to stay indoors or in bed. Exchanges with neighbours were common over children's clothes in particular, recycling down the generations, and children playing in the street without shoes or stockings was widespread into the 1940s. Flat cloth caps, suits and perhaps a scarf, with no tie, characterized the basic dress of the working man between the wars, and their wives were never seen without an apron or a pinafore, but head coverings like caps and bonnets indoors remained only on old women.[15]

In the fashion industry, of course, the seamstresses, hairdressers and salesgirls strove very hard to attain the current look, wearing cloche hats and clutch coats in the Twenties, and long skirts in the Thirties. A great many uniforms followed fashion. H.J. Heinz of Pittsburgh's 57 varieties were bottled in the Edwardian period by girls in long striped blue dresses with gigot sleeves, white aprons, and large white caps edged with elastic to conceal their hair. Come the Twenties, uniforms in food factories changed to shorter skirts and lower waists, and in the Thirties the waists went up and the hems went down as part of the return to a more feminine look. It puts companies to a lot of expense, but workers did not like to look dated when the cinema made them even more conscious of changes in the mode.

The impact of things American could be seen in films and heard on the wireless, and the Edwardians were annoyed about the casual style of the USA, where lounge suits were called 'business suits', and soft trilbies were preferred to hard bowlers. It was considered a bad influence on the young: the crooners Rudy Vallee and the Connecticut Yankees, Paul Whiteman's Rhythm Boys of 1927, Bing Crosby, Harry Barris and Al Rinker who, horror of horrors, performed in lounge suits, not evening dress! In British bands the players wore dinner jackets and black ties, and the leader white tie and tails (with the exception of Ivy Benson's all-girl band).

Black jazz was called barbaric and the bands upset people. When Duke Ellington and his band appeared at the London Palladium in 1933 they wore white evening jackets and coloured trousers, with white shoes! Their English imitators went even further, performing in polo-necked sweaters in white or black with lounge suits, or sports jackets and grey trousers, at jazz meccas like the Nest in Kingly Street, where black jazz musicians introduced marijuana as an alternative to the traditional drugs of opium and alcohol.

Outside on the street the slop suit so common on farms was also worn by road workers when mending the highway, or in 1939 for starting to dig up the tram lines for the war effort. These canvas or cotton suits were often worn on top of the ordinary working suit, along with the now traditional cloth cap. Of course, in a heat wave it was possible to wear only the slop suit, but there were few signs of that, as it would have been considered improper.

A disappearing craft was that of the flint knapper. At Brandon in Suffolk in 1927 H.V. Morton met Mr Edwards. 'A young man was sitting on a low stool with a stout leather guard strapped above the knee of his left leg. On this guard he held a great nodule of flint, which he hit sharply with a short-necked hammer.' The flints were exported mostly to Africa for the flint-lock guns which were lingering there, but there were only six knappers still working in Brandon.[17] Leather knee guards were worn by thatchers for kneeling on ladders, and as late as 1985 I saw a worker laying concrete wearing a pair of knee pads. Leather hand guards were worn by cobblers when sewing stout skins.

Once the USA entered the Second World War and clothes rationing existed in the UK, American garments were desirable extras. The Canadian lumberjacket was adopted in Britain and airmen's leather flying jackets were highly prized. Denim and jeans materials were European, and the advent of American jeans was post-war. Windcheater jackets were adopted by dockyard labourers straight off the Liberty ships. For the girls, anything: underwear, nylon stockings, scented soaps, blouses, were welcome gifts from GIs. Great Aunt Minnie in Boston sent us food parcels, but I was not old enough to ask for nylons. Evelyn Waugh was annoyed by the shabbiness of London by 1943, with girls with filmstar hairdos, slacks and high heels all going out with soldiers. The hair was the only item most girls could afford to be fanciful with, and slacks saved precious stockings, so they appeared in a huge number of jobs.

During the Second World War, of course, women once again had to run much of the country, working for Air Raid Precautions (ARP), for the Auxiliary Fire Service (AFS), for the Auxiliary Ambulance Service (AAS), and Rescue Shoring/Demolition (RSD). The ARP received overalls and tin hats; the AFS navy blue coats and slacks (that is, trousers); the AAS had to wait seven months before they received a drill overall worth 11/–, and complained that they still needed their own clothes and coats in winter, when a navy blue British Warm would have been ideal. Rationing made people reluctant to risk their own clothing. The RSD were also given tin hats and overalls, but their superintendent said they were not warm in winter, and the women superintendents were very annoyed that they were paid only £2 a week while the male stretcher bearers under their command got £3. In fact the Industrial Court in April 1939, just before the war, agreed to a complaint from women bus and tram conductors that they ought to receive equal pay for the same job, but authority kept making excuses that men were heads of families, regardless in fact of their married state, and whether the working woman was head of her family. (An Equal Pay Act was passed in 1970 and enacted from 1975, the same year as the Sex Discrimination Act, but a lot of employers redefined jobs to deny women equal pay, and by 1979 there were complaints about the acts failing.)

Women building Wellington bombers in 1940 received two caps, a pair of gloves, and a pair of dungarees per year as their working allowance, as they drilled, riveted, and sewed on the canvas frame. Portsmouth claimed to have the first women bus drivers on double-deckers in 1941, who were dressed exactly like men in grey jackets and trousers, shirts, ties and peaked caps, with the corporation badge. In railway workshops it was either dungarees and a slop jacket or the boiler suit, the all-in-one form of overall, for the women mechanics. Dungarees and boiler suits were common on women shipbuilders and repairers, electricians, painters, and carpenters. Lighter work like making camouflage nets was done mostly by older women who wore what they liked: usually pinafores, overall coats, and sometimes dungarees. Films made turbans very fashionable, and these were widely adopted by women workers, to keep the hair out of the way.[18]

The Women's Voluntary Service, the WVS, was founded in 1938 at the approach of war, remembering Queen Mary's volunteers of 1914, and members were called 'the girls in green' from the colour of their uniform with its hat and coat with the badge. They turn out to offer succour during disasters down to this day, and were also employed on campaigns during the war like the Save Fuel drive in 1942, riding about on bicycles without tyres, as rubber went to military vehicles first. Large numbers of women also worked as auxiliary nurses, clerks, civil servants, telephonists and

83. Victor Stewart, 'Mrs E. Hunt and Mrs E. Devine, the first women to drive doubledecker buses, at Portsmouth', 1941. Male dress for masculine jobs. There is nothing feminine on the outside except the size of the shoes and the hair, and only a hint of shape. As in the First World War, any woman doing a masculine job could be given shirts and ties. In the Second World War, however, trousers were supplied instead of skirts to a greater degree. Keeping cheerful in adversity was a British characteristic.

OPPOSITE ABOVE
84. Anon., 'Civil Defence Workers' Parade at Wembley Stadium, London', October 1942. The Home Secretary and Minister for Home Security, Herbert Morrison, takes the salute. The nurses all have white uniforms of overalls and aprons with capes. The veil type of cap appeared during the Edwardian period, but some of the nurses wear the newer cap that was round without a veil at the back. They are followed by the WVS, the 'girls in green', in their coats and hats with a badge. The most common dress for the rest are the overalls and tin hats, some with overcoats, and of course their gas masks over the shoulder.

administrators, often wearing slacks when they could both for warmth (given the fuel cuts) and to save stockings.

Industry and the sea

The Great Western Railway prided itself upon its smartness and looks, which characterized just how much companies expected their servants to represent the corporate image. The GWR rule book of 1933 stated: 'When on duty be neat in appearance, and, where supplied, wear uniform, number, and badge . . . When an employee leaves the service he must deliver up his uniform, and all other articles belonging to the Company.' Missing articles would have to be paid for. Similar rules were laid down by the Great North of Scotland Railway in 1908: 'Every servant receiving uniform must, when on duty, appear in it clean and neat, with the number and the badge perfect.' The GWR published its *Standard List of Uniform Clothing* in 1907. It made it clear that only men who had entered its service before 1868 could receive boots. Balmoral boots were issued every two years to station masters, chief inspectors, station inspec-

tors, ticket collectors, passenger guards, messengers, and telegraphists. Blücher boots, with nails or without, were given every two years to signalmen, goods yard police, foreman porters, yard foremen, shunters, and number takers. The company livery was blue, and was usually presented in May. The first-class station master had a dark blue superfine cap, with a slightly ball-shaped crown, a full peak with three-quarters of an inch of gold embroidery, a mohair oak leaf band and braiding, and a badge at centre front in gold embroidery stating GWR. He received a dark blue beaver overcoat with a velvet collar, cloth buttons, and horizontal pockets, every two years. His normal wear was a dark blue frock coat in superfine serge, with braided borders, ornamental braided cuffs, and cloth buttons, replaced every nine months. His vest/waistcoat was dark blue superfine serge and also had braided borders and cloth buttons, renewed every nine months. The trousers were dark blue serge with one inch of braid down the sides, and were replaced twice a year, in May and November. The Principal Station Master at Paddington received a new silk top hat every six months. Various inspectors received dark blue cloth caps of the type number 16 with an overlapping crown, five-eighths of an inch of gold embroidery around the edge, and oak leaf embroidery around the GWR badge in front. They too received dark blue overcoats in cloth with cloth buttons and horizontal pockets every two years. Every May a frock coat in dark blue superfine serge, with a braided collar and back skirts, and ornamental braid on the cuffs, was supplied, along with a matching vest in dark blue superfine serge. Trousers in plain dark blue serge were replaced six-monthly, in May and November.

Lower down the scale, staff had red piping on the dark blue. Passenger guards had dark blue cloth caps bearing the GWR badge in front with gilt thread, renewed every May, and an overcoat in dark blue cloth with GWR buttons every two years, but they did not receive frock coats. Instead they received a dark blue serge jacket with a turn-down collar, an open front, red piping on the edges, a breast pocket and two flap pockets, and the word 'guard' in gilt thread on either side of the collar. Under it went a vest of dark blue serge with red piping, and both were supplied in May. Two pairs of trousers a year had red piping down the sides on the dark blue serge. The porters' caps, in dark blue cloth with red piping, had GWR on the front in red worsted. Their dark blue serge jackets had 'porter' written on the collars, GWR buttons, flap pockets, and the number badge on the right sleeve, embroidered in red worsted. The vest in dark blue serge had linen sleeves, GWR buttons, and the trousers in dark blue serge had red piping down the sides. Dark blue overcoats, caps, jackets, trousers and vests were also given to sleeping-car attendants and train attendants. The GWR also employed its own omnibus drivers, who sported the dark blue frock coat, with the GWR buttons and badge and red piping, renewed yearly. In bad weather they wore short overcoats in rough pilot cloth with GWR in red worsted. The company also had its own fire service who had brass helmets for fires, and dark blue cloth caps otherwise. Their overcoats were dark blue cloth, as were the tunics which had red cloth ends on the collars. The vest was in dark blue cloth, as were the trousers. Top

boots were also supplied. The GWR also had two new categories of drivers, the road motor car conductors, and the motor car drivers, who looked very different from the railway staff, for the former wore a grey tweed overcoat, cap and suit, with black leather puttees and gilt buttons, while the drivers were in black leather caps, with either a black oilskin for wet weather given every two years, or a summer overcoat in light brown canvas with GWR on the collar in red worsted, a black leather jacket with a cloth surface collar, and black leather puttees. The puttees reflect the wearing of riding breeches by early chauffeurs, which some continued into the 1960s. Those employed by individuals were dressed in dark blue or grey liveries, with the peaked cap that Edward VII gave to his first chauffeur; however, Hollywood film stars liked their chauffeurs in white liveries with white automobiles. Gradually from the 1930s, trousers began to replace riding breeches, so the result was the lounge suit, with only the cap indicating service.[19]

In the mill towns, 'the first sound in the mornings was the clumping of the mill-girls' clogs down the cobbled street', wrote Orwell in 1937. Clogs continued into the war, along with the tartan shawl, the calf-length skirt and dark stockings. In the cotton factory their now-traditional pinafores continued as the principal form of protection, but in the Woollen and Worsted Textile Regulations of 1926 overalls and head coverings were made compulsory in textile factories. Priestley pondered the problem at Blackburn Technical College, in the heart of the cotton-weaving mills, where Japanese students were taught British techniques and then went home to imitate them and undercut the

85. Victor Stewart, 'A Mechanic on Southern Rail', November 1942. 'Somewhere in southern England' a mechanic keeps the railways running. The one-piece overall with side pockets has become the fundamental garment against industrial dirt. Women wore it in aircraft factories, bomb factories, artillery factories, shipyards and chemical works. The beret is a more feminine touch, smaller than the male kind, but most men still sported cloth caps. The neckcloth has been copied from male workers.

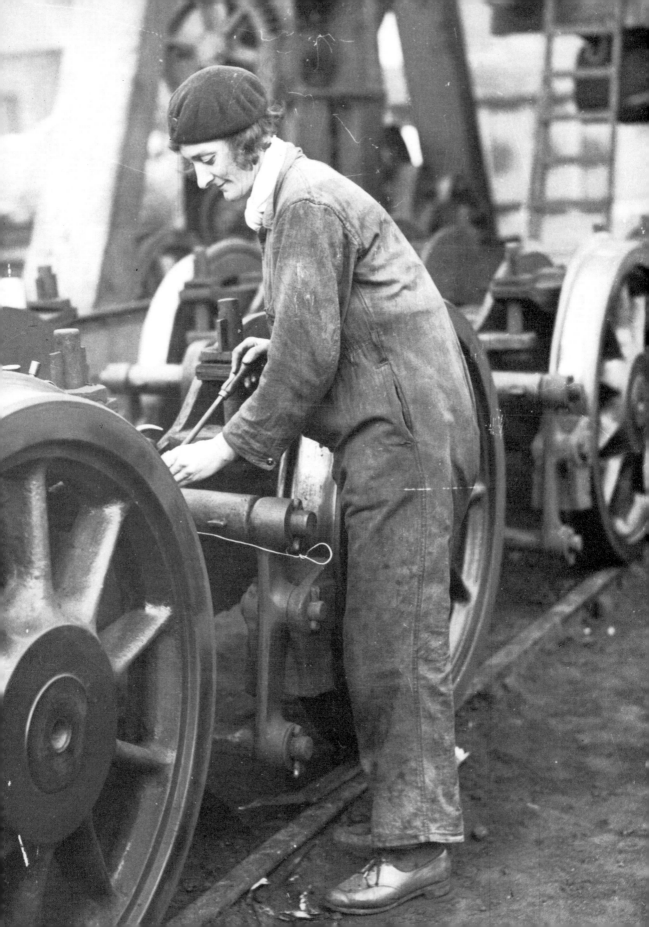

British prices with cheap labour and no safety regulations. Where, he asked, was the sense in training rivals? Perhaps he felt that the British should have kept the secrets of the Industrial Revolution to themselves. Blackburn was also suffering because of Gandhi's ban on importing English cloth as part of his independence campaign, so the mass production of dhootie cloth for India ground to a halt. Kilbarchan claimed to be the last centre for hand loom weaving of tartan in Scotland, when H.V. Morton went there in 1933. Whereas there had been 800 looms in the last century, now it was only 20 and no apprentices could be found. The weavers were all women aged from 50 to 80 and one old man. They argued that durable kilts had to be made of handwoven cloth and vegetable dyes.[20]

At leadmines fustian was the traditional wear because of its dense quality which made it pretty waterproof. Long footless stockings coming up to the thigh were common wear in wet weather, as the oily wool helped to repel rainwater. In the Northern Dales these traditional footless stockings were called 'loughrams', and were hand knitted, mainly in Swaledale and Wensleydale. They also acted as knee protectors when kneeling underground. Cornish leadminers had a hard hat of compressed felt impregnated with resin until carbide lamps appeared in 1910, but they were less common in the north. Down coal mines Orwell found a new helmet in 1937: '. . . wooden crash helmets – a comparatively recent invention – are a godsend. They look like a French or Italian steel helmet, but they are made of some kind of pith and very light, and so strong that you can take a violent blow on the head without feeling it.' He noticed that height was a disadvantage down mines, so small men were common, and nudity could still appear: 'In the hotter mines they wear only a pair of thin drawers, clogs, and knee pads; in the hottest mines of all, only the clogs and knee pads.' Helmets were still not compulsory; older miners resisted them as 'soft' and stuck to caps, so sensitive are men about their concept of masculinity. Orwell said that British mines were mostly very old-fashioned. Less than one in three had pithead baths and lockers, so

that miners could wash and change at work. Most miners still trudged home in their dirty clothes and had their food first, then bathed in the tin tub and changed. Many had blue noses and necks from coal dust entering the pores, and needed a gargle as soon as they got to the surface to clear the dust from their throats. Their average wage in 1934 was £115 11s.6d. a year, but most suffered lay-offs which reduced that. There were still women alive, Orwell noticed, who had pulled coal wagons underground before 1842, presumably centenarians of great toughness who had begun work as children. On the surface women were still active, although they no longer worked at night shifts. Sorting coal was still their sphere, a very ancient one. Covering the hair against coal dust continued to be essential, and sacking aprons and skirts had at last replaced trousers in the Wigan mines. In the mines trousers for women made a come-back during the Second World War as slacks, now that stockings were a problem to obtain, but this time there was no nonsense about vestigial skirts to half-conceal the trousered legs and middle. The slacks were worn boldly on their own. On the heads of the younger women went coloured turbans à la Carmen Miranda (but without the fruit) to keep the hair clean, instead of the traditional shawls or 1920s dust caps. The older surface women workers were disgusted, of course, having gone over to skirts, and called them brazen, but all over the country working women had donned slacks for convenience. In 1948 the mines were nationalized and every mine now had to have pithead baths and canteens. Mechanical sorting of coal from muck was introduced, and the male-dominated National Union of Mineworkers in Lancashire negotiated with the new National Coal Board that women should be excluded as mechanization was introduced from the 1950s, for the same weary argument that hard work was unfeminine. In the meantime it was argued that elderly or disabled male miners should have the sorting jobs, even though they were less robust and strong than the women. Thus women were ousted from the traditional work they had been doing at mines and with iron ore for centuries, if not millennia.

Nobody made a fuss, because the whole of government propaganda was aimed at getting women out of jobs to make room for the men returning from the war.

In the 1960s the NCB began to introduce compulsory helmets in plastic or fibreglass, but the miners did not like them as they did not mould themselves to the head in the same way as the pith helmets that Orwell had seen. For working underground the men liked old clothes.[21]

The first factory act required adequate clothing for apprentices, but thereafter the law concerned itself with hours worked, safety regulations, dangerous machinery and pay, rather than clothing. By the end of the century, however, as more chemicals were being used, protective clothing had to be considered. The Factory and Workshop Act of 1891 contained many special rules for dangerous occupations, which applied into the next century. The chemical works special rules required that 'Suitable respirators shall be provided for the use

86. James Jerché, 'Welsh Miners Underground', from H.V. Morton's *In Search of Wales*, 1932. The first flashlight photograph taken underground means that nobody dared move. The miners show their resistance to safety measures like helmets and stick to cloth caps. Old clothes were most common underground, when clothes were worn at all, and two of these men are working in vests.

of the workers in places where poisonous gases or injurious dust may be inhaled.' The special rules for handling of dry and drysalted hides and skins imported from China or from the west coast of India stated:

Suitable overalls, protecting the neck and arms, as well as ordinary clothing, add materially to the safety of the workmen, and should be provided and worn, where practicable, if dangerous hides are handled. They should be discarded on cessation of work. Similarly, for the protection of the hands, gloves should be provided and worn where the character of the work permits.

This was to guard against the danger of anthrax in the dust. Paint manufacture also came under the 1891 Act:

They shall provide suitable respirators and overall suits, kept in a cleanly state, for all workers engaged in any department where dry white lead, or arsenic is used in the manufacture or paint mixing, and overall suits for those engaged in grinding in water or oil, and for all workers in Milan red, vermilionette, Persian red, wherever dust is generated.

The enamelling of iron plates involved arsenic, so here the special rules said, 'They shall provide suitable respirators, overall suits and head coverings, for all workers employed in the processes of grinding, dusting and brushing.' Lucifer match factories also came under the 1891 rules: 'The occupier shall provide and maintain sufficient and suitable overalls for all workers employed in phosphorous processes, except for persons employed only as boxers.'

It has often been claimed that it was working in munition factories in the First World War which put women into trousers on a wide scale. Special rules for manufacturing explosives also were laid down in 1891:

Overall suits and head coverings shall be supplied to all workers in shops where di-nitro-benzole is used, these suits to be taken off or well brushed before meals, and before leaving the works, and to be washed at least once a week.

Suitable respirators (capable of being washed), folds of linen, or woollen material of open texture, or other suitable material, shall be supplied to those workers liable to inhale dust, and the wearing of such respirators shall be urged where the workers derive benefit . . .

The overall suits meant the short smock top and trousers in canvas, so when women took over the

87. 'Billingsgate Fish Porters', c.1910. For carrying boxes of fish on their heads the porters devised these reinforced flat-topped caps. The white overall dominates this area of work, but after the First World War the long sleeve was shortened, as most men rolled it up. Canvas trousers and boots complete the outfit. The strong family likenesses in the men shows how jobs were kept in the family.

work they had to wear the suits. A munition worker said that they were usually in blue or khaki, but the overseers had coats in red, yellow, green or blue, often with a red bandana to lighten the scene. There were three munition factories in Britain before 1914, rising to 4,800 during the war, so huge numbers of women were called into force to make high explosives, shells and fuses, and to be tool setters and testers, reaching a total of 700,000 employees. They were also summoned into HM dockyards as painters, electricians and carpenters, so here overalls, dungarees and aprons were worn. On the eve of another war in 1939 H.V. Morton visited a TNT works and had to strip to his underclothes to put on their safety clothing like oversized pyjamas in white felt, with a cap with a number stencilled on it, and rubber overshoes. No nailed boots were allowed because of the danger of sparks, and everyone had to walk slowly. Thus in the explosives industry trousers became a tradition for women along with the men.

Some special rules were revised over the years 1901–3, and those engaged in the manufacture of yellow lead had to have 'respirators and overall suits and head coverings'. For bottling aerated water, the revised rules stated:

They shall provide all bottlers with face-guards, masks, or veils of wire gauze.
They shall provide all wirers, sighters, and labellers with face-guards, masks, or veils of wire gauze, or goggles.
They shall provide all bottlers with full-length gauntlets for both arms.
They shall provide all wirers, sighters, and labellers with gauntlets for both arms, protecting at least half of the palm and the space between the thumb and forefinger.

It was made clear that while the employer should strive his best to enforce the wearing of such protective clothing, the ultimate responsibility lay with the worker.

In 1909 'suitable overalls and head coverings' were required for the china biscuitware industry. The 1912 regulations for bronzing ruled: 'There shall be provided – Suitable overalls for all persons employed in *bronzing*, and head coverings for females employed in *bronzing*, which shall be

collected at the end of every day's work, and be washed or renewed at least once every week.' The 1913 rules for the manufacture and decoration of pottery required overalls and aprons:

The occupier shall provide and maintain suitable aprons of a waterproof or similar material which can be sponged daily, for all dippers, dippers' assistants, and ware cleaners; provided that, if the front of the overall supplied to any such worker in pursuance of these regulations is made of a material which can be sponged daily, no separate apron need be provided for that worker.

Two sets of regulations were issued for the tanning industry; first the 1918 Tanning (Two-Bath Process) Welfare Order, which ruled:

The occupier shall provide and maintain in good condition for the use of all persons coming into contact with chrome solutions, rubber or leather aprons and bib, and rubber boots, or leather leggings which will protect open tops and laceholes of clogs or boots, and for those who are continually immersing their hands in the solution, loose-fitting rubber gloves of suitable length.

This was modified slightly by the Tanning Welfare Order of 1930, which said:

The apron and leg coverings shall be such as to afford effective protection from the wet or damp of the process in which the worker is engaged. Leg covering shall include vamps, spats, or other efficient means to prevent water entering the uppers of the workers' footwear. The gloves shall be of rubber or leather, except where leather is specified by the Schedule.

As well as protective clothes, employers had to provide accommodation for the workers' own clothes, as is made clear in the order of 15 August 1919 for the welfare of employees in the fruit preservation industry:

The occupier shall provide and maintain in good condition suitable protective clothing for the use of all persons employed in the processes of preparing and boiling fruit, filling, finishing and covering filled vessels, spinning on tops, and in any wet process.
The occupier shall provide and maintain for the use of all persons employed in the factory suitable accommodation for clothing put off during working hours, with adequate arrangements for drying the clothing if wet.

88. 'A Carmarthenshire Cocklewoman', from Gertrude Jekyll's *Old English Household Life*, 1925. The survival of breeching into the twentieth century, with the skirt tied between the legs. A sacking apron is pulled up to act as an extra container. Her jacket is probably a sort of bedgown, and she shows the Welsh habit of wearing a hat over a headscarf or shawl. The clogs were just as common at the mills in Lancashire.

The welfare of laundry workers was considered in the order issued in 1920:

The occupier shall provide and maintain in good and clean condition, for the use of all persons employed in processes involving exposure to wet, suitable protective clothing, including waterproof boots or clogs, and also, for persons engaged in sorting soiled linen, suitable overalls or aprons with bibs and armlets from wrist to elbow.

The Hollow-ware and Galvanizing Welfare Order of 1921 required 'suitable protective clothing for all persons employed in wet processes, including for persons coming into contact with acid or acid solutions, finger stalls (or where necessary) gloves of rubber or other suitable material, aprons of acid-proof material, and clogs'.

The glass-bevelling industry was instructed in March 1921 to provide cloakrooms for the workers' clothes and for the aprons they worked in. Lead compound manufacturers also received orders in that year to provide 'sufficient and suitable overalls and head coverings, and clean respirators, and . . . cause them to be worn as directed in Regulation 25.' The Vehicle Painting Regulations for 1926 required that 'Every person employed in *painting* shall wear an overall which he shall remove before partaking of food or leaving the premises.' The Asbestos Industry Regulations of 1931 required breathing apparatus to be worn in chambers with loose asbestos, when cleaning cylinders and filling asbestos insulating mattresses, and also, 'There shall be provided and maintained for the use of all persons employed in the cleaning of dust settling and filtering chambers, tunnels and ducts, suitable overalls and head coverings.' Finally, the Factories Act of 1938 set new rules for bottling. 'There shall be provided and maintained in good condition for the use of persons engaged in filling bottles or syphons (*a*) suitable face guards to protect the face, neck and throat, and (*b*) suitable gauntlets for both arms to protect the whole hand and arm.'

At long last the welfare of workers was given serious thought. While the early rules above indicate only protective overalls, by 1918 the regulations had become more detailed, indicating what garments and footwear were required, and this was to be the model afterwards. The early respirators were simply pieces of cloth, but by the 1930s breathing apparatus was common. No longer was the responsibility for protecting themselves left entirely to the workers who could resort only to leather or canvas aprons, clogs or, by the later nineteenth century, to overall suits. They could not tell what the long-term effects of new industrial techniques would have on them, so at last the government accepted responsibility, after campaigning by the Liberals and then the new Labour Party. The collation of all the acts, regulations and rules for special industries was undertaken by Alexander Redgrave in 1878, and his work continues today with frequent new editions by judges and lawyers, as the bible for industry.[22]

Conservative coastal communities tried to resist change. In Wales in 1932 H.V. Morton found that 'Old women, who look as though they are waiting for Rembrandt to come and paint them, sit in the Saturday market in Swansea. They wear black hats, shawls, and aprons. Their gnarled hands rest on baskets full of boiled cockles.' On the Gower Peninsula summer was cockle time, and winter mussel time, and their harvesting was entirely women's work, as it had been for centuries. The beds were four to five miles out in the bay, so at low tide at Pen Clawdd 200 women, mostly on donkeys, congregated and galloped out to sea to start digging. They looked like Arabs, as they tied their shawls about their heads with a band. Short skirts, coarse black stockings without feet, and rubber-soled light shoes completed the attire. When Morton produced a camera the old women hid their faces, for they still considered photography to mean bad luck. In 1925 Gertrude Jekyll said that the cockle women in Carmarthenshire looked like those of the east coast of England, pulling their skirts up to tie with string between their legs, and wearing clogs, thick stockings, and shawls with low hats on top. She did wonder why they did not wear short skirts, as it was 1925, but old habits die hard. Breeching skirts lasted into the twentieth century.[23]

For fishermen and sailors alike it was a time of great sadness as they witnessed the death of the wind-powered ships – the China tea clippers and the square riggers on the Australian wheat run which numbered 140 in 1921 but shrank to 20 by 1933 – as coal and oil-powered vessels ousted them from the trade routes. Traditional fishing craft were replaced by steam trawlers, and the barges began to lose trade to powered vessels, railways and roads. Frank Mason drew the Deal luggers, scoffies, Fraserburgh herring boats of Fifie type, Mounts Bay luggers, North Sea bawleys, Essex smacks, Thames barges, beach yawls, Yorkshire cobles and herring mules, zulus, Lowestoft drifters, billyboy schooners and coasting ketches for Frank Carr's aptly named *Vanishing Craft* in 1934.

Merchant seamen and fishermen both had to pay for their own clothes, so as soon as a sailor was hired it was off to the seaman's tailor for a pair of rubber sea boots, a blue jersey, overalls or dungarees, heavy clothing like pilot coats for going round the Horn, oilskins in yellow, towels, soap, blankets and bedding.[24] Jim Uglow, bargemaster, worked on the Thames barges between the wars, the last period of their commercial survival. Cement was carried from Chatham and Maidstone cement works to London Docks for the export trade. The works (including one owned by my grandfather's uncles) were gradually bought up by Associated Portland Cement, so the cement conveyance began to depend on one employer's wishes. Sweaters, canvas trousers, oilskins, and either the cloth cap of the ordinary working man, or a peaked cap or a woolly hat, constituted the costume. Uglow bought his first navy blue suit when he was 14. One thing he learnt the hard way was that when loading pitch it was advisable to cover the face and hands with muslin, because it stuck to the skin. On fishing boats the long knitted stockings and footless leg warmers continued as essential wear for fishing off Iceland. The barges often crossed the Channel to take pitch, cement and stone to the Continent, and plied along the coast to Portland and Plymouth. During both wars the Navy from Harwich and Portsmouth directed when and where barges and fishing boats could travel. The

89. James Jerché, 'The Cocklewomen of Penclawdd', from H.V. Morton's *In Search of Wales*, 1932. Two hundred women rode out to the cockle beds at low tide, their faces wrapped up against the cold wind and spray, which caused people to say that they looked like Arabs. The only suggestion of 1932 is the glimpse of a stocking in artificial silk, rather than wool. Shawls and mantles were still used as protection against the weather despite the invention of mackintoshes.

Germans often laid mines under cover of fog, and the German fleet shelled Hartlepool, Scarborough and Whitby in December 1914 from the fog, killing 100 civilians. There could be some arguments between old salts and flashy young naval officers about sailing orders, and Uglow remembered one such with the officer of an MTB who zoomed about wearing his peaked officer's cap and striped pyjamas. The most widespread garment of naval origin made its appearance in the 1890s, when the Navy started to introduce destroyers. These fast vessels lacked amenities and an extra stout weather coat was devised, using duffel cloth in a shapeless form with a hood and toggle fastening, loose enough to fit over the uniform. The earliest example I have found was in a naval photograph of 1897. While it did not spread to civilians in large numbers until after the Second World War, it was in existence some 50 years earlier, and is now called the duffle coat. This typifies the increasing casualness in naval dress, which the merchant navy of course imitated. Frock coats were now worn only for levées and royal visits to the fleet. Monkey jackets, to the hip, appeared in 1889 as undress, and in 1891 mess jackets for evening were allowed. The former reflected the civilian lounge suit; the latter passed over into civilian fashion for evening in the 1930s and were adopted by some dance bands like Joe Loss at the Astoria. They were termed Park Lane mess jackets, and retained the naval epaulettes. When bargemaster Uglow was

awarded the MBE he was told to report to the Palace dressed in the uniform of a captain in the merchant navy, which he considered a great expense, so afterwards he took the gold braid off to convert it into his Sunday best dark blue lounge suit. The very fact that this was possible shows just how close the uniform and civilian suit had become, unlike earlier periods when frock coats distinguished superior from inferior. It also reflected the gradual democratization of the services, with officers no longer coming exclusively from titled families.[25]

Servants

The early twentieth century saw an enormous change in the tradition that wealth meant land, huge houses and vast numbers of servants. The agricultural depression had reduced the value of land, and many landowners suffered as a result and had to sell up or else economize and reduce their staff. Those families whose ancestors had spread their money into property, mines, minerals, banks and shares, survived better and could still maintain a large establishment, but even here difficulties arose. The First World War killed off almost a whole generation, so there was a shortage of young men to act as footmen, grooms, stableboys or gardeners. Moreover, this meant that traditional male jobs in town like secretaries, clerks and shop assistants, were available for women in large numbers. Those who had done such work during the war preferred its regular hours to the long days and late nights in service, so there was also a shortage of girls to become housemaids. In 1894 the Liberals introduced death duties as the first attack on inherited wealth, and the demolition of

90. 'American lard being unloaded into barges from the Liberty ship Charles E. Eliot', 1944. These dockers at the Royal Docks wear dungarees, but one has adopted an American windcheater jacket and henceforth many American casual garments were going to be introduced into Britain and Europe. The Liberty ships were simple mass-produced carriers that ferried supplies across the Atlantic.

91. Victor Stewart, 'Assault boat builders at Ranelagh Yacht Yard, Wootton, Isle of Wight', 1945. These ladies can look forward to the end of the war, and have evidently saved their precious make-up for the photographer. They sport a mixture of all-in-one overalls with trousers, dungarees, and overall coats. Clogs and shoes can be seen, while fashionable hairstyles were not rationed.

Hamilton Palace by its Duke was one in a series of reductions of country seats.

Thus servants could now pick and choose to some extent, and demanded labour-saving devices such as vacuum cleaners, electric light, gas cookers, and even central heating, which all helped to reduce the labour involved in running a house. The First World War also caused shortages; hair powder based on flour went out, as the flour was needed for bread, and silk stockings were difficult to import, so footmen had to wear trousers. The eighteenth-century finery was now brought out only for very special occasions. New wealth from furs and property like that of the Astors could maintain an old-style establishment, but there were now fewer of them. In 1928 their five homes comprised Cliveden in Buckinghamshire; 4 St

James's Square, London; Rest Harrow at Sandwich, Kent; 2 Elliot Terrace, Plymouth; and Tarbert Lodge on Jura in the Inner Hebrides. These were run by the controller, accountant and two assistant accountants in London. Cliveden was maintained by a staff of 25, including a part-time clockwinder. The gardens employed 20 men. Three foresters and two gamekeepers worked on the estate, the stables had four grooms, the garage five chauffeurs, and a boatman. The home farm had 27, including the stud. The domestic staff amounted to 32. As the Astors were a political family there was a total of seven secretaries spread throughout the houses. The maintenance staff at Sandwich amounted to three, at St James's Square to eight, at Plymouth to four, and at the Jura to seven. Additional staff would be hired when giving dinner parties or garden parties.

The tailor for the household liveries was Robert Lillico of Maddox Street in London. The butler wore a navy blue tail coat, black kneebreeches, black stockings and black pumps as his dress livery, but everyday livery was evening dress. The footmen's everyday livery was a brown suit with brass buttons with red and yellow piping down the side of the trousers, and a waistcoat striped with yellow and white. For dress livery they retained the coat and waistcoat, but wore kneebreeches, white stockings and black pumps. The valet and groom of the chambers wore morning dress during the day with black coats and tails, stiff shirts, black waistcoats and striped trousers, and in the evening donned black tie and tails. Many families liked the 'pepper and salt' grey and white pinhead suiting for morning suits for male servants. The Astors' liveried male servants were entitled to long johns under their trousers, but if they did not care for them the tailor gave them a glass of whisky in lieu (and probably still charged for them). The nanny at Cliveden wore a white blouse and grey skirt in the morning, and a dark grey dress for afternoons. She repaired the children's clothes, in the same way that the lady's maid had to look after the mistress's clothes. In Lady Astor's case it was Rose, Rosina Harrison, whose mother wisely sent her to a dressmaker's at 16 to learn the skills, so she made some of her mistress's clothes in addition to repairing, ironing, cleaning, and organizing them, as well as being responsible for the jewellery. The official dressmaker was Madame Rémond of Beauchamp Place, but sometimes Rose was sent to Marks and Spencer's. It was still a case of print frocks for morning and black dresses for afternoon for maids, although they grew slightly shorter into the Twenties. The lady's maid, however, was still allowed to look more fashionable like her mistress, with a twin-set and skirt during the day, and a dark dress in the evening. One string of pearls or beads and a watch were the limit for jewellery, and no make-up. It was still the custom for maids to receive the mistress's old clothes to wear or sell.[26]

Liveries were still given, as in the mediaeval tradition, in spring and autumn, usually March/April and October for everyday livery, and once a year for evening livery, overcoats, and tweed suits. The most unfortunate were still the scullery maids, scrubbing away with soda that made their hands and arms red, as nobody gave them rubber gloves. In the kitchens whites ruled for coats, aprons, hats, and jackets.

The pattern of entertaining changed. Long visits

for weeks at a time had been the tradition when travel was difficult and expensive, but the advent of the motor car brought about the weekend visit. If guests did not bring their own servants, footmen and maids had to take them on in addition to their normal duties. Picnics were popular at such weekends in the summer, with the employers lounging about in casual dress, but waited on by menservants in black suits and bowler hats, or housemaids in black frocks with white collar and cuffs and the white cap, looking decidedly out of place in the open country. The servant was expected to look smart at all times, regardless how 'undressed' the master was.

On farms with servants, the dress was usually very simple. When Mrs Watkins was servant on a farm in Herefordshire around 1920, she wore a blouse and skirt, red flannel petticoats, thick black stockings, and had a coat for going out. Sacking aprons, called 'harden aprons', mattered in that county, for the boiled flour bags were very white, and a freshly washed apron was the sign of the hardworking woman. It was still the tradition for whole families to enter service, often in the same department, so that Alfred Tinsley followed his father and grandfather into the hunting stables at Melton in Yorkshire, and became a gentleman's groom. He received every year a stable suit of jacket, kneebreeches and leggings, and a hunting suit of black jacket, Bedford cord kneebreeches, hunting boots and a bowler hat. He was very proud of his turn-out, for what other members of the working class got new clothes every year? In 1931 one million people were still in service, but another mass call-up was looming ahead that would sweep them into the army or the factories.[27] The biggest change was yet to come, but working dress will last as long as the human species does.

92. 'It is going to take more than Hitler's bombs to shift this lady from her pitch', c.1944. Clothes rationing imposed the same quality of clothes for all, so this Piccadilly flower seller is better dressed than any of her predecessors, with an overcoat and stylish hat instead of an apron and shawl. She is closer to fashion than would have been thought possible before the war.

Range of occupations, 1500–1700

Actors
Animal keepers
Apothecaries
Artists
Authors
Barbers and barber surgeons
Bargees
Basketmakers
Bath house attendants
Bishops
Blacksmiths
Boat builders
Bonnet makers
Booksellers and binders
Brass merchants
Brewers and brewsters
Butlers
Button and buckle makers
Candle makers
Cannon casters
Carpet weavers
Carters
Charcoalmen
Cheesemen
Chess makers
Chimney sweeps
Clergymen
Clerks
Clock makers
Coach builders
Coachmen
Cooked meat sellers
Copper merchants
Dancers
Dancing masters
Dentists
Designers
Diplomats
Dockers
Doctors
Domestics

Drawing masters
Dressmakers
Drovers
Dustmen and garbagers
Embroiderers
Engravers
Ferrymen
Fishermen
Fishmongers
Fishwives
Footmen
Fruiterers
Furniture makers
Furriers
Gardeners
Gilders
Glaziers
Goldsmiths
Gravediggers
Greengrocers
Grocers
Gunsmiths
Hairdresssers
Heralds
House builders
Innkeepers
Ironmongers
Joiners
Journeymen
Lace makers
Launderers
Lawyers
Linen drapers
Locksmiths
Maids
Managers
Mariners
Mattress makers
Mercers
Merchant tailors
Midwives

Milkmaids
Nurses
Ostlers
Painters
Pamphleteers
Paper makers
Parchment makers
Pastrycooks
Paviors
Pedlars
Pin makers
Pipe makers
Playwrights
Polishers
Pork butchers
Prostitutes
Ratcatchers
Roadmenders
Scribes
Scriveners
Secretaries
Silversmiths
Simplers
Spinsters and spinners

Stationers
Street traders
Tavern keepers
Teachers
Toy makers
Translators
Upholsterers
Vintners
Wagoners
Wainwrights
Washerwomen
Water carriers
Watermen
Wax chandlers
Woodmongers
Wool carders
Wool merchants
Wool packers

Watch makers spread during the sixteenth century.
Imports from the New World led to the introduction
of tobacconists, and exploration saw Indian/exotica
shops opening up.

APPENDIX II

Some women warriors

For thousands of years women have done 'masculine' jobs. This applied in particular to tribal leaders.

Sparetha of the Scythians led her people against the Persians, about 500 BC.

Tomyris, Queen of the Massagetae, defeated the Persian Emperor Cyrus the Great and cut his head off in 528 BC.

Queen Artemisia commanded five ships from Halicarnassus, Cos, Nisyra, and Calydna in the fleet of Xerxes, and was his naval consultant, in 480 BC.

Boudicca, Queen of the Iceni, tried to drive the Romans out of Britain in 61 AD.

King Alfred the Great's daughter, Aethelflaed, Lady of the Mercians, was commander-in-chief for the defence of the West Coast, and liberated Derby in 917 and Leicester in 918 from the Danes, and blocked the Vikings' raids.

Duchess Gaita of Lombardy rode to war with her husband Duke Robert, and wore full armour in 1080.

An unnamed woman was in charge of the defence of Otranto when it was being besieged in 1107.

Scores of women were left in charge of estates during the Crusades when the men were away.

The Rijksmuseum, Amsterdam, has a portrait of Kenau Simonsdr Hasselaer, aged 47, armed to the teeth in 1573 (cat. A502). She led her Women's Brigade to defend the walls of Haarlem during the Spanish attack on 31 January 1573.

During the English Civil War Charlotte, Countess of Derby, defended Lathom House against the Roundheads in 1643–4, and the Isle of Man in 1651.

During the French Civil War (La Fronde), Anne Marie Louise, Duchess de Montpensier, took Orléans, and fired the cannons of the Bastille against the royalists.

For the pirates Mary Read and Ann Bonny, see chapter 3.

All the above women appeared in their own clothing, but there have been examples of women pretending to be men in order to join the Army or Navy, or work at labouring or on merchant ships: see chapter 5.

Glossary of terms not explained in the text

Callimanco   Scottish glossy surface cloth where
    pattern is not visible from other side
Dornick   Table linen and towels used in Scotland
Fingrims   Fingroms, Aberdeenshire woollen
    worsted cloth
Pottage   Any food boiled in a pot
Scrip   Bag or satchel as carried by shepherds
Temmin   Temming, a coarse thin cloth

Notes

1 Before 1600

1 John Aubrey, *Brief Lives*, ed. O. Lawson Dick, Penguin English Library, 1972, p. 95.
2 William Langland, *Piers Ploughman*, ed. Stella Brook, Manchester University Press, 1975, *passim*.
3 Sir James Murray, *A New Dictionary of English based upon historical principles*, Clarendon Press, Oxford, 1928.
4 Paul Hentzner, *A Journey into England in the Year 1598*, trs. ed. Horace Walpole, Strawberry Hill, 1757, p. 79.
5 *The Life and Times of Anthony à Wood, antiquary of Oxford 1632–1695*, described by himself, ed. Andrew Clark, Clarendon Press, Oxford, 1891, vol. II, pp. 84–5.
6 Charles Clode, *Memorials of the Guild of Merchant Tailors*, Harrison & Sons, 1875, p. 208.
7 *England as seen by Foreigners in the days of Elizabeth and James the First*, ed. William Brenchley Rye, John Russell Smith, 1865, p. 69.
8 Mary Bateson, *Records of the Borough of Leicester 1327–1509*, Clay & Sons, 1901, vol. II, pp. 154, 291.
9 William Gates, *An Illustrated History of Portsmouth*, intro. Sir William Besant, *Hampshire Telegraph*, 1900, p. 167.
10 Aubrey Burstall, *A History of Mechanical Engineering*, Faber & Faber, 1963, p. 145.
11 Fynes Moryson, *Itinerary*, trs. from Latin by himself, John Beale, Aldersgate Street, 1617, vol. I, p. 45.
12 Christopher Lloyd, *The British Seaman*, Collins, 1968, *passim*; *The Oxford Companion to Ships and the Sea*, ed. Peter Kemp, OUP, 1979, pp. 741–4.
13 F. Furnivall, *The Records of Chaucer*, Kegan Paul, Trench, Tubner, 1900, pp. 1–4.
14 *Ibid.*, pp. 64–8.
15 *Statutes at Large*, ed. Danby Pickering, Cambridge, 1762 onwards, 110 volumes, 1225–1869.
16 David Blewitt, 'Records of Drama at Winchester and Eton 1397–1576', *Theatre Notebook*, XXXVIII, no. 3, 1984, pp. 135–43.
17 *England as seen by Foreigners, op. cit.*, pp. 13, 196–7.

2 The Seventeenth Century

1 John Aubrey, *op. cit.*, p. 41.
2 Samuel Pepys, *Diary*, transcribed R. Latham & W. Matthews, Bell, 1970, vol. VIII, 14 July 1667.
3 Roger North, *Autobiography*, ed. A. Jessop, David Nutt, 1887, p. 131.
4 Celia Fiennes, *Illustrated Journeys c.1682–1712*, ed. C. Morris, Macdonald, Webb & Bower, 1984, p. 196.
5 Fynes Moryson, *op. cit.*, vol. III, pp. 180–1.
6 Anthony Count Hamilton, *Memoirs of Count Gramont*, ed. A. Fea, 1906, p. 285; John Ives, *Select Papers relating chiefly to English Antiquities*, 1773, p. 39.
7 Fynes Moryson, *op. cit.*, vol. I, p. 199, vol. III, pp. 177–9.
8 Pepys, *op. cit.*, vol. I, 23 May 1660.
9 Fynes Moryson, *op. cit.*, vol. III, pp. 177–9.
10 Gervase Markham, *The English Huswife, contayning the inward and outward vertues which ought to be in a compleat woman*, John Beale for Roger Jackson, at the Great Conduit Fleet Street, 1615, *passim*.
11 *The House and Farm Accounts of the Shuttleworths of Gawthorpe Hall Lancashire*, ed. J. Harland, Chetham Society, 1856, pp. 132, 148.
12 *Rural Economy in Yorkshire in 1641, Farming & Account Books of Henry Best of Elmswell in the East Riding*, ed. C. Robinson, Surtees Society, 1857, pp. 133–4.
13 Diana de Marly, 'Some Aristocratic Clothing Accounts of the Restoration Period in England', *Waffen und Kostümkunde*, Munich, 1976, pp. 105–17.

14 Fynes Moryson, *op. cit.*, pp. 185–6, 197, vol. I.

15 Elizabeth Cellier, *A Scheme for a Royal Hospital*, June 1687, Harleian Miscellany, vol. IV, T. Osborne, 1754, pp. 136–40; Jane Sharp, *The Compleat Midwife's Companion*, 1671, reprinted 1725, John Marshall, *passim*.

16 John Aubrey, *op. cit.*, p. 314.

17 Samuel Pepys, *op. cit.*, 26 July 1664.

18 John Aubrey, *op. cit.*, p. 338.

19 Diana de Marly, 'The Status of Actors under Charles II of Great Britain: an Examination of the Livery Accounts of the Great Wardrobe', *Theatre Research (Recherches Théatrales)*, vol. XIV, 1980, pp. 45–53.

20 Count Lorenzo Magalotti, *Travels of Cosmo the Third Grand Duke of Tuscany through England during the Reign of Charles the Second in 1669*, anon. trs. 1821, pp. 323, 295. The original is in the Laurentian Library, Florence.

21 Ned Ward, *The London Spy*, 1698–1700, vol. II, p. 168.

22 *Ibid.*, pt. 2, p. 27.

23 Diana de Marly, 'Fashionable Suppliers 1660–1700, Leading Tailors and Clothing Tradesmen of the Restoration Period', *The Antiquaries' Journal*, vol. LVIII, part II, 1979, pp. 333–51.

24 John Aubrey, *The Natural History and Antiquities of the County of Surrey*, 1673–92, E. Curl, 1719, intro. 1st vol. by John Evelyn.

25 Thomas Savery, *The Miner's Friend; or an Engine to raise Water by Fire*, 1702, pp. 6–7, 62–3.

26 Guy Miège, *The New State of England under Their Majesties King William and Queen Mary*, 1691, pp. 18–19.

27 Fynes Moryson, *op. cit.*, vol. III, p. 78.

28 Celia Fiennes, *op. cit.*, p. 165.

29 Alice Clark, *Working Life of Women in the Seventeenth Century*, 1919, reprint Routledge & Kegan Paul, 1982, pp. 228–9.

30 Christopher Lloyd, *op. cit.*, pp. 64, 99.

31 George Everett, *Encouragement for Seamen and Mariners*, 1695, Harleian Miscellany, vol. IV, T. Osborne, 1745, pp. 370–80.

32 John Evelyn, *The Diary*, ed. de Beer, Oxford, 1959, pp. 71, 92–3.

33 Ned Ward, *op. cit.*, vol. II, 'A Frolick to Horn Fair'.

34 Thomas Morer, *A Short Account of Scotland*, Thomas Newborough at the Golden Ball, St Paul's churchyard, 1702, pp. 7–13.

35 Janet Arnold, *Lost from her Majesties Back*, the Costume Society, 1980, pp. 24, 36.

36 Pepys, *op. cit.*, 2 September 1667.

37 Aubrey, *op. cit.*, p. 308.

38 Bundle 910, the Lauderdale accounts, Leicester, courtesy of Sir Humphry Tollemache Bt.

39 Diana de Marly, *op. cit.*, 'Status of Actors'.

40 Public Record Office E/101/435/6, pp. 2–3.

41 Aubrey, *op. cit.*, pp. 461–2.

3   1700–1795

1 *The Purefoy Letters 1735–53*, ed. G. Eland, Sidgwick & Jackson, 1931, II, p. 318, no. 473; II, p. 321, no. 479.

2 Daniel Defoe, *A Tour thro' the whole Island of Great Britain*, 2nd edn, 1738, II, p. 237.

3 César de Saussure, *A Foreign View of England in the Reigns of George I and George II*, trs. Mme van Muyden, John Murray, 1902, p. 219; *Purefoy* above, II, p. 308, no. 457.

4 Duke François de La Rochefoucauld, *A Frenchman in England in 1784*, trs. S. Roberts from his *Mélanges sur l'Angleterre*, intro. Jean Marchand, Cambridge, 1933, p. 4.

5 William Marshall, *The Rural Economy of Norfolk*, T. Cadell, 1787, I, p. 40.

6 Samuel Curwen, *Letters and Journals*, ed. G. Ward, New York, 1842, p. 389.

7 Sophie von La Roche, *Sophie in London in 1786*, trs. Clare Williams, intro. G.M. Trevelyan, Jonathan Cape, 1933, p. 90.

8 Saussure, *op. cit.*, pp. 190–1.

9 *Ibid.*, p. 289.

10 Jo Haynes, *A View of the Present State of the Clothing Trade in England with Remarks on the Causes and Pernicious Consequences of its Decay*, 1706, pp. 23–36, and *Great Britain's Glory*, 1715.

11 Ann Buck & Harry Matthews, 'Pocket Guides to Fashion', *Costume*, XVIII, 1984, pp. 35–58.

12 Carl Philip Moritz, *Travels through various Parts of England*, 1782, vol. IV of Mavor's *The British Tourist*, 1798, E. Newbery, p. 82.

13 Battista Angeloni, *Letters on the English Nation*, anon. trs. 1755, I, p. 34.

14 John Macky, *A Journey through England*, J. Hooke at the Flower de Luce, Fleet St, 1722, II, p. 238.

15 Daniel Defoe, *The Complete English Tradesman*, Charles Rivington at the Crown & Bible, St Paul's Churchyard, 1727, pp. 287–303.

16 John Gay, *Trivia: or, The Art of Walking the Streets of London*, S. Powell, Castle Lane, Dublin, 1727, *passim*.

17 Saussure, *op. cit.*, p. 277.

18 *Ibid.*, pp. 233, 323; de Marly, *op. cit.*, 'Fashionable Suppliers'.

19 Frances Burney, *Evelina, The History of a Young Lady's Entrance into the World*, 1778, ed. Bloom, OUP, 1968, p. 27.

20 S. La Roche, *op. cit.*, p. 93.

21 Jonas Hanway, *A Sentimental History of Chimney Sweepers in London and Westminster*, Dodsley Pall Mall, Sewell Cornhill, 1785, pp. xx–xxi, 27.

22 Angeloni, *op. cit.*, II, p. 219; Jean Le Blanc, *Letters on the English and French Nations*, Richard James, Dublin, 1757, I, p. 13.

23 Barrie Trinder, *The Industrial Revolution in Shropshire*, Phillimore, 1973, p. 21 *et seq.*

24 Zacharias Conrad von Uffenbach, *London in 1710*, trs. W. Quenel & M. Mare, Faber & Faber, 1934, pp. 54–5.

25 Roger North, *op. cit.*, p. 183.

26 Historical Commission on Manuscripts 15th Report, appendix VI, p. 345.

27 Frank Atkinson, *Some Aspects of the 18th-century Woollen and Worsted Trade in Halifax*, Halifax Museum, 1956, intro.

28 G. Miège, *The Present State of Scotland*, J. Brotherton, A. Bettesworth, C. Hitch, G. Strahan, W. Mears, R. Ward, E. Syman, J. Clark, 1738, pp. 20–40.

29 John Macky, *A Journey through Scotland*, J. Pemberton at the Buck & Son, J. Hooke, 1723, p. 194.

30 Charles Hadfield, *British Canals*, seventh edn, David & Charles, Newton Abbot, 1984, p. 32.

31 Arthur Young, *Six Month's Tour throughout the North of England*, 1771, IV, pp. 321–2.

32 Frances Burney, *The Early Diary 1768–1778*, ed. A. Ellis, George Bell & Sons, 1889, I, pp. 204, 238.

33 Burney, *op. cit.*, pp. 268–9.

34 Daniel Defoe, *General History of the Robberies and Murders of the Most notorious Pyrates*, C. Rivington at Bible & Crown, St Paul's Churchyard, J. Lacey at the Shop Temple Gate, J. Stone next Crown Coffee House Gray's Inn, 1724, p. 117.

35 Christopher Lloyd, *op. cit.*, pp. 235–6.

36 *Ibid.*, pp. 258–61.

37 Commander W.E. May R.N., *The Dress of Naval Officers*, National Maritime Museum, HMSO, 1966, p. 4.

38 Giles Jacob, *The Country Gentleman's Vade Mecum*, William Taylor at the Ship, Paternoster Row, 1717, pp. 44 *et seq.*

39 C.H. & M. Baker, *The Life and Circumstances of James Brydges, First Duke of Chandos*, Clarendon Press, Oxford, pp. 175–204.

40 La Rochefoucauld, *op. cit.*, pp. 25–6.

41 Thomas Seaton, *The Conduct of Servants in Great Families*, Tim Godwin at the Queen's Head, St Dunstan's Fleet St, 1720, pp. 159–60.

42 Pierre Grosley, *A Tour to London: or, New Observations on England*, trs. Dr Nugent, Lockyer Davis, 1772, I, pp. 74–5.

43 Moritz, *op. cit.*, p. 97.

44 Daniel Defoe, *Everybody's Business*, T. Warner at the Black Boy, Paternoster Row, 1725, pp. 4–15.

45 Count Frederick Kielmansegge, *Diary of a Journey to England 1761–2*, trs. Countess Kielmansegg, Longmans Green & Co., 1902, pp. 53–4.

46 Jonas Hanway, *An Essay on Tea*, 1757, p. 272.

47 Jonas Hanway, *Letters on the Importance of the Rising Generation*, 1767, II, p. 173.

48 Robert Dodsley, *Servitude: A Poem*, T. Worrall, at Judge's Head, St Dunstan's, 1728, pp. 21–8.

49 Grosley, *op. cit.*

50 *Purefoy Letters*, *op. cit.*, II, p. 308, no. 456, p. 310, no. 461.

51 Revd. William Cole, *The Blecheley Diary 1765–7*, ed. F. Stokes, Constable, 1931, pp. 70–1, 150.

52 Timothy Burrell, *Journal and Account Book 1683–1714*, ed. R.W. Blencoe, Sussex Archaeological Society, 1850, XXXIV, pp. 136–7.

53 Thomas Newte, *A Tour in England and Scotland*, 1785, vol. IV of Mavor, p. 157.

54 J. Jean Hecht, *The Domestic Servant in Eighteenth Century England*, Routledge & Kegan Paul, 1980, p. 56.

4 The Industrial Revolution 1795–1845

1 John Housman, *Topographical Description of Cumberland, Westmorland, and Lancashire*, Francis Jollie, Carlisle, 1800, pp. 70–1.

2 Francis Heath, *Peasant Life in the West of England*, Sampson, Low, Marston, Searle, Rimington, 1880, pp. 53–4.

3 *Ibid.*, pp. 228–30.

4 Richard Warner, *A Walk through Wales in August 1797*, E. Cruttwell, Bath, 1798, pp. 32, 162, 181.

5 Arthur Aikin, *A Journal of A Tour through North Wales*, J. Johnson, 1797, p. 81.

6 Samuel Bamford, *Early Days*, Simpkin, Marshall & Co., 1849, pp. 5, 99, 111, 143–8, 183.

7 Samuel Bamford, *Tawk o' Seawth Lankeshur*, 1850, p. 7.

8 Donald Ross, *The Glengary Evictions*, W.G. Blackie, Glasgow, 1853, *passim.*

9 William Cobbett, *Rural Rides*, ed. G.D. & M. Cole, Peter Davies, 1930, vol. I, pp. 13, 17, 36, 78, 93, 159.

10 Carl Philip Moritz, *op. cit.*, p. 68.

11 Samuel Bamford, *Early Days*, pp. 81, 67.

12 Charles Dickens, *Sketches by Boz*, Chapman & Hall, 1839, p. 79.

13 See my *Fashion for Men*, Batsford, 1985, chapters IV & V.

14 Henry Hanson, *The Canal Boatmen 1760–1914*, Allan Sutton, Gloucester, 1984, p. 166.

15 K. Pennant, *A Tour in Scotland*, third edition, W. Eyres, Warrington, 1774, pp. 117, 190–3.

16 William Cobbett, *op. cit.*, vol. III, p. 818.

17 Charles Vancouver, *General View of the Agriculture of the County of Devon*, Richard Phillips, 1808, p. 385.

18 Samuel Smiles, *The Life of George Stephenson*, John Murray, 1864, pp. 250–2.

19 *First Report of the Commissioners*, Children's Employment Commission; Mines, W. Clowes, HMSO, 1842, pp. 26–47, 162.

20 Benjamin Silliman, *Journal of Travels in England, Holland and Scotland, in 1805–6*, S. Converse, Newhaven, 1820.

21 Henry Mayhew, *London Labour and the London Poor*, 1851–62, vol. II.

22 Dr Frederick Wendeborn, *A View of England*, G. & J. Robinson, 1791, p. 120; George Nicholls, *Eight Letters on the Management of the Poor*, S. & J. Ridge, Newark, 1822, p. 19.

23 Anne Born, *South Devon*, V. Gollancz, 1983, p. 126.

24 Stephen Deuchar, *Paintings, Politics and Porter; Samuel Whitbread and British Art*, Catalogue of Museum of London exhibition, 1984, p. 43.

25 Christopher Lloyd, *op. cit.*, pp. 208, 272; Brian Hall, *Mr Midshipman Clark*, BBC Scotland, Radio 4, broadcast on 6 April 1985.

26 Henry Angelo, *Reminiscences*, Kegan Paul, Trench, Trubner & Co., 1904, p. 221.

27 C. Vancouver, *op. cit.*, p. 388; Portsmouth Chamber of Commerce, centenary catalogue, 1979.

28 W. Gates, *op. cit.*, p. 537.

29 William Austin, *Letters from London*, W. Pelham, Boston, 1804, p. 10; Silliman, *op. cit.*, pp. 218–19.

30 Wendeborn, *op. cit.*, p. 359.

31 John Macdonald, *Travels*, 1790, ed. E. Ross & E. Power, Routledge & Son, 1927, *passim*.

32 Johann Archenholz, *Picture of England*, Dublin, 1791, p. 207.

33 Adeline Hartcup, *Below Stairs in the Great Country Houses*, Sidgwick & Jackson, 1980, pp. 85–7.

34 Merlin Waterson, *The Servants' Hall*, Routledge & Kegan Paul, 1980, illustrations 71, 86, 95.

5   The Heavy Industrial Age

1 Kenneth Hudson, *Patriotism with Profit, British Agricultural Societies*, Hugh Evelyn, 1972, pp. 53–7, 123.

2 Joseph Arch, *The Story of his Life*, preface by the Countess of Warwick, Hutchinson, 1898, p. 31.

3 Richard Jefferies, *Wild Life in a Southern County*, no date, Collins, p. 113.

4 Gertrude Jekyll, *Old West Surrey*, Longman, Green & Co., 1904, p. 258.

5 Edwin Grey, *Cottage Life in a Hertfordshire Village*, preface by Sir E. Russell, Fisher Knight & Co., Gainsborough Press, St Albans, 1934, pp. 30–1.

6 John Atkinson, *Forty Years in a Moorland Parish*, Macmillan, 1891, p. 112 n.

7 Nancy Mitford, ed., *The Stanleys of Alderley, letters 1851–65*, Chapman & Hall, 1939, p. 2, letter 1.

8 Thomas Hardy, *The Dorset Farm Labourer Past and Present*, Dorset Agricultural Workers' Union, 1884, pp. 8–9.

9 Joseph Arch, *op. cit.*, p. 69.

10 *Mineral Map & General Statistics of New South Wales*, Thomas Richards, Sydney, 1876, unpaginated.

11 Edwin Grey, *op. cit.*, pp. 34 *et seq.*

12 Benjamin Malkin, *Scenery, Antiquities and Biography of South Wales*, Longman, Hurst, Rees & Orme, 1807, pp. 106–16.

13 Anne Beale, *The Vale of the Towey*, Long, Brown, Green & Longman, 1844, pp. 23, 25, 109–16.

14 Edward Jones, *The Bardic Museum*, 1802, p. xvi.

15 John T. Dunbar, *History of Highland Dress*, Batsford, 1978, p. 129.

16 National Museum of Antiquities of Scotland files on the Isles, and Alexander Fenton, 'Farm Servant Life in the 17th–19th Centuries', reprinted by Scottish Country Life Museum Trust, 1975.

17 Thomas Hardy, *op. cit.*, p. 9.

18 Hippolyte Taine, *Notes on England*, trs. W. Rae, Strahan & Co., 1872, p. 371.

19 Thomas Hardy, *op. cit.*, p. 5.

20 John Hollingshead, *Underground London*, Groombridge & Sons, 1862, p. 60.

21 Thomas Wright, *Some Habits and Customs of the Working Classes*, Tinsley Bros., 1867, p. 187.

22 Henry Mayhew, *London Labour and the London Poor*, Griffin, Bohun & Co., 1861, I, p. 368.

23 *Ibid.*, III, p. 313.

24 Benjamin Rowntree, *Poverty: a study of town life*, Macmillan, 1901, p. 381, Appendix C.

25 John Thomson, *Particular Account of John Thomson a journeyman plasterer*, no publisher, Edinburgh *c.*1820; Elizabeth Longford, *Eminent Victorian Women*, Weidenfeld & Nicolson, 1981, pp. 227–48.

26 Sarah Tooley, *Life of Florence Nightingale*, S. Bousfield, 1904, p. 119 *et seq.* Florence Nightingale scrapbook, *Newspaper Reports and Cuttings*, the British Library.

27 Sir Rickman Godlee Bart., oration *Lister and his work*, University of London Press, 1927, p. 11.

28 John Hollingshead, *Ragged London in 1861*, Smith, Elder & Co., pp. 46–9; Henry Mayhew, *op. cit.*, IV, p. 357.

29 Joanna Trollope, *Britannia's Daughters, Women of the British Empire*, Hutchinson, 1983, p. 175.

30 C.H. Ward-Jackson, *A History of Courtaulds*, Curwen Press private circulation, 1941, p. 56.

31 George Smith, *Our Canal Population*, Haughton & Co., 1876, pp. 55, 76.

32 Welsh Industrial & Maritime Museum, Cardiff.

33 *Railways and Railway Men*, W.R. Chambers, 1892, pp. 53, 76–7.

34 Public Record Office, Kew, RAIL 667/545; RAIL 56/22; RAIL 410/1333; RAIL 1017/1.

35 Michael Hiley, *Victorian Working Women*, Gordon Fraser, 1979, pp. 52–60; Wanda Neff, *Victorian Working Women*, Historical & Literary Study of Women in British Industries and Professions, 1832–50, Allen & Unwin, 1929, p. 39.

36 David Griffith, *Griffith Jones Ffotograffydd cynnar o'r Felinheli*, Gwynnedd Archives Services, Caernarfon, 1980.

37 Sara Stevenson, *David Octavius Hill and Robert Adamson*, catalogue of their calotypes, Scottish National Portrait Gallery, National Galleries of Scotland, 1981, pp. 196–9.

38 James Bertram, *The Harvest of the Sea*, John Murray, 1865, p. 429, and *The Unappreciated Fisher Folk*, W. Clowes & Sons, Great International Fisheries Exhibition, 1883, frontispiece.

39 Peter Anson, *Fisher Boats and Fisher Folk on the East Coast of Scotland*, Dent, 1930, p. 54.

40 Christopher Lloyd, *op. cit.*, pp. 274–83.

41 Isabella Beeton, *Household Management*, Ward, Lock & Co., revised edition, 1880, pp. 7, 1004.

42 John James, *The Memoirs of a House Steward*, Bing, Holt, 1949, pp. 19, 97.

43 H. Taine, *op. cit.*, p. 49.

44 Michael Hiley, *op. cit.*, pp. 120–8.

45 Eugène Herbodeau and Paul Thalamas, *George Auguste Escoffier*, Practical Press, 1955, p. 77; Marie Louise Ritz, *César Ritz, Host to the World*, Harrap, 1938, p. 100; Paul Levy, 'Scandal at the Savoy', on staff commissions, *The Observer*, 19 May 1985.

6 Into the Twentieth Century 1900–1945

1 Barclay Wills, *Shepherds of Sussex*, foreword by the Duke of Norfolk, Skeffington & Son, 1938, pp. 57, 63, 70, 80, 124.

2 W.H. Hudson, *A Shepherd's Life*, Methuen, 1910, pp. 55, 72; H.V. Morton, *I saw Two Englands*, Methuen, 1942, pp. 131–2.

3 Arthur Randell, *Fenland Memories*, ed. Enid Porter, Routledge & Kegan Paul, 1969, pp. 33–4, 82.

4 *Traditional Working Clothes of Northern England*, The Bowes Museum exhibition catalogue, 1983.

5 G.K. Montgomery, *The Maintenance of the Agricultural Labour Supply*, International Institute of Agriculture, Rome, 1922, pp. 51–68.

6 J.B. Priestley, *An English Journal*, W. Heinemann & Victor Gollancz, 1934, pp. 369–70, 401.

7 Charles Kightly, *Country Voices, Life and Lore in Farm and Village*, Thames & Hudson, 1984, pp. 22, 45.

8 Gordon Honeycombe, *Selfridges*, Selfridges Ltd, 1985, illustrations pp. 63, 144, 194, 201, 208.

9 *The Times History of the War*, vol. IV *The Times*, 1915, p. 242; H.J. Usborne, *Women's Work in War Time*, preface Lord Northcliffe, Warner Laurie, 1917, *passim*.

10 Helen Fraser, *Women and War Work*, Arnold Shaw, New York, 1918, pp. 236–55.

11 Priestley, *op. cit.*, p. 411.

12 George Orwell, *Down and out in Paris and London*, Victor Gollancz, 1933, p. 174.

13 *Ibid.*, p. 91.

14 H.V. Morton, *What I saw in the Slums*, The Labour Party, 1933, pp. 11–45.

15 George Orwell, *The Road to Wigan Pier*, foreword Victor Gollancz, pub. Victor Gollancz, special edition for Left Book Club, 1937, *passim*.

16 Sid Colin, *And the Bands played on*, foreword George Chisholm, Elm Tree, 1980, pp. 66–7.

17 H.V. Morton, *In Search of England*, Methuen, 1927, p. 206.

18 Elaine Burton, *What of the Women? A study of women in wartime*, Frederick Muller, 1941, pp. 55, 59, 70–7.

19 Great Western Railway & Great Central Joint Railway, *Rules for Observance by Employees*, 1933, p. 6; Great North of Scotland Railway, *Book of Rules and Regulations*, John Avery, Aberdeen, 1908, p. 2; PRO RAIL 253/139 GWR *Standard List of Uniform Clothing*, 1907, *passim*.

20 Priestley, *op. cit.*, p. 275; H.V. Morton, *In Scotland Again*, Methuen, 1933, p. 133.

21 Dave Douglas, 'The Durham Pitman', part 4 of *Miners, Quarrymen and Saltworkers*, ed. F. Kirk, Butterworth, Shaw & Sons, 1972, pp. 121–4.

22 Alexander Redgrave, *The Factory Acts*, 11th edition by Charles Lloyd, revisions W. Peacock, 1909, 14th edition Joseph Owner, 1931, 17th edition John Thompson and Harold Rogers, 1949, all pub. Shaw & Sons and Butterworth.

23 H.V. Morton, *In Search of Wales*, Methuen, 1932, p. 230; Gertrude Jekyll, *Old English Household Life*, Batsford, 1925, p. 139.

24 Basil Lubbock, *Round the Horn before the Mast*, John Murray, 1902, p. 11.

25 Captain Jim Uglow, *Sailorman, a Bargemaster's Story*, Conway Maritime Press, 1975, *passim*.

26 Rosina Harrison, *Rose: My Life in Service*, Viking Press, New York, 1975, *passim*.

27 Charles Kightly, *op. cit.*, pp. 147, 165.

Bibliography

AIKIN, Arthur, *A Journal of a Tour through North Wales*, J. Johnson, 1797.

ANGELO, Henry, *Reminiscences*, Kegan Paul, Trench, Trubner, 1904.

ANGELONI, Battista, *Letters on the English Nation*, 1755.

ANSON, Peter, *Fisher Boats and Fisher Folk on the East Coast of Scotland*, Dent, 1930.

ARCH, Joseph, *The Story of his Life*, preface the Countess of Warwick, Hutchinson, 1898.

ARCHENHOLZ, Johann, *Picture of England*, Dublin, 1791.

ARNOLD, Janet, *Lost from Her Majesties Back*, Costume Society Extra Series, no. 7, 1980.

ATKINSON, Frank, *18th century Woollen and Worsted*, Halifax Museum, 1956.

ATKINSON, John, *Forty Years in a Moorland Parish*, Macmillan, 1891.

AUBREY, John, *Brief Lives*, ed. O.L. Dick, Penguin English Library, 1972.

AUSTIN, William, *Letters from London*, W. Pelham, Boston, 1804.

BAKER, C.H. & M., *First Duke of Chandos*, Clarendon Press, 1949.

BAKER, J.H., 'History of the Gowns worn at the English Bar', *Costume*, vol. IX, 1975.

BAMFORD, Samuel, *Early Days*, Simpkin, Marshall, 1849.
    Tawk o' Seawth Lankeshur, 1850.

BATESON, Mary, *Records of the Borough of Leicester, 1327–1509*, Clay & Sons, 1901.

BEALE, Anne, *The Vale of the Towey*, Long, Brown, Green & Longman, 1844.

BEETON, Isabella, *Household Management*, Ward, Lock & Co. revised edn, 1880.

BERTRAM, James *The Harvest of the Sea*, John Murray, 1865.
    The Unappreciated Fisher Folk, W. Clowes & Sons, Great International Fisheries Exhibition, 1883.

BEST, Henry, *Rural Economy in Yorkshire in 1641, Farming and Account Books of H. Best of Elmswell in East Riding of Yorkshire*, ed. C. Robinson, Surtees Society, 1857.

BLEWITT, David, 'Records of Drama at Winchester and Eton 1397–1576, *Theatre Notebook*, XXXVIII, no. 3, 1984.

BLITH, W., *The English Improver Improved*, John Wright, 1655.

BLYTHE, Ronald, *Akenfield, Portrait of an English Village*, Penguin, 1969.

BORN, Anne, *South Devon*, Victor Gollancz, 1983.

BUCK, Ann, and MATTHEWS, Henry, 'Pocket Guides to Fashion', *Costume*, XVIII, 1984.

BUCKLAND, Kirstie, 'The Monmouth Cap', *Costume*, XIII, 1979.

BURNEY, Fanny, *Evelina*, ed. Bloom, OUP, 1968.
    The Early Diary 1768–1778, ed. A. Ellis, George Bell & Sons, 1889.

BURRELL, Timothy, *Journal and Account Book 1683–1714*, ed. R. Blencoe, Sussex Archaeological Society, 1850.

BURSTALL, Aubrey, *A History of Mechanical Engineering*, Faber & Faber, 1963.

BURTON, Elaine, *What of the Women?*, Frederick Muller, 1941.

Calendar of State Papers Domestic Series, of the Reign of Charles 1, ed. John Bruce, Longman, Brown, Green, Longman and Robert, 1858.

CAMPBELL, Beatrix, *Wigan Pier Revisited*, Virago, 1984.

Cases in the Courts of Star Chamber and High Commission, ed. S. Rawdon Gardiner, Camden Society, 1886.

CELLIER, Elizabeth, *A Scheme for a Royal Hospital*, 1687, Harleian Miscellany, vol. IV, T. Osborne, 1745.

CLARK, Alice, *Working Life of Women in the Seventeenth Century*, 1919, reprinted Routledge & Kegan Paul, 1982.

CLODE, Charles, *Memorials of the Guild of Merchant Taylors*, Harrison & Sons, 1875.

COBBETT, William, *Rural Rides*, ed. G.D. and M. Cole, Peter Davies, 1930.

COLE, William, *The Blecheley Diary 1765–7*, ed. F. Stokes, Constable, 1931.

COLIN, Sid, *And the Bands Played On*, foreword George Chisholm, Elm Tree, 1977.

CRITCHLEY, Julian, 'The Tory Party in the Two-Button Era', *The Observer*, 25 August 1985.

CURWEN, Samuel, *Letters and Journals*, ed. G. Ward, New York, 1842.

DEFOE, Daniel, *Everybody's Business*, T. Warner, 1725.
   A Tour Thro' the Whole Island of Great Britain, 1738.
   The Complete English Tradesman, Charles Rivington at the Crown & Bible, St Paul's Churchyard, 1727.
   General History of the Robberies and Murders of the Most Notorious Pyrates, Charles Rivington at the Crown & Bible, J. Lacey at the Shop Temple Gate, J. Stone next Crown Coffee House Gray's Inn, 1724.

DE MARLY, Diana, 'The Status of Actors under Charles II', *Theatre Research/Recherches Théatrales*, vol. XIV, 1980.
   'Fashionable Suppliers, 1660–1700, Leading Tailors and Clothing Tradesmen of the Restoration Period', *The Antiquaries Journal*, vol. LVIII, 1979.
   'Some Aristocratic Clothing Accounts of the Restoration Period', *Waffen und Kostümkunde*, 1976.
   Fashion for Men, Batsford, 1985.

DE ROUVRAY, Louis, Duc de Saint Simon Vermandois, *Mémoires*, ed. A. de Boislisle, 43 vols, Les Grands Ecrivains de France, 1879–1930.

DE SAUSSURE, César, *A Foreign View of England in the Reigns of George I and George II*, trs. Mme van Muyden, John Murray, 1902.

DEUCHAR, Stephen, *Paintings, Politics and Porter: Samuel Whitbread and British Art*, Museum of London, 1984.

DICKENS, Charles, *Sketches by Boz*, Chapman & Hall, 1839.

Dictionary of National Biography.

DODSLEY, Robert, *Servitude*, T. Worral at the Judge's Head, St Dunstan's, 1728.

DOUET D'ARCQ, Louis, *Comptes de l'Argenterie des Rois de France au XIVe Siècle*, Jules Renouard, Paris, 1851.

DOUGLAS, Dave, 'The Durham Pitman', part 4 of *Miners, Quarrymen and Salt-workers*, ed. R. Samuel, Routledge & Kegan Paul, 1977.

DUNBAR, John Telfer, *History of Highland Dress*, Batsford, 1979.

EVELYN, John, *The Diary*, ed. E.S. de Beer, OUP, 1959.

EVERETT, George, *Encouragement for Seamen and Mariners*, 1695, Harleian Miscellany, T. Osborne, 1745.

FAHY, John, 'Employment in Retailing', GLC Strategic Planning for London, Conference, 26 April 1985.

FIENNES, Celia, *Journey*, ed. C. Morris, foreword G.M. Trevelyan, Cresset Press, 1949.
   The Illustrated Journeys, ed. C. Morris, Macdonald, Webb & Bower, 1984.

First Report of the Commissioners, Children's Employment Commission: Mines, W. Clowes, HMSO, 1842.

FITZHERBERT, John, *Book of Husbandrie*, I.R. for Edward White at the little North Door of St Paul's Church at the Sign of the Gunn, 1598.

FRASER, Helen, *Women and War Work*, Arnold Shaw, New York, 1918.

FURNIVALL, F., *The Records of Chaucer*, Kegan Paul, Trench, Tubner, 1900.

GATES, William, *An Illustrated History of Portsmouth*, intro. Sir W. Besant, Hampshire Telegraph, 1900.

GAY, John, *Trivia; or, The Art of Walking the Streets of London*, S. Powell, Castle Lane, Dublin, 1727.

GODLEE, Sir Rickman, Bt, *Lister and his Work*, University of London Press, 1927.

GREAT NORTH OF SCOTLAND RAILWAY, *Book of Rules and Regulations*, John Avery, Aberdeen, 1908.

GREAT WESTERN & GREAT CENTRAL JOINT RAILWAY, *Rules for Observance by Employees*, 1933.

GREY, Edwin, *Cottage Life in a Hertfordshire Village*, preface Sir E. Russell, Fisher Knight & Co., Gainsborough Press, St Albans, 1934.

GRIFFITH, David, *Griffith Jones ffotograffydd cynnar o'r Felinheli*, Gwynned Archives Services, Caernarfon, 1980.

GROSLEY, Pierre, *A Tour to London; or, New Observations on England*, trs. Dr Nugent, Lockyer Davis, 1772.

HALL, Brian, *Mr Midshipman Clark*, BBC Scotland, 6 April 1985.

HAMILTON, Anthony Count, *Memoirs of Count Gramont*, ed. Allan Fea, 1906.

HANSON, Henry, *The Canal Boatmen 1760–1914*, Allan Sutton, Gloucestershire, 1984.

HANWAY, Jonas, *A Sentimental History of Chimney Sweepers in London and Westminster*, Dodsley Pall

Mall, Sewell Cornhill, 1785.
  An Essay on Tea, 1757.
  Letters on the Importance of the Rising Generation, 1767.
HARDY, Thomas, *The Dorset Farm Labourer Past and Present*, the Dorset Agricultural Workers' Union, 1884.
HARRISON, Rosina, *Rose: My Life in Service*, Viking Press, New York, 1975.
HARTCUP, Adeline, *Below Stairs in the Great Country Houses*, Sidgwick & Jackson, 1980.
HASBACH, W., *A History of the English Agricultural Labourer*, trs. Ruth Kenyon, preface Sidney Webb, King & Son, 1908.
HAYNES, Jo, *A View of the Present State of the Clothing Trade in England with Remarks on the Causes and Pernicious Consequences of its Decay*, 1706.
  Great Britain's Glory, 1715.
HEATH, Francis, *Peasant Life in the West of England*, Sampson, Low, Marston, Searle, Rimington, 1880.
HECHT, Jean, *The Domestic Servant in Eighteenth Century England*, Routledge & Kegan Paul, 1980.
HENTZNER, Paul, *A Journey into England in the Year 1598*, trs. Horace Walpole, Strawberry Hill, 1757.
HERBODEAU, Eugène and THALAMAS, Paul, *George Auguste Escoffier*, Practical Press, 1955.
HILEY, Michael, *Victorian Working Women*, Gordon Fraser, 1979.
HOLLINGSHEAD, John, *Underground London*, Groombridge & Sons, 1862.
  Ragged London in 1861, Smith, Elder & Co.
HONEYCOMBE, Gordon, *Selfridges*, Selfridges, 1984.
HOUSMAN, John, *Topographical Description of Cumberland, Westmorland, and Lancashire*, Francis Jollie, Carlisle, 1800.
HUDSON, W.H., *A Shepherd's Life*, Methuen, 1910.
IVES, John, *Select Papers chiefly relating to English Antiquities*, 1772.
JACOB, Giles, *The Country Gentleman's Vade Mecum*, William Taylor at the Ship, Paternoster Row, 1717.
JAMES, John, *The Memoirs of a House Steward*, Bing, Holt, 1949.
JEFFERIES, Richard, *Wild Life in a Southern County*, no date, Collins.
JEKYLL, Gertrude, *Old West Surrey*, Longman, Green & Co., 1904.
  Old English Household Life, Batsford, 1925.
JONES, Edward, *The Bardic Museum*, 1802.
KANEFSKY, John, 'The Development of the British Coal Industry', *Coal: British Mining in Art 1680–1980*, Arts Council/National Coal Board, 1982–3.
KIELMANSEGGE, Frederick, Count, *Diary of a Journey to England 1761–2*, trs. Countess Kielmansegg (sic), Longmans, Green & Co., 1902.
KIGHTLY, Charles, *Country Voices: Life and Lore in Farm and Village*, Thames & Hudson, 1984.
LANGLAND, William, *Piers Ploughman*, ed. Stella Brook, Manchester University Press, 1975.
LA ROCHE, Sophie von, *Sophie in London in 1786*, trs. Clare Williams, intro. G.M. Trevelyan, Jonathan Cape, 1933.
LA ROCHEFOUCAULD, François Duc de, *A Frenchman in England in 1784*, trs. S. Roberts, from *Mèlanges sur l'Angleterre*, intro. Jean Marchand, Cambridge, 1933.
LE BLANC, Jean, *Letters on the English and French Nations*, Richard James, Dublin, 1757.
LLOYD, Christopher, *The British Seaman*, Collins, 1968.
LUBBOCK, Basil, *Round the Horn before the Mast*, John Murray, 1902.
MACDONALD, John, *Travels*, 1790, ed. E. Ross and E. Power, Routledge & Son, 1927.
MACKY, John, *A Journey through England*, J. Hooke at the Flower de Luce, Fleet St, 1722.
  A Journey through Scotland, J. Pemberton at the Buck & Son, J. Hooke, 1723.
MAGALOTTI, Lorenzo, Count, *Travels of Cosmo the Third Grand Duke of Tuscany through England during the Reign of Charles the Second in 1669*, anon. trs., 1821.
MALKIN, Benjamin, *Scenery, Antiquities and Biography of South Wales*, Longman, Hurst, Rees, Orme, 1807.
MARKHAM, Gervase, *The English Huswife, contayning the inward and outward vertues which ought to be in a compleat woman*, John Beale for Roger Jackson at The Great Conduit in Fleet St, 1615.
MARSHALL, William, *The Rural Economy of Norfolk*, T. Cadell, 1787.
MAY, W.E., Commander RN, *The Dress of Naval Officers*, National Maritime Museum, HMSO, 1966.
MAYHEW, Henry, *London Labour and the London Poor*, Griffin, Bohun & Co., 1861.
MIÈGE, Guy, *The New State of England under Their Majesties King William and Queen Mary*, 1691.
  The Present State of Scotland, J. Brotherton, A. Bettesworth, C. Hitch, G. Strahan, W. Mears, R. Ward, E. Syman, J. Clark, 1738.
Mineral Map & General Statistics of New South Wales, Thomas Richard, Sydney, 1876.
MITFORD, Nancy, ed., *The Stanleys of Alderley, Letters 1851–65*, Chapman & Hall, 1939.
MONTGOMERY, G.K., *The Maintenance of the Agricultural Labour Supply*, International Institute of Agriculture, Rome, 1922.

MORER, Thomas, *A Short Account of Scotland*, Thomas Newborough at the Golden Ball, St Paul's Churchyard, 1702.

MORITZ, Carl, *Travels through various parts of England, 1782*, E. Newberry, 1798.

MORTON, H.V., *In Search of England*, Methuen, 1927.
In Search of Wales, Methuen, 1932.
In Scotland Again, Methuen, 1933.
What I saw in the Slums, Labour Party, 1933.
I Saw Two Englands, Methuen, 1942.

MORYSON, Fynes, *Itinerary*, trs. from Latin by himself, John Beale, Aldersgate Street, 1617.

MURRAY, Sir James, *New English Dictionary on Historical Principles*, Oxford, 1919.

NEFF, Wanda, *Victorian Working Women*, Historical and literary study of women in British industries and professions 1832–50, Allen & Unwin, 1929.

NEWTE, Thomas, *A Tour in England and Scotland, 1785*, E. Newberry 1798.

NICHOLLS, George, *Eight Letters on the Management of the Poor*, S. & J. Ridge, Newark, 1822.

NORTH, Roger, *Autobiography*, ed. A. Jessop, David Nutt, 1887.

ORWELL, George, *Down and Out in Paris and London*, Victor Gollancz, 1933.
The Road to Wigan Pier, foreword Victor Gollancz, Victor Gollancz for Left Book Club, 1937.

PENNANT, K., *A Tour in Scotland*, W. Eyres, Warrington, 1774.

PEPYS, Samuel, *The Diary*, transcribed R. Latham and W. Matthews, Bell, 1970.

PRIESTLEY, John Boynton, *An English Journal*, W. Heinemann & Victor Gollancz, 1934.

Purefoy Letters 1735–53, ed. G. Eland, Sidgwick & Jackson, 1931.

RANDELL, Arthur, *Fenland Memories*, ed. E. Porter, Routledge & Kegan Paul, 1969.

REDGRAVE, Alexander, *The Factory Acts*, 9th ed. H. Scrivener, Shaw & Sons, Butterworth, 1902.
The Factory and Truck Acts, 11th ed. C. Lloyd, revisions W. Peacock, Shaw & Sons, Butterworth, 1909.
Factory Acts, 14th ed. J. Owner, Butterworth, 1931.
Factory, Truck and Shops Acts, 17th ed. J. Thompson & H. Rogers, Shaw & Sons, Butterworth, 1949.
Factory Acts, 22nd ed. Judge I. Fife and A. Machin, consultative editor F. Kirk, Shaw & Sons, Butterworth, 1972.

RIMBAULT, Edward, *The Old Cheque Book or Book of Remembrance of the Chapel Royal from 1561–1744*, Camden Society, 1874.

RITZ, Marie Louise, *César Ritz, Host to the World*, Harrap, 1938.

ROSS, Donald, *The Glengary Evictions*, W.G. Blackie, Glasgow, 1853.

ROWNTREE, Benjamin, *Poverty: a study of town life*, Macmillan, 1901.

RYE, William Brenchley ed., *England as seen by Foreigners in the days of Elizabeth and James the First*, John Russell Smith, 1865.

SEATON, Thomas, *The Conduct of Servants in Great Families*, Tim Godwin at the Queen's Head, St Dunstan's Fleet St, 1720.

SHARP, Jane, *The Compleat Midwife's Companion; or, The Art of Midwifery Improv'd*, 1671, reprint John Marshall, 1725.

SHUTTLEWORTHS, *The House and Farm Accounts of*, ed. John Harland, Chetham Society, 1856.

SILLIMAN, Benjamin, *Journal of Travels in England, Holland and Scotland in 1805–6*, S. Converse, Newhaven, USA, 1820.

SMITH, George, *Our Canal Population*, Haughton & Co., 1876.

SMITH, Peter, *The Turnpike Age*, Luton Museum & Art Gallery, 1970.

SMILES, Samuel, *The Life of George Stephenson*, John Murray, 1864.

Statutes at Large, ed. Danby Pickering, Cambridge, 1762.

Statuti Populi et Communis Florentiae, ed. Fribourg, 1774–83.

STEVENSON, Sara, *David Octavius Hill and Robert Adamson*, catalogue of calotypes, Scottish National Portrait Gallery, 1981.

TAINE, Hippolyte, *Notes on England*, trs. W. Rae, Strahan & Co., 1872.

THOMSON, John, *Particular Account of John Thomson a journeyman plasterer*, anon. pub. Edinburgh, c.1820.

Times History of the War, *The Times*, 1915 onwards.

TOOLEY, Sarah, *Life of Florence Nightingale*, S. Bousfield, 1904.
History of Nursing in the British Empire, S. Bousfield, 1906.

TRINDER, Barrie, *The Industrial Revolution in Shropshire*, Phillimore, 1973.

TROLLOPE, Joanna, *Britannia's Daughters, Women of the British Empire*, Hutchinson, 1983.

UFFENBACH, Zacharias Conrad von, *London in 1710*, trs. W. Quenell and M. Mare, Faber & Faber, 1934.

UGLOW, Jim, *Sailorman, a Bargemaster's Story*, Conway Maritime Press, Greenwich, 1975.

USBORNE, H.U., *Women's Work in War Time*, Preface Lord Northcliffe, Warner Laurie, 1917.

VANCOUVER, Charles, *General View of the Agriculture of the County of Devon*, Richard Phillips, 1808.

VIGEON, Evelyn, 'Clogs or Wooden-Soled Shoes', *Costume*, XI, 1977.

WARD, Ned, *The London Spy*, 1698–1700.

WARD–JACKSON, C.H., *A History of Courtaulds*, Curwen Press, 1941.

WARNER, Richard, *A Walk through Wales in August 1797*, E. Cruttwell, Bath, 1798.

WATERSON, Merlin, *The Servants' Hall*, Routledge & Kegan Paul, 1980.

WEIDITZ, Christophe, *Das Trachtenbuch von seinen Reisen nach Spanien 1529 und des Niederlanden 1531–32*, intro. Dr Theodore Hampe, Walter de Gruyster, Berlin & Liepzig, 1927.

WENDEBORN, *A View of England*, G. & J. Robinson, 1791.

WILLS, Barclay, *Shepherds of Sussex*, foreword the Duke of Norfolk, Skeffington & Son, 1938.

WOOD, Anthony à, *The Life and Times of, 1632–1695*, ed. A. Clark, Clarendon Press, Oxford, 1891.

WRIGHT, Thomas, *Some Habits and Customs of the Working Classes*, Tinsley Bros, 1867.

YOUNG, Arthur, *Six Months Tour throughout the North of England*, 1771.

YOUNG, Toby, 'Saturday Afternoon Fever', *The Observer*, 2 June 1985.

Manuscripts

British Library: Add. Ms.21,950, Bills and Accounts of Charles Stuart, Duke of Richmond.

Hatfield House, Household Accounts vol. VII, coll. the Marquess of Salisbury.

Leicestershire Archives Office, Accounts of the first Duke of Lauderdale.

Public Record Office Chancery Lane, E./101/435/6 Account of John Viscount Purbeck, Master of the Wardrobe, 1620.

Public Record Office, Kew, RAIL 667/545 Stockton & Darlington Railway.

    RAIL 56/22 Blythe and Tyne Railway Co.
    RAIL 410/1333 London and North West Railway.
    RAIL 1017/1 South Eastern Railway.
    RAIL 253/139 Great Western Railway.
    all relating to uniforms.

Index

actors' liveries 31
agricultural labourers 8–11, 21–7, 47–54, 76–85,
    105–15, 137–49
agricultural societies 105
Aiken, Arthur 80
America 18, 62, 68, 85, 94, 115
Angeloni, Battista 53, 60
Anson, Peter 132
apprentices 13, 31, 55, 64
aprons 10 and *passim*
Arch, Joseph, founder of Agricultural
    Labourers' Union 105–10
Archenholz, Johann 103
Army, modern 82, 122
Army, Roman 15, 17, 30
Army followers 28, 79
artisans 11, 15, 32, 37, 55, 61, 65–6, 70, 116,
    125, 151
Astors 169–70
Atkinson, Revd John 107
Aubrey, John, antiquarian 7, 21, 25
Austin, William 96, 102
Australia 110, 123

Bamford, Samuel, radical 80, 99
bargemen/watermen 43
Barry, Miranda, Army surgeon 120–21
Beale, Anne, novelist 112
bedgowns 79–89, 110–12, 131
Beeton, Isabella, journalist 133
Best, Henry, gentleman farmer 25–6, 35–6
Blyth & Tyne Railway Company 125–6
bondagewomen 113, 140
bonnets, black satin 54, 78, 138
    sun 77, 113–14, 138

    tunnel 78, 138
    uglies 113, 138
Bonny, Ann, American pirate 67–8
books on dress 79
breeching, by women 39–40, 66–7, 100, 130
brewers 37, 98
brewsters 37
Bridgewater, *see* Egerton
Bronze Age 8
Brummell, George ('Beau') 87
Brydges, James, first Duke of Chandos 70–72
Burney, Fanny, novelist 58, 66–7, 100
Burrell, Timothy, lawyer 74
Busby, T.L., artist 79, 87
butchers 30, 56

canal folk 15, 65–6, 93, 124
carpenters 10, 15, 37, 66
Charles I 24
Charles II 24–5, 41
chauffeurs 158
Children's Employment Commission 95–6
chimney sweeps 56, 59–60
Clark, Alice, economist 37
clogs 25, 95, 149, 154, 158
cloth industry 8, 17, 35–6, 62–5, 91–2, 96,
    123–4, 158–9
coachmen 30, 47, 74, 87, 135
Cobbett, William 84–5, 91
cocklewomen 126–7, 166
Cole, Revd William 74
constables
    male 12, 98
    female 151–2
Cosmo (Cosimo) III 31, 32

cow boys, English 25
Cullercoats 131
Cullwick, Hannah, general servant 136
Curwen, Samuel, judge 49–50

Darby, Abraham I, industrialist 61
Darby, Abraham III, industrialist 64
Defoe, Daniel 49, 55, 67–9, 73–4
department stores 115–16, 151
Dickens, Charles 86
doctors 28, 54, 122
'doctresses' 30, 81, 111, 120–21
Dodsley, Robert, footman poet 73–4
'dressing down' of British upper classes 9, 55–
    60, 66, 73, 87
drift to town 11, 27, 84, 146, 149
dustmen/garbagers 56, 88

Edward II, household of 18–19
Edward III
    statute on dress (1337) 8–9
    statute on labourers (1350) 9–10
Edward IV
    household of 19–20
    statute on dress (1463) 9
Egerton, Francis, third Duke of Bridgewater 15,
    65–6
Elizabeth I
    act on employment (1562) 11–12
    clothes given to servants 41
    her tailor 13
    Poor Laws 11
engineers 35, 66, 93, 125–6, 161–6
Escoffier, chef 136
Evelyn, John, diarist 35, 39
Exchange
    the New 31
    the Old Royal 13, 31
executioners 30

Factory and Workshop Acts 161–6
firemen 55–6, 88, 158
fisherlassies 132
fishermen 17, 38–9, 98–9, 132, 166
fishwives 39–40, 66–7, 130–32
Fitzherbert, John 10

flint knappers 155
frocks
    coats 10, 47, 74–5
    priestly 10
    see also smock frocks

galley slaves 39
gamekeepers 25, 70, 113
Gay, John 55–7
Gramont, Count 23
Great North of Scotland Railway 157
Great Wardrobe 13, 41
Great Western Railway 157–8
Grey, Edwin 107–9
Grosley, Pierre 72–4
Guild of Merchant Tailors and Linen
    Armourers 12

Hall, Elizabeth, Lady Llanover, 112
Hanway, Jonas, 56, 59–60, 73
Hardy, Thomas, 107–9, 114
Harrison, Rose, lady's maid 170
Hartlepool 100
hats
    doghair 137
    felt 7, 30, 37
    general 59, 111–13, 126
    straw 23, 37, 56, 111–13
    taffeta 50, 59
    top 104, 109, 111–14, 123, 149, 157
Haynes, Jo, wool factor 52
Heath, Francis 76–8, 109
Henry IV, statute on livery (1411) 20
Hentzner 11, 89
hoods 37, 57, 127, 138
homespun clothing 10–11, 25, 47, 85
housewife's cloth (linen) 35–6, 63
housewives 10–11, 25, 56
Housman, John 76
Hudson, W.H. 137–8

industrial developments 15, 35, 61, 64–5, 92,
    123–5, 158–66. See also Factory Acts
Irish dress 23
Irish rugs 39
iron ore workers 15, 17, 34, 124

Jacob, Giles 70
James, John, footman 133–4
Jeffries, Richard 105, 139
Jekyll, Gertrude, garden designer 105–7, 114,
    138, 166
Jews 58
jockeys 51–2

Kalm, Pehr, horticulturist 52
Kiechel, Samuel 12
Kielmansegge, Count 53, 73
kitchen staff 79, 103, 136, 153–4

La Roche, Sophie von 50, 59
La Rochefoucauld, François Duc de 49, 72
Le Blanc, Jean 61
Leicester 13
Lister, Joseph, first baron 122
livery, for servants 19–20, 41–6, 70–75, 102–4,
    133–6, 169–70. See also railway companies
London & North Western Railway 126

Macdonald, John, postillion, cook, and valet
    103
Macky, John 54, 63, 69
mantles 8, 13, 21–3, 39, 51
Markham, Gervase 25
Mayhew, Henry 116–23
mercers 55
Meteren, Emanuel van, Dutch consul 12–13
midwives 29–30
Miège, Guy 63–4
milkmaids 50, 90
milliners 58, 96–8
miners, both sexes 15, 34–5, 61–2, 94–6, 126–30,
    160–61
Monmouth caps 18, 21, 38
Moritz, Carl Philip 53, 72–3
Morton, H.V., journalist, 154–5, 160, 164, 166
Moryson, Fynes 23–4
Munby, Arthur, lawyer 118, 128, 136
musicians 14–15, 87, 155

National Union of Miners 127
navvies (navigators) 66, 93–4, 125
Newhaven 131–2

Nicholls, George, Poor Law Commissioner 97
Nightingale, Florence 121–2
nurses 30, 99, 121–2, 151

Orwell, George 149, 153–4, 158, 160–61
overall
    as industrial garment 124, 144, 161–6
    as overcoat 8, 26, 62, 83

peasantry, British, imitation of upper-class
    fashion 23–4, 40, 72, 103, 114, 133–4, 145
pedlars 35, 37, 62
Pennant, K. 90
Pepys, Samuel, civil servant 21, 28, 30, 41
Pigot, James 78
pirates, female 67–8
plaids/plodds 23, 35, 39–41, 63–4, 90, 112–13
Plymouth 100–102
Portsmouth 17, 37, 69, 93, 100–102
postmen 32, 88
press-ganging 17, 37, 68, 133
Priestley, J.B. 145–6, 153
prisoners 39, 57, 123
professions 12–13, 28, 54–5, 64–5, 69, 86, 92,
    114, 124, 149
protective clothing 17, 124, 161–6
Protestant Clothing Ethic 12, 25, 28, 54, 86–7
prostitutes 14, 33, 57, 123
Purefoys, family 47, 74
Pynne, William 79

Quakers 57–8

railways 35, 92–4, 125–6, 157–8
Randell, Arthur, 138–9
Read, Mary, English pirate 67–8
ready-made clothes 8, 15, 18, 35, 37
Redgrave, Alexander 166
Roman Navy 17
Ross, Donald 84
Rouvray, Louis, Duc de Saint Simon
    Vermandois 28
Royal Navy 17–18, 37–8, 68–70, 99–100, 133,
    166–8

Saussure, César de 49, 56–8, 69

Savery, Thomas 35
Scottish dress 23, 40–41, 63–4, 75, 90, 112–13
second-hand clothes 14, 28, 96, 116
secretaries 28, 135, 169
servants 18–20, 41–6, 70–75, 102–4, 133–5, 168–70
Shakespeare, William 11, 31
shepherds 7–9, 21, 82, 105–9, 137–8
shirtmakers 34, 72, 98
shoddy cloth 96, 149
shrimp girls 100, 130
Silliman, Benjamin 102
slate quarrymen 130
Smiles, Samuel 93
Smith, George 124
smock frocks 10, 26, 47, 77, 84, 105–9
smugglers 52, 102
South Eastern Railway 126
Stanley, Lady Josepha 107
Stockton & Darlington Railway 92–3
sweaters (knitted shirts) 132–3

tailors 12–13, 32, 44, 47, 55, 71–2, 125–6, 141, 169–70
Taine, Hippolyte 114, 135
teachers and dons 12, 28, 85–6
trousers
    on men 8, 17–18, 27, 62, 82, 104, 109–10, 169
    on women 18, 67–8, 126–8, 141, 151, 155–6, 160
tunics 8–9, 15, 17, 132
Tusser, Thomas 11

Uglow, Jim, bargemaster 166–8

underground sewermen 116
unemployment 11, 125, 153–4

Vancouver, Charles 92, 100–102

Ward, Ned 30–33, 39
Warner, Revd Richard, 79–80
washerwomen 14
watermen 43
weavers 17, 35–6, 62–3, 92, 160
Weiditz, Christophe, artist 10, 18
Welsh dress 23, 79–80, 111–12
Wenderborn, Dr Frederick 97, 102
West, Nan, housekeeper 74
White, William Johnstone 82–4
wigs 32–3, 52, 58, 86, 103
    hair powder in lieu of 103, 134, 169
Wills, Barclay 137
women, attitudes towards 67, 95, 127–8, 155–6
women working as men
    anonymous 18, 99
    Miranda Barry 120–21
    Ann Bonny 67–8
    Helen Bruce 120
    Helen Oliver 120
    Mary Read 67–8
Women's Land Army 144, 147
woollen drapers 32
Woolley, Hannah, governess 28
workhouses 97–8, 118
Wright, Thomas, journeyman engineer 116

Young, Arthur 66